MAKING AMERICANS

MAKING AMERICANS

JEWS AND THE BROADWAY MUSICAL

ANDREA MOST

HARVARD UNIVERSITY PRESS
Cambridge, Massachusetts
London, England
2004

★

Designed by Gwen Nefsky Frankfeldt

Pages 241–245 constitute an extension
of the copyright page.

Library of Congress Cataloging-in-Publication Data

Most, Andrea.
Making Americans : Jews and the Broadway musical /
Andrea Most.
p. cm.
Includes index.
ISBN 0-674-01165-1 (alk. paper)
1. Musicals—United States—History and criticism.
2. Jews—United States—Music—History and criticism.
I. Title.
ML1711.M74 2003
782.1′4′089924073—dc21
2003056636

★

FOR ALAN

★ ★ ★ ★ ★

★ ★ ★ ★ ★ ★ ★ ★ ★ ★ ★ ★ ★ ★ ★ ★ ★ ★ ★ ★
★   ★
Acknowledgments
★   ★
★ ★ ★ ★ ★ ★ ★ ★ ★ ★ ★ ★ ★ ★ ★ ★ ★ ★ ★ ★

I am deeply indebted for the intellectual and financial support I received while writing this book, in particular to Jonathan Sarna, Joyce Antler, Eugene Goodheart, and Michael T. Gilmore. A Leo Wasserman Research Fellowship from the American Jewish Historical Society, Brandeis University, gave me the opportunity to conduct initial research for the project. My thanks also to the University of Toronto Dean's Travel, Connaught Start-Up, and English Department SIG funds for assistance with photo-research and manuscript-preparation costs. A Summer Fellowship from the National Endowment for the Humanities allowed me the time to complete the manuscript.

Many archivists and librarians helped me research my subject. I am particularly grateful to the librarians at the Music Division of the Library of Congress, to Jeremy Megraw and the staff of the Billy Rose Theater Collection of the New York Public Library, and to Marty Jacobs and Marguerite Lavin at the Museum of the City of New York. Sargent Aborn of Tams-Witmark, Inc., and Theodore Chapin of the Rodgers and Hammerstein Organization kindly supplied me with original scripts from their archives. Robin Walton of the Rodgers and Hammerstein Organization, Kate Darling of Williamson Music, and Rosemarie Gawelko of Warner Brothers all assisted me in securing text and lyrics permissions.

Generous colleagues read the book at various stages of completion. Rose Rosengard Subotnik has been an extraordinary resource; her limitless knowledge of the musical theater, abundant energy, and meticulous readings were instrumental in the shaping of the book. Felicia Herman and Rona Sheramy provided essential feedback, emotional sustenance, and delicious dinners. I have been inspired, provoked, challenged, and supported by long conversations with Richard Rabinowitz about Jews, America, culture, and the theater. My thanks to David Savran for taking the time to read the whole manuscript and to David Román for his feedback on my *South Pacific* chapter. Both are avid and invaluable supporters of the field of musical theater scholarship. I was fortunate to reconnect with my old friend Jonathan Warren, whose rigorous close reading and generous intellect helped me to refine my project. Our conversations also provided inspiration and ideas for my analysis of *Annie Get Your Gun.* Thanks as well to Lauren Berlant, Pamela Klassen, and Sarah Wilson for comments on specific chapters.

My thanks to Lindsay Waters, Thomas Wheatland, and Maria Ascher at Harvard University Press for carefully shepherding the manuscript through the publishing process, to Alexa Selph for indexing, and to Laure Baudot for assistance with proofreading.

Finally, I wish to acknowledge those whose patience and love sustained me as I wrote this book. Knowing that my children were in Edlyn Noel's capable hands gave me the time and peace of mind essential to my work. My parents, Arnold and Deborah Most, and my sister, Jennifer Most Delaney, have been a constant source of support and encouragement. My children have profoundly shaped my life and my work. I finished the first chapter while in labor with my son, Max, and am completing my revisions as my one-year-old daughter, Alice, plays next to my desk. Max, a.k.a. "Cowboy Will," kept *Oklahoma!* perpetually alive for me with his famous tap-dancing performances of "Kansas City." My husband, Alan Ackerman, is my intellectual role model. Without his own inspired scholarship on the theater, his rigorous readings of my manuscript, and his unswerving faith in me, this book would not exist. I dedicate it to him.

Contents

Overture 1

1
Acting American
Jews, Theatricality, and Modernity 12

2
Cantors' Sons, Jazz Singers, and Indian Chiefs
The Invention of Ethnicity on the Musical Comedy Stage 32

3
Babes in Arms
The Politics of Theatricality during the Great Depression 66

4
"We Know We Belong to the Land"
The Theatricality of Assimilation in *Oklahoma!* 101

5
The Apprenticeship of Annie Oakley
Or, "Doin' What Comes Natur'lly" 119

6
"You've Got to Be Carefully Taught"
The Politics of Race in *South Pacific* 153

Coda
"I Whistle a Happy Tune" 183

Notes 203   Credits 241

Index 247

Illustrations

1. Gieber Goldfarb (Willie Howard) as the taxi driver in *Girl Crazy* (1930). 4

2. Gieber Goldfarb (Willie Howard) as the sheriff in *Girl Crazy*. 5

3. George Jessel, Dorothy Raymond, and Sam Jaffe in Samson Raphaelson's play *The Jazz Singer* (1925). 37

4. George Jessel as Jakie Rabinowitz in *The Jazz Singer*. 38

5. Eddie Cantor's multiple identities in *Whoopee,* as imagined by Alfred Frueh in *The New Yorker* (1929). 40

6. Cartoon by Al Hirschfeld caricaturing performers in *Girl Crazy*. 41

7. Eddie Cantor and his shadow in *Whoopee,* ca. 1929. 55

8. Eddie Cantor as Henry Williams in Indian disguise, with Jeanette Reade as Nurse Custer, in *Whoopee*. 56

9. Gieber Goldfarb (Willie Howard) with Chief Eagle Rock (played by Chief Rivers) in *Girl Crazy*. 57

10. Willie Howard, John McGowan, and Ginger Rogers in *Girl Crazy*. 61

11. Performing "Youth Will Arrive" from *Babes in Arms* (1937). 68

12. The Nicholas Brothers dancing in the finale of *Babes in Arms*. 89

13. The Nicholas Brothers and others in a typical minstrel routine from *Babes in Arms*. 91

14. Joseph Buloff and Celeste Holm as Ali Hakin and Ado Annie in *Oklahoma!* (1943). 109

15. Jud Fry (Richard Gordon) and Curly (James Alexander) almost come to blows in *Oklahoma!* 112

16. Invitation to first-anniversary party for *Oklahoma!*   115

17. Finale of *Oklahoma!* in the 1943 production.   117

18. Annie (Ethel Merman) stands beside her image in *Annie Get Your Gun* (1943).   120

19. Annie's chest full of jewels.   133

20. "Living curtain" at the end of *Annie Get Your Gun.*   135

21. Annie (Ethel Merman) after being adopted into Sitting Bull's tribe.   137

22. Bloody Mary (Juanita Hall), Liat (Betta St. John), and Joe (William Tabbert) in the 1949 production of *South Pacific.*   161

23. Nellie Forbush (Mary Martin) "washing that man right out of her hair."   163

24. Nellie Forbush (Mary Martin) and Luther Billis (Myron McCormick) in "Honey Bun."   167

25. Nellie (Mary Martin) gazes admiringly at Emile (Ezio Pinza).   171

26. The nuclear family in the finale of *South Pacific.*   182

27. The King (Yul Brynner) and Anna (Celeste Holm) perform "Shall We Dance" in the 1952 production of *The King and I.*   195

28. The multi-ethnic cast of *A Chorus Line* (1975).   198

29. Press release for the four-thousandth performance of *A Chorus Line* (1985).   198

30. Poster for *A Chorus Line.*   199

★ ★

What care I who makes the laws of a nation
Let those who will take care of its rights and wrongs.
What care I who cares
For the world's affairs
As long as I can sing its popular songs.

—Irving Berlin, "Let Me Sing and I'm Happy"

We know we belong to the land
And the land we belong to is grand.

—Oscar Hammerstein, "Oklahoma"

★ ★

Overture

A WONDERFUL story is told about the Jewish comic Willie Howard. During the Philadelphia tryout of the 1930 Gershwin musical *Girl Crazy*, he sang "But Not For Me" with the female lead. Then, in an effort to cheer her up, he sang the song again, pretending he was Maurice Chevalier. The trick was effective, so he impersonated Al Jolson, then Eddie Cantor, then George Jessel. The audience went wild and began shouting out requests. He obliged, performing encore after encore and, as one reviewer noted, becoming anybody they wanted him to be.[1] Willie Howard's character in the play— Gieber Goldfarb—was a funny but marginal Jewish taxi driver. But in his song, Howard was able to stop being *just* Gieber and to become a whole array of sexy, glamorous celebrities. What the crowd experienced during this number was essentially a collective religious experience. In watching Howard reinvent himself over and over again on the stage, the audience was reenacting a key sacrament of American Jews—indeed, of all believers in the American Creed.[2] His impersonations were a demonstration of the power and possibility of performance for newcomers to American culture.

Focusing on American musicals produced in the years 1925 to 1951, this book shows how first- and second-generation American Jewish writers, composers, and performers used the theater to fashion their own identities as Americans. In the musical, they discovered a theatrical form particularly well suited to representing the complexity of assimilation in America. In its songs, dances, plots, and characters, the midcentury musical theater expressed both anxiety about difference and delight in the apparently limitless opportunities America afforded for self-invention. The Broadway stage was a space where Jews envisioned an ideal America and subtly wrote themselves into that scenario as accepted members of the mainstream American community. Remarkably successful, the Jewish creators of the Broadway musical established not only a new sense of what it means to be Jewish (or "ethnic") in America but also a new understanding of what "America" itself means. Through song, dance and shtick, these Jewish artists invented characters and stories that came to be closely identified with the "real" America. The boundary between the theatrical and the real is a permeable one in this story. As Stephen Greenblatt notes, "Self-fashioning derives its interest precisely from the fact that it functions without regard for a sharp distinction between literature and social life. It invariably crosses the boundaries between the creation of literary characters, the shaping of one's own identity, the experience of being molded by forces outside one's control, the attempt to fashion other selves."[3] The process of imagining Americans on the musical stage is, I argue, indistinguishable from the story of America itself. In this book, America is a place of the imagination, and the myths invoked in these American musicals resonate beyond the geographic borders of the United States. Though the musicals themselves were created by artists living and working in the United States, they appeal to audiences around the world, particularly those in English-speaking multicultural societies like Canada.

This book weaves together two narratives—the story of Jewish acculturation in America and of the development of the American musical—showing that they are inextricable. *The Jazz Singer,* the first play addressed here, is a case in point. Just as Jakie Rabinowitz and Jack Robin are two names for the same person, their biographies form two aspects of a single narrative: the story of leaving behind the religious, Old World, Jewish life of the immigrant family is inseparable in the play from the story of becoming an American musical theater star. The fact that Jewish writers and composers are ubiquitous in the annals of the Broadway musical is due to more than just serendipity.[4] I discuss the influence of those whose work defined the genre during the years before, during, and after World War II: Irving Berlin, Eddie Cantor, Dorothy and Herbert Fields, George and Ira Gershwin, Oscar Hammerstein, Lorenz Hart, and Richard Rodgers. Other well-known Jewish figures include Jerome Kern, Kurt Weill, George S. Kaufman, Moss Hart, Frank Loesser, Frederick Loewe, Alan Jay Lerner, Yip Harburg, Leonard Bernstein, Betty Comden, Adolph Green, Jerry Ross, Richard Adler, Jerry Bock, Sheldon Harnick, and Stephen Sondheim (the only notable exception was Cole Porter).[5] The works that are the subject of this study epitomize how the Broadway musical form shaped, and was shaped by, the shifting status of Jewishness in American cultural life. The complex narrative of Jewish socioeconomic mobility in twentieth-century America is a crucial subtext of these shows. In plays such as *Whoopee, Girl Crazy, Babes in Arms, Oklahoma!, Annie Get Your Gun, South Pacific,* and *The King and I,* the topics of ethnic identity, racialist ideology, and antisemitism in particular were represented, debated, and discussed on the Broadway musical stage.[6]

We will focus here on the nature and significance of the relationship between ethnicity and cultural form. The musical theater offered an array of techniques for defining community, encoding otherness, playing roles, and defining the boundaries of the self. Jewish writers and composers developed a new genre of musical theater, best described as *musical comedy*, which uses comic structure, love plots, tacit and overt ethnic characters, and the distinct separation of dialogue and song to respond to and represent theatrically the experience of Jewish assimilation in America.[7] In surprisingly complex and culturally dense theatrical ways, this group of plays encodes, in both content and form, the concerns of a group intensely eager for acceptance into a new community. The plays vary widely in subject matter and setting, but the plot of each musical comedy conveys a set of common themes.

First, each tells a story about difference and community. In each play, there are outsiders who need to be converted, assimilated, or accepted into the group.[8] In *Girl Crazy* (1930), for example, the Jewish comic is at first out of place in the Wild West, but by the end has become the sheriff of the town. In *South Pacific* (1949), the Frenchman Emile, who is an object of McCarthy-style suspicion in the first act, becomes a war hero about to marry an American woman by the end of the show. Indeed, the experience of being an outsider— even one not explicitly Jewish—comes to be defined by a narrative trajectory from exclusion to acceptance, a trajectory codified by Jewish writers of musicals. For all sorts of outsiders, the way to become American is, in other words, a Jewish way, and those who follow that path perform—wittingly or unwittingly—a Jewish story, which is to say, an American story, indeed *the* American story.

Second, each of the plays articulates a vision of a utopian liberal society, which by the end of the play is perceived as more tolerant, egalitarian, or just than the status quo. This trajectory is overt in *Whoopee*, in which the lovers are united in spite of the wishes of a domineering father; in *Babes in Arms*, when the children are given independence and autonomy; in *South Pacific*, which celebrates a moral victory over racial prejudice; and in *The King and I*, which concludes with the implied conversion of a monarchy to a democracy.

Finally, each play articulates the values of this liberal society through the device of a love story. By defining appropriate mates for the central characters, circumscribing and containing desire, and eradicating obstacles to the sanctioned love relationships, these works dramatize the values of the musical's utopian liberal society through the conventions of the romantic love story.[9] When, in the recognition scene at the end of *Whoopee*, the Indian chief reveals that Wanenis is not Indian but white, and therefore an appropriate match for Sally, the play dramatizes the values of the society it seeks to per-

1. Willie Howard as Gieber Goldfarb in *Girl Crazy* (1930). At the beginning of the play, Goldfarb is a taxi driver. Photo by the White Studio. Courtesy of the Billy Rose Theatre Collection, New York Public Library for the Performing Arts; Astor, Lenox and Tilden Foundations.

petuate. In another powerful reversal, at the end of *Oklahoma!* Jud Fry's death allows Curly and Laurey to marry, again dramatizing the boundaries of acceptable society imagined in the play. Musicals that are central to the American musical theater tradition but clearly *not* a part of the musical comedy genre were not included in this study; I do not discuss in detail shows without a coherent "book," like the vaudeville-style revues of the Ziegfeld Follies or Irving Berlin and Moss Hart's hit show *As Thousands Cheer,* though I do use them occasionally as a reference point from which to understand the innovation of the musical comedy. *Of Thee I Sing,* a Pulitzer Prize–winning show with songs by George and Ira Gershwin, while closer in musical form to the musical comedies, is a political satire and not a romantic comedy. Similarly, *The Cradle Will Rock* (a work of musical agitprop) and *West Side Story* (a musical tragedy) each represent a distinct genre that deserves a full-length study of its own.

One of the goals of this book, then, is to examine the ways the genre of musical comedy constructs "America" in its narratives, characters, and songs. There is no single vision of America in musical comedy. Rather, "America" becomes what Sacvan Bercovitch calls "a rhetorical battleground, a symbol that has been made to stand for diverse and sometimes mutually contradictory outlooks."[10] In musical comedy, there is often a gap between the stated (or sung) ideals of the community and the values dramatized by the action of the love story. For example, in *South Pacific* the song "You've Got to Be Carefully Taught" describes a society that has the capacity to eradicate its own racism. This song serves as an anthem for the play; it is meant to argue for the liberal

2. Willie Howard as Gieber Goldfarb in *Girl Crazy* (1930). By the play's end, Goldfarb has become the sheriff of the town. Photo by the White Studio. Courtesy of the Billy Rose Theatre Collection, New York Public Library for the Performing Arts; Astor, Lenox and Tilden Foundations.

worldview of its creators. But, as we shall see in Chapter 6, the love plots in the play contradict, and at times reject, these liberal values in ways that reinscribe some of the racism the song argues against. A closer look at the utopian liberal communities described on the musical comedy stage, therefore, reveals them to be less than straightforward. They cannot fully resolve the complex web of tensions and contradictions that characterized the society with which the play opened. This book contributes to a lively ongoing debate about the problematic role of race in the Jewish production of popular culture.

In writing about Jews and race, however, I have found that although the problem of race is central to my project, it cannot fully explain the celebratory energy of the American musical theater. Musical comedy communities mask troubling aspects of American society, and without question these need to be brought to light and carefully understood. But the necessary process of unmasking should not erase the significance of the utopian vision itself, which is, after all, given dramatic pride of place. In *Love and Theft*, Eric Lott paved the way for a more nuanced understanding of racist representation in popular culture by arguing for the "contradictory racial impulses at work" in blackface minstrelsy. The "theft" of black humanity that minstrelsy represented did not cancel out the "love" white audiences felt for black culture.[11] Rather, the two impulses worked reciprocally to create a highly complex social structure. Likewise, the racism of the love stories in *South Pacific* does not render meaningless the utopian liberal vision of "You've Got to Be Carefully Taught." Both impulses exist in the play, and both must be taken into account. They are, in fact, profoundly intertwined. As Bercovitch argues, American ideology is not "a system of ideas in the service of evil" but rather "a system of ideas wedded for good *and* evil to a certain social and cultural order."[12] The popularity of Broadway musicals cannot be explained *exclusively* as a culture's desire to reinforce its own racism. Such an account avoids direct discussion of several crucial elements: the role of self-invention in the utopian musical community, the active role of the audience in a musical, and the imaginative and expressive potential of song and dance. When, in *Whoopee,* Eddie Cantor bursts out of a stove with his face blackened by coal dust and begins to sing "My Baby Just Cares for Me," he is unquestionably using and manipulating the dynamics of American race relations in his performance. But he is also a Jew hiding in the stove in order to avoid detection by a posse of cowboys. So his ability to transform himself with blackface can also be read as a triumph of Jewish escapism or American self-invention. And his song and dance delights the audience so much that they demand an encore. So the better he sings, the longer he can remain safe behind his disguise. None of these factors cancel the racism of the scene, but they add levels of understanding and analysis that offer a more complex account of the show's power.

Eddie Cantor's blackface Jewishness is an example of the ways in which these plays teach us how to see Jews in the context of modern American culture and racial ideology. The question of who counts as a Jew in this book—where biological and theological definitions are beside the point—is one that must be answered on a case-by-case basis. This book considers as Jewish both those who identified themselves as Jews and those who were perceived as Jewish by others (regardless of their status under Jewish law). In a story about the theater and race, perception is crucial. This book is about the *perceived* role of Jews in American culture (from the perspective of both Jews and non-Jews), and not about Jews in any essential or theological way.[13] I am less interested in demonstrating overtly Jewish content in the plays I have selected than in exploring how the anxiety of being perceived as a Jew (or as un-American) informed the work that the characters in these plays created. To this end, I focus on such issues as the creation of Jewish political liberalism in *Babes in Arms,* race and ethnicity in *Oklahoma!,* and McCarthyism in *South Pacific.* Because the book is about assimilation as much as anything else, overt Jewish characters and themes actually *disappear* as the decades progress. But a crucial part of my argument is that the experience of Jewishness does not always manifest itself openly and obviously. The secular Jews who created the musical theater were still affected by their position *as Jews* in American culture, even when they were no longer creating overtly Jewish characters.

Since the early twentieth century, scholars of American culture have been puzzled by the apparent preponderance of Jews in American theater and film. They have wondered why Jews were attracted to the performing arts, and why the forms developed under Jewish auspices appealed so broadly and successfully to the American public.[14] In his history of American Jews in the interwar period, for example, Henry Feingold observes: "Why American Jewry produced a disproportionate number of such interlocutors [of American culture], especially in the film and entertainment industries, remains a mystery."[15] The widespread use of the term "disproportionate" to characterize Jewish involvement in popular culture relies on two problematic assumptions. First, the word implies that there is some norm of "proportionate" representation—that the various groups constituting American society would each participate in the production of American culture in proportion to their numeric representation in the population as a whole. The fact that there are a "disproportionate" number of Jews is then posed as a problem: Jews have somehow displaced others and established an abnormal level of influence over a particular field. So although the connotations are clearly not intended by most of those who use it, this term carries traces of antisemitism. Indeed, for much of the twentieth century, beginning in the 1920s with the publication of *The International Jew* in Henry Ford's *Dearborn Independent,* antisemites have been setting the terms of the debate over the role of Jews in popular culture.[16] Second, the term "disproportionate" implies that one can separate Jews from American popular culture—that there is a popular culture that exists before and outside Jewish involvement—and also that there is an "American Jew" who exists outside popular culture. I argue instead that we have learned how to "see" Jews by seeing musical theater and that the musical theater exists because of the unique historical situation of the Jews who created it. The social reality of being a Jew in America is fundamentally inscribed in the form of the American musical theater.

Some historians have attributed Jewish involvement in popular entertainment to the lack of a preexisting corporate structure in the American entertainment industry, an absence that allowed Jews to advance quickly, unhampered by prejudice. Irving Howe, in *World of Our Fathers,* notes that in addition to the absence of antisemitism, the theater was a place where true meritocracy reigned: "Here . . . people asked not, who are you? but, what can you do?" Howe acknowledges that there must have been "other, deeper reasons for the Jewish plunge into entertainment," and he argues that the immigrant streets themselves fostered the theatrical spirit. He sees Jewish success in the theater as an explosion of "long-contained vulgarity"—"a challenge to rabbinic denial and shtetl smugness." While persuasive at times, Howe's argument that theater represents "a rebellion against the respectability of immigrant Jewish life" is reductive and ultimately unsubstantiated. His rationale explains neither the predominant position of Jews in European theater nor the presence of the many Ivy League–educated, "uptown" Jews who succeeded on the Broadway stage, including Richard Rodgers, Lorenz Hart, Oscar Hammerstein, and Alan Jay Lerner. Others have viewed "culture" as a portable commodity which Jews were able to transport with them from Europe, or have pointed to the Yiddish theater as a possible training ground for the production of popular culture. These speculations, while all partially correct, do not address the facts of *theater* itself that are crucial to understanding the Jewish relationship to the performing arts.[17]

Theatrical elements such as celebratory self-invention, active audience participation, and expressive singing and dancing are all vital features of the unique formal structure of the musical comedy. The plays discussed in this book represent a particular relationship between the two primary elements that make up a musical comedy: song and story. The role of music—or, perhaps more accurately, song and dance—in the theater can be understood on a continuum. At one end is strict dramatic realism, which uses songs and dances rarely, and then only as they might realistically be heard or seen in the situation being represented—for example, when a radio is turned on and a couple dances in the living room, or when a housewife hums as she hangs laundry.[18] At the other end is opera and ballet, where all words are sung or all action is danced. The plays discussed in this book fall in the middle of this continuum. In musical comedy there is an equal division of labor between the book, which consists of spoken scenes, and the musical numbers, which consist of songs and dances.[19] The two modes of performance are distinctly separated.[20] Dialogue is not sung. Numbers have clear beginnings, when a character begins to sing, and endings, when the audience applauds. The role of applause—or, more accurately, of the audience—is central to musical comedy. Audiences form a crucial component of the new community that is described and celebrated in the play. The separation of musical numbers from scenes allows audiences to participate in the play by applauding and even determining some of the course of the play by calling for encores.[21]

At the same time that this new theatrical form was developing in America, Bertolt Brecht was experimenting with what he called the "epic theater." His theoretical writings from the time offer a useful context for understanding the structure of the musical comedy form. He too was interested in the separation between story and song in the musical theater and saw the "separation of the elements" as a crucial characteristic that differentiated the epic theater from opera. In 1930, when the American musical comedy was entering its most successful period, Brecht described the epic theater as a reaction to and defense against the Wagnerian notion of the *Gesamtkunstwerk,* the total or integrated work of art:

> So long as the expression *Gesamtkunstwerk* means that the integration is a muddle, so long as the arts are supposed to be "fused" together, the various elements will all be equally degraded, and each will act as a mere "feed" to the rest. The process of fusion extends to the spectator, who gets thrown into the melting pot too and becomes a passive (suffering) part of the total work of art. Witchcraft of this sort must of course be fought against. Whatever is intended to produce hypnosis, is likely to induce sordid intoxication, or creates fog and has got to be given up.[22]

Brecht abhorred the effects of *Gesamtkunstwerk,* which he saw as promoting proto-fascism and obstructing the goals of the Communist revolution. He argued for the separation of the elements because he saw it as a crucial tool for producing the "alienation effect" (*Verfremdungseffekt*) in the theater—a strategy which forces audience members to stand outside the action, to remain conscious of the play *as play,* to resist being emotionally swept up in the action on the stage, and to retain their critical faculties. Brecht's theories of the theater have an interesting, if complex, relationship to American theatrical forms. Brecht himself, like a number of other German émigrés to America between the wars, was largely dismissive of American popular culture and stayed only a short time in the United States. *The Threepenny Opera* was received harshly by critics in New York, and ran only twelve performances on Broadway in 1933. One of Brecht's disciples, Marc Blitzstein, dedicated his American agitprop musical *The Cradle Will Rock* to Brecht, but the form never took off in America. Brecht's musical partner, Kurt Weill, became a relatively successful Broadway composer when he paired up with Ira Gershwin in the 1940s, but his style had changed dramatically from the days of *The Threepenny Opera* and *Mahagonny.* As we will see, when Broadway musical composers and writers began to refashion themselves as "artists" in the postwar period by integrating songs with dialogue, they turned not to Brecht but to Wagner for their inspiration.[23]

The separation of the elements in musical comedy presents a complicated challenge to Brecht's theory. Musical comedy is distinctly *not* realist, and the advent of a musical number—the switch in theatrical modes—does, like Brecht's alienation effect, remind the audience that they are in a theater. But this reminder does not create the alienation effect Brecht describes. Quite the opposite. We might call the result of the separation of elements in musical comedy an *assimilation effect.* The assimilation effect combines the self-consciousness provoked by the separation of elements on the musical stage with emotional response and communal celebration. The Jewish creators of musical comedy resisted Brecht's dislike of the sung expression of feeling, by showing how such expression can be empowering instead of entrapping. To explain how this process works, I must hark back to the initial discussions that inspired this book. In a seminar on Freud, Foucault, and Oscar Wilde led by Paul Morrison at Brandeis University in 1996, my fellow students and I read *Teleny,* a work of pornography attributed to Wilde and his friends, and discussed how the two central elements of the book—the love story and the sex scenes—offered two radically different ways of understanding identity. We read the love story in terms of Freudian notions of sexuality, and interpreted the sex scenes, which were always set off from the story, as Foucauldian spectacle. In short, we drew a distinction between sex as truth and sex as spectacle. We were then able to draw crude but useful oppositions between realism and theatricality, essence and performance, character and action, being and doing—oppositions which helped us to understand Wilde's work. The two elements of *Teleny* always remain distinct, but at first the central character has trouble distinguishing between them. He confuses surfaces with truth—interpreting the orgy scenes naturalistically, for example, and assuming that men in drag are actually women. Wilde, who was deeply resistant to Freudian, essentialized notions of identity, insisted on removing the blinders from his character's eyes. The education of the central character, then, is a *theatrical* one as much as a sexual one: he learns to reject essential truths and to accept performed ones.[24] It occurred to me that the same tension—between performed and essential notions of self—was present in the musical theater in the division between story and song. Musical comedies, I came to realize, were narratives of a desperate Jewish desire to resist essentialized (or racialized) identity through the powerful language of theatricality.

When a character begins to sing, the actor gives birth to a new self. As the music swells, the actor drawing in breath is pregnant indeed. Each song offers the performer the opportunity to create somebody new, somebody *different* from the character in the dialogue scenes. The collective thrill the audience experiences is the joy of watching not just a character but also an actor invent him or herself. The musical comedy is a celebration of acting, and particularly of American acting, of the marvelous freedom Jews felt in America to invent themselves anew. This effect is indeed what Brecht hoped the separation of elements would achieve: "Character is alterable and able to alter."[25] But in the musical comedy, this moment of alteration, of self-fashioning, does not lead to alienation. Rather, it is an experience of, and a dramatization of, *assimilation.*

Let us think of the musical comedy not just as an enormously popular theatrical genre, but as a canon of sacred texts and songs that reveal the passionately felt convictions of secular American Jews. That moment when a character goes from speaking to singing in a musical comedy is a quasi-religious one. The eyes of audience members well up with tears not because of sentimental feelings, but because of a sense of fullness that requires release, of connection that demands expression. The desire to sing along, to participate in the self-invention that is taking place on stage, is almost irrepressible. Musicals, unlike dramatic plays, tend to be revived frequently and to attract repeat visitors. So the audience for a musical is often made up of people who know the songs very well, anticipate them, and—privately or publicly—imagine themselves in the role of the singer.[26] Encapsulated in that exquisite moment of recognition is the story of Jewish assimilation in America, indeed the story of midcentury America in flux, of a country carefully balanced on the edge of enormous change.

Acting American

Jews, Theatricality, and Modernity

> They carried my great-grandmother's coffin down in one of those elevators that
> started and stopped when the elevator man tugged at a steel cable running
> through the car. The coffin was a plain pine box and had lain on a bed of ice on
> the floor for only a few hours before it was taken away. The ice took the place
> of embalming, strictly forbidden, and the body had to be removed almost
> immediately. This hurried ritual was the end of orthodox Judaism in our family.
> The next step was known as Reform, and even this faded after the bar mitzvah
> of my brother and me as a gesture to my grandfather on my mother's side.
> From that time on, my parents, my brother and I were Jewish for socioethnic
> reasons rather than because of any deep religious conviction.
>
> —Richard Rodgers, *Musical Stages*

I N THE opening paragraph of his memoirs, quoted above, Richard Rodgers asserts first and foremost that he is not a *religious* Jew.[1] He then launches into a discussion of his childhood home and his earliest memories of playing music and attending the theater. Aside from an offhand mention of the rabbi who officiated at his wedding, Rodgers never returns to the topic of Judaism or Jewishness in the book. The paragraph thus appears to be an irrelevant vignette in an account of a career in the musical theater. Yet its placement indicates a specific choice on the part of the author. It is a striking disclaimer, an answer to an unspoken question. Rodgers seems aware that some connection between Jewishness and a life on Broadway is assumed, and he disposes of it as early and as neatly as possible. He clearly chooses to distance himself from Orthodox Judaism; and whether or not he represents his family's attitude accurately, his decision to place the statement so prominently at the beginning of his book indicates that he has a large stake in this distancing. His need to address Jewishness at the outset indicates not only that the issue is present in Rodgers' mind but also that it has a particular relationship to the story he wishes to tell. Rodgers indicates that religious Judaism had essentially "played itself out" in his family by the time he was a young boy and was replaced by a "socioethnic" identification with Jewishness. He makes it clear that the Orthodox Judaism of his great-grandmother is distinctly out of place in his life story; his socioethnic identity, on the other hand, appears to have fundamentally shaped who he is. Equally important, the description of his adoption of socioethnic Judaism flows into his reminiscences of his first encounters with the theater, as if asserting a vital relationship between the two: secular Jewish identity is fundamentally related to a life in the theater.

★   ★   ★   ★   ★

The juxtaposition of secular Jewishness and the theater is vital to understanding the role of Jews in the performing arts.[2] Jews self-consciously used performance, in all of its manifestations, to negotiate their emergence into modern, cosmopolitan, non-Jewish societies. Jewish assimilation into mainstream American culture in particular can be viewed as a largely theatrical venture. Since for Jews "otherness" was not part of their external identity, as it was for African- and Asian-Americans, they could convincingly adopt alternate personas, playing the role of "American" (or "German" or "Russian") and passing as nonmarginal subjects. Theater was, for Jews, both a metaphor for the presentation of self in everyday life and a cultural form in which they participated in large numbers.

Gershom Scholem maintained that we can locate the beginning of modern Jewish self-consciousness in sixteenth-century Marrano culture, and in the seventeenth-century Sabbatian movement that sacralized the marranic split between inner belief and outer identity. Arguing that Jewish modernity begins with Sabbatianism, Scholem wrote: "Within the spiritual world of the Sabbatian sects . . . the crisis of faith which overtook the Jewish people as a whole upon its emergence from its medieval isolation was first anticipated." Sabbatianism sacralized "necessary apostasy"—essentially formalizing in religious terms the paradoxical Marrano condition of believing one thing while practicing another. Scholem saw both historical and metaphorical parallels between the Sabbatian split consciousness and the modern sense of self developed by the eighteenth-century *maskilim* ("enlightened Jews").[3] This tension between "inner" and "outer"—eloquently formulated by the *maskil* Judah Leib Gordon when he exhorted Russian Jews to be a "man abroad and a Jew in your tent"—became pervasive in the modernizing Jewish world.

Sigmund Freud was perhaps the first to analyze systematically the Jews' wide acceptance of this double mode of behavior. In his study of jokes and the unconscious, he uses a number of Jewish jokes to demonstrate how humor reveals the workings of the psyche. One joke he cites is a particularly revealing comment on the way Jews developed two modes of behavior, one for the Jewish and one for the non-Jewish world:

A Galician Jew was travelling in a train. He had made himself really comfortable, had unbuttoned his coat and put his feet up on the seat. Just then a gentleman in modern dress entered the compartment. The Jew promptly pulled himself together and took up a proper pose. The stranger fingered through the pages of a notebook, made some calculations, reflected for a moment and then suddenly asked the Jew: "Excuse me, when is Yom Kippur [the Day of Atonement]?" "Oho!" said the Jew, and put his feet up on the seat again before answering.[4]

The humor of the joke resides in the acknowledgment that one must perform a role in the non-Jewish, modern world, but can simply relax and be oneself around other Jews. Underlying the light-hearted nature of the joke, of course, is the very real threat of persecution, which drove Jews to adopt this double standard of behavior. Mary Antin, whose autobiography describes her experience as an immigrant from Russia, indicates the dangers that fostered this sense of split consciousness: "In your father's parlor hung a large colored portrait of Alexander III. The Czar was a cruel tyrant,—oh, it was whispered when doors were locked and shutters tightly barred, at night,—he was a Titus, a Haman, a sworn foe of all Jews,—and yet his portrait was seen in a place of honor in your father's house. You knew why. It looked well when police or government officers came on business."[5] Antin makes a distinct effort to distinguish this sort of behavior from either lying or hypocrisy. This performance of patriotism was necessary for survival: "'It is a false world,' you heard, and you knew it was so, looking at the Czar's portrait. . . . 'Never tell a police officer the truth,' was another saying, and you knew it was good advice."[6]

Antin openly acknowledges the doubleness of the Jewish moral and behavioral code: "A Jew could hardly exist in business unless he developed a dual conscience, which allowed him to do to the Gentile what he would call a sin against a fellow Jew."[7] This sense of split consciousness is akin to W. E. B. DuBois's notion of black "double-consciousness" in America: "this sense of always looking at one's self through the eyes of others, of measuring one's soul by the tape of a world that looks on in amused contempt and pity. One ever feels his twoness,—an American, a Negro."[8] But whereas DuBois emphasizes the ways in which the internal development of the black American is crippled by this double consciousness, Jewish writers more often highlight individuals' sense of control over their contrasting modes of behavior in the internal (Jewish) and external (non-Jewish, secular) worlds and the way in which they even draw strength from their ability to "outwit the Gentile." In fact, all of the major groups involved in developing the American musical theater lived with this experience of doubleness: not only Jews and blacks, but also the Irish and homosexuals. A detailed look at the way in which this performative doubleness functioned in the evolution of American popular theater is beyond the scope of this study, but the example of the Jewish experience lays the groundwork for further exploration.[9]

The sort of self-conscious role-playing demanded by modernizing societies led Jews to develop talents that were highly suitable for the theater. Offering a commercially viable place to employ role-playing skills, the theater was also an arena in which Jews and non-Jews alike could experiment with the shifting identity boundaries so characteristic of the modern world. In early modern Europe, the emergence of Jewish culture outside a religious context was nearly always accompanied by significant Jewish production of theater. As early as the sixteenth century, cosmopolitan Jews (mostly escaped Marranos) were beginning to write secular drama in Amsterdam and Italy, much of it in Spanish with occasional works in Hebrew.[10] By the eighteenth century, members of Moses Mendelssohn's circle of *maskilim* in Berlin found the theater to be a particularly effective medium for conveying their ideas about enlightenment, Romanticism, and assimilation. Writers such as Isaac Euchel and Aaron Wolfsohn-Halle used Yiddish, French, German, and Hebrew to dramatize differences among the various sectors of eighteenth-century German-Jewish society.[11] In America as well, in the late eighteenth and early nineteenth centuries, Jewish playwrights and producers, notably Mordecai Manuel Noah, Isaac Harby, and Jonas B. Phillips, were engaged in the struggle to define a new American theater.[12] Jewish playwright David Belasco, writing around the turn of the twentieth century, popularized a number of American stories, many set to music by Puccini, such as *The Girl of the Golden West* (1905) and *Madama Butterfly* (1900). Famous mid-nineteenth-century actresses, such as Adah Isaacs Menken and Sarah Bernhardt, were Jewish, and the figure of the Jewish actress became a prominent trope in nineteenth-century novels such as George Eliot's *Daniel Deronda* and Henry James's *The Tragic Muse*.[13]

By the late nineteenth century, as Jews fully entered the modern world, entertainment created by Jews flourished in the cabarets, music halls, and operettas of England, France, Germany, Russia, and Poland, and in the circuses, vaudeville shows, melodramas, and operas of North America. Jewish impresarios such as Otto Brahm in Germany, Max Reinhardt in Austria, and Oscar Hammerstein I in the United States fundamentally shaped the art and business of the theater in those countries.[14] The music publishers Witmark and Sons, run by three German-Jewish brothers, dominated the U.S. music publishing business, popularizing the songs of late nineteenth-century American vaudeville and operetta. U.S. theaters, too, were largely built and owned by Jews— the "Syndicate," a group of seven Jewish theatrical promoters, determined most of the shows that were presented around the country, until their power was broken by another Jewish team of producers—the Shubert Brothers.[15]

At the beginning of the twentieth century, mass culture in North America was on the verge of explosive growth and Jews were uniquely positioned to seize this opportunity. The arrival of great numbers of Jewish immigrants coincided with rampant urbanization. From the 1880s to the 1920s cities grew at a tremendous rate, and the burgeoning populations created an ideal audience for popular culture. Workers abandoned the countryside in quest of employment in factories and sweatshops. Thousands of southern blacks moved to northern cities to escape the Jim Crow laws and to pursue greater social mobility than was possible for them in the South. And millions of immigrants arrived from around the globe.[16] Construction of new buildings was constant during these years, but no amount of new housing could meet the demand. Overcrowding in working-class neighborhoods was the rule, with families often squeezed into one- and two-room tenement apartments that had little light, inadequate ventilation, and only a few, shared toilets.[17] Desperate for diversion and seeking escape from uncomfortable living quarters, city dwellers formed an eager audience for all forms of mass culture.

While poverty was the reality in the homes of most urban newcomers, images of new wealth, consumption, prosperity, and progress were everywhere on the streets and in popular culture. Economist Thorstein Veblen described the practice of "conspicuous consumption" in which the newly wealthy displayed their possessions and clothing as a sort of performance—a means of showing off their financial status. Members of the lower economic classes imitated the wealthy, purchasing with their often extremely limited incomes items that made them *seem* more financially established. Clothing, therefore, perpetuated the split between appearance and reality, often serving to hide rather than reveal a person's origins. The dramatic effect of new and ostentatious clothing was particularly apparent at Ellis Island. Numerous stories are told of recently landed wives who could not recognize their well-dressed, Americanized husbands, though they had been separated only a brief time. In Abraham Cahan's novella *Yekl,* for example, the snappily dressed Jake, who has been in America for only three years, appears at Ellis Island to meet his wife, Gitl. "Gitl . . . was overcome with a feeling akin to awe. She . . . could not get herself to realize that this stylish young man—shaved and dressed as in Povodye is only some young nobleman—was Yekl, her own Yekl, who had all these three years never been absent from her mind."[18] Gitl, whose experience has been limited almost entirely to the shtetl, is not yet attuned to the kinds of discrepancies between appearance and reality fostered by the American marketplace.

The burgeoning advertising industry also propagated the ideology of conspicuous consumption and increased the disjunction between appearance and reality. By the early twentieth century, advertisements were appearing everywhere in the modern city. Even human bodies became props for advertising: boys were hired to parade in front of shops wearing sandwich boards proclaiming the latest products. Andrew Heinze describes the process by which a simple cracker became a popular product through ingenious advertising and packaging. The campaign for Uneeda Biscuit showed "that even the lowly soda cracker could be rescued from the barrel and made into something with position and prestige in the world."[19] The new architecture of the city also resembled a confusion of surfaces seemingly disconnected from the interiors of the buildings they masked. Department stores, for example, often resembled cathedrals or palaces. "Architecture," Alan Trachtenberg notes, "furthered the sense of discontinuity in everyday life: discontinuity and fracture between what façades and interiors implied, between allusions of visible design and invisible organizations of life performed in the building."[20]

For immigrants and rural workers, accustomed to surroundings in which appearance was more congruent with reality, life in the twentieth-century city demanded a new set of skills. City dwellers quickly learned to be skeptical observers of the world around them—to look carefully at surfaces and never assume that these corresponded to reality. People who never developed such skills were taken in by con men, false advertising, or unscrupulous bosses.[21] Formed by the conditions of Jewish life in Europe, many Jewish immigrants brought with them these very skills of critical observation, and so had a particular advantage in negotiating the new urban scene. Central and eastern European Jewish immigrants also brought with them the experience of an inner/ outer split in consciousness, particularly those who came from rapidly modernizing European urban centers. This inner/outer split not only equipped many Jews to distinguish between surface and reality, but also made them particularly self-conscious about this process. As they settled into their lives in the New World, immigrants passed the memory of this double role on to their children. Although the harsh outward conditions of the European Jewish experience may have been muted in America, parents still felt it necessary to prepare their children inwardly to live two lives simultaneously, the Jewish and the American.[22] This self-consciousness about acting, role playing, and spectating in the urban landscape, a consciousness that the children of immigrants developed in the home, was conducive to a life in the theater.

The large numbers of German Jews active in nineteenth-century North American theater also opened doors for newly arriving eastern European Jews (though tensions certainly existed between the wealthier, Americanized German Jews who ran the nineteenth-century opera and vaudeville houses and their newly arriving coreligionists).[23] As in the garment industry, the early presence of Jews in the theater and music business encouraged newly arriving Jews to join their ranks. When songwriters such as Irving Berlin first tried to peddle their wares on Tin Pan Alley in the early twentieth century, the businessmen they encountered were invariably Jewish. Additionally, many Protestants viewed the theater as sinful, and so the arena was considerably more open to Jews (as well as Irish Catholics) than were many other public institutions. Residual Puritan prejudices against the theater meant that Jews and other outsiders could enter the field and develop it while facing relatively little religious or ethnic discrimination.[24]

Jews created theater not only in non-Jewish venues, but also for specifically

Jewish audiences, in Jewish languages, and with Jewish themes. Many important Zionist activists, such as Theodor Herzl and Israel Zangwill, wrote plays.[25] Another Zionist, Martin Buber, not only tried his hand at playwriting but also developed an entire Jewish theory of human interaction based on his experience with the drama.[26] Zionists eventually developed a sophisticated Hebrew-language theater company, Habimah; founded in Moscow in 1918, it soon moved to Palestine, where it is active today.[27] More commercial and less ideological, the Yiddish theater, begun in Romania in the 1860s, quickly gained popularity and spread throughout the Yiddish-speaking world. By the turn of the twentieth century, Yiddish theaters flourished in Poland, Russia, Germany, England, the United States, Canada, and South America.[28]

In the United States, particularly in New York City, the Yiddish theater was a central institution of immigrant life, attracting five thousand to seven thousand patrons per night—in 1900, eleven hundred performances were given before an estimated two million patrons.[29] Theater was a consuming passion for thousands of inhabitants of the Lower East Side in Manhattan, and one of their favorite ways of spending the few hard-earned dollars they could spare. Even those living at the poverty line often found a way to scrape together the twenty-five, fifty, or seventy-five cents needed to purchase a ticket. In a 1902 study of Lower East Side immigrant neighborhoods, journalist Hutchins Hapgood noted that "many a poor Jew, man or girl, who makes no more than ten dollars a week in the sweatshop, will spend five dollars of it on the theater."[30] In the early part of the century, at least three (and at times as many as twelve) full-time professional companies flourished on the Lower East Side, offering performances seven evenings a week, with matinees on Saturday and Sunday as well.[31] Yet despite the initial success of Yiddish theater, the phenomenon was short-lived, catering largely to the needs of a transitional immigrant community.[32] Serving as an alternative to the shtetl marketplace, the shul (religious school), the rebbe (rabbi), and the traditional Jewish texts, Yiddish theater facilitated the immigrants' psychological, emotional, moral, and educational transition to a new, American way of life while also enabling them to maintain a connection with the old.[33] As immigrants became acclimated to American life, they switched their allegiance from the Yiddish theater to the English-language theaters, also run by their coreligionists. The Yiddish theater offers a fascinating window onto a specific period in American Jewish history, but its focus was necessarily on the internal workings of the community, and its impact on the future of Jewish life in America remained limited.

The Broadway theater, on the other hand, has retained its powerful myth-making status to the present day. The Jews who created the Broadway musical invented an entire language of symbols, gestures, sounds, costumes, and narrative forms that came to be closely identified with the "real" America. So successful were they in tapping into the American mythological imagination that their work permeated not only the major urban and cultural centers of the country but also every small town and railroad stop in between. Few Americans, even today, reach adulthood without at least one experience of performing in or witnessing a production of a Broadway musical originally written by Jews, whether in high school, college, or amateur theater, or by attending performances of a touring professional company.[34] One can scarcely enter a shopping mall without hearing the songs—now called jazz standards—originally written by Jewish composers for the musical theater. And video stores across the country rent the film versions of almost all of the major midcentury musicals I discuss in this book.

* * * * *

"To name a period," writes historian Michael Denning, "is already to argue about it."[35] I have chosen to begin this book in 1925 with the opening of *The Jazz Singer* on Broadway and to end it in 1951 with the first performances of *The King and I.* During these years, the great musical writers—Irving Berlin, Jerome Kern, George and Ira Gershwin, Rodgers and Hart, Rodgers and Hammerstein, Cole Porter, and Kurt Weill—did their best work. This was the period when Broadway stars—Al Jolson, Eddie Cantor, Ethel Merman, Mary Martin, Alfred Drake, Bert Lahr, and Ray Bolger, to name a few—were household names and show tunes were synonymous with popular music. But most important, the Broadway musicals of these years represented a significant element in the American cultural landscape. They trace a set of transformative arcs in American culture. Within the brief space of twenty-five years, American politics, racial dynamics, and popular culture changed dramatically and fundamentally, and Broadway musicals reflected these changes from a uniquely American Jewish perspective.

During the 1920s, 1930s, and 1940s, economic and political crises radically transformed American society. The boom of the late 1920s, followed by the Depression and a phenomenal wartime recovery, shaped the economic mindset of the American people for years afterward. Deeply isolationist in the 1920s and 1930s, America emerged from World War II as a new world leader, shouldering the responsibility of "keeping the world safe for democracy" and out of the hands of the Soviet Union. For American Jews, World War II was not just a fight against fascism but an urgent struggle against the genocidal Nazi regime. They shared in the postwar triumphalism, further magnified by the glory of the founding of the State of Israel in 1948.

Americans also reacted strongly to their country's experiment with leftist politics in the 1930s. While the structures of the liberal New Deal still remained largely in place in the early 1950s, the tenuous left-wing alliance that had brought about the New Deal was shattered by the efforts of Cold War

hawks like Senator Joseph McCarthy. Jews, in particular, were affected by the left's defeats. In the late 1920s and early 1930s, many of them belonged to Socialist and Communist organizations and worked within the labor union movement, especially in the garment industry. From 1935 to 1939, the Communist Party joined with other liberal organizations to fight fascism under the auspices of the Popular Front. American Jews, who were overwhelmingly liberal in those years (more than 90 percent of them voted Democrat), formed a significant force within Popular Front organizations.[36] Jews involved in the arts tended to be active in Popular Front activities and, as we shall see in *Babes in Arms,* represented these activities in their cultural work. After the Nazi-Soviet nonaggression pact was signed in 1939, many disillusioned Jewish Communists rejected the party and became active anti-Communists. During the postwar Red Scare, however, their disaffection was largely irrelevant in the eyes of the congressional investigating committee. "Are you now or *have you ever been* a member of the Communist Party?" the House Un-American Activities Committee asked. Much of the anti-Communist activity of the early Cold War years was tinged with antisemitism, and Jews (Communist or not) feared the subpoena that could mean the loss of job, livelihood, and hard-won social status. But perhaps even more significant, Jews in the postwar era were stunned that after their faultless demonstrations of loyalty in fighting the war, they still were not accepted as the patriotic Americans they knew themselves to be. The musicals discussed in this book reveal the complexities of Jewish political commitment during these years, tracing a path from New Deal liberalism to jingoistic patriotism to ambivalent anti-Communism.

The American racial landscape also changed dramatically during these years. In the mid-1920s, the science of eugenics distinguished a wide variety of races which included "Negroes" and "Anglo-Saxons," as well as "Mediterraneans," "Asiatics," "Celts," "Semites," "Tartars," and "Teutons." When Congress established immigration restrictions in the mid-1920s, its goal was to keep Anglo-Saxon America "safe" from racial multiplicity—specifically from those races emigrating from southern and eastern Europe. By the late 1940s, however, as the horrors of the Nazi Holocaust were exposed, racial science was largely discredited. Anthropologists replaced the hundreds of races on prewar charts with three: "Caucasian," "Negroid," and "Mongoloid." Americans were primarily concerned with only two categories: "black" and "white." Fighting side by side with "Anglo-Saxons" in the foxholes of World War II, descendants of southern and eastern European immigrants became "white" ethnics. Segregated in the army and still burdened by Jim Crow laws in the South, American Negroes became "blacks." The term "race relations" came into use to describe encounters between "black" and "white" people.[37] Whiteness, in fact, became largely invisible and race issues tended to refer to the concerns of blacks.[38]

American Jews were deeply threatened by the racialized debates over immigration and were personally affected when European Jews were all but barred from entering the United States after 1924. The Jews creating musical theater during the 1920s, 1930s, and 1940s confronted a dilemma of identity as race became a central topic of concern in American intellectual and political circles. With so many apparently different racial types populating the country in the 1910s and early 1920s, academics and politicians began to express concern about who was "really" American, and thus worked to limit the perceived dilution of the national character through immigration restriction. Lothrop Stoddard, author of the influential book *The Rising Tide of Color against White World-Supremacy* (1920), warned that "the Nordic native American has been crowded out with amazing rapidity by these swarming, prolific aliens, and after two short generations he has in many of our urban areas become almost extinct."[39] Charles W. Gould, in *America: A Family Matter* (1922), argued that "American" was an endangered racial category, one that could not be learned but could only be inherited. He exhorted his readers to "repeal our naturalization laws, secure our children and our children's children in their legitimate birthright."[40]

This nativist racism was often explicitly antisemitic. Drawing on racist rhetoric prevalent in Europe, nativist writers considered Jews to be particularly dangerous to American racial purity because of the very same inner/outer split described above, but now refracted through an antisemitic lens to imply insidious intent. The Jew, these writers claimed, could appear to be a "real American" while secretly diluting the stock with a different racial strain. In *America Comes of Age* (1927), André Siegfried characterized Jewish immigrants with deep distrust: "They appear to assimilate at the lowest melting point, but even after three generations one finds them still with their national traits unaffected. . . . The Jew passes through the first phase of his Americanisation with disconcerting rapidity—there is something suspicious about his excessive zeal. . . . Caught suddenly into the rhythm of the New World, he is soon more American than the Americans themselves."[41] Yet because of their "race traits," Jews never fully assimilate, and this leads to prejudice: "The knowledge that the Americans have encountered something which they cannot assimilate has long stirred up an anti-Semitic feeling which accounts for the aloofness of the Jew in his American environment."[42]

Being both marginal Americans *and* creators of mainstream American popular culture gave Jews a particular visibility that landed them in an assimilatory paradox. On the one hand, according to those who were suspicious of their influence, Jews were such good Americans that they became "more American than the Americans." On the other, they still retained traces of racial difference that, even if imperceptible to the Gentile eye, made them a threat to the "American environment." Walter Benn Michaels argues that much of the American modernist literary canon is infused with this nativist and antisemitic rhetoric: "Twenties nativism made anti-Semitism an element of American cultural citizenship and therefore an essential aspect of American identity, regardless of how one felt personally about individual Jews."[43] Michaels looks at Jewish outsider figures in major works by F. Scott Fitzgerald *(The Great Gatsby)*, Ernest Hemingway *(The Sun Also Rises)*, William Faulkner *(The Sound and the Fury)*, and Willa Cather *(The Professor's House)*, and concludes that Jewish male characters in these novels function as a stand-in for all that was perceived as endangering American purity and supremacy.[44]

In the early 1920s, patrician race thinkers joined political forces with trade union members anxious about jobs lost to new immigrants, and with the Populists of the South and West (where the most intense racial animosities were being expressed), to bring the topic of immigration restriction to the floor of Congress. The Johnson-Reed Act of 1924 finally satisfied these factions, effectively closing the door to any significant immigration from southern and eastern Europe. The act used the 1890 Census, rather than the 1910 Census, as a guide to ethnic distribution and limited the quotas for each group still further. Remaining in effect throughout the 1930s and early 1940s, the Johnson-Reed Act had disastrous consequences for Jews attempting to escape Nazi and Soviet atrocities.[45]

Jewish musical theater artists (as well as most other Americanizing Jews) were deeply threatened by this exclusive and intolerant national ethos, and they responded to it directly in the shows they created. Yet in the early years of the century, rather than repudiating racial language they often celebrated racial multiplicity. In Israel Zangwill's 1908 play *The Melting Pot,* the protagonist, a Jewish composer named David Quixano, explains the idea behind his new American symphony: "America is God's Crucible, the great Melting-Pot where all the races of Europe are melting and re-forming. . . . God is making the American."[46] Samson Raphaelson continued Zangwill's racialized image of the Jewish musician in his 1925 play *The Jazz Singer.* In a 1915 essay Horace Kallen, another Jewish intellectual, disputed the assimilationism of the melting-pot image but did not reject its racial assumptions. Labeling his model "cultural pluralism," Kallen saw the United States as a canopy for a wide variety of racially defined immigrant groups who could retain their particularity while functioning under a shared political umbrella. Kallen, like many of his colleagues of the time, saw racial background as immutable: "Men may change their clothes, their politics, their wives, their religions, their philosophies, to a greater or lesser extent: they cannot change their grandfathers."[47] By positing culture as an inherited biological trait, even Kallen, who was rightly suspicious of racially based policies like the restrictive immigration laws, contributed to the notion that Jews constituted a race, rather than a nation or a religious group.

Opponents of racial science also contributed to the discussion. Jewish writers in particular created assimilationist models for American citizenship, arguing vehemently for open immigration policies and alternative visions of the new American. Mary Antin, in *The Promised Land* (1912), described her transformation, via the American public school system, from eastern European ghetto dweller to successful American citizen. She defined herself not as a member of the Jewish race, but as an American-in-process, capable of learning, changing, and adopting the American value system. Using her own life as an example, she argued that immigrants are the lifeblood of America, the spirit that reinvents the country: "We are the strands of the cable that binds the Old World to the New. . . . Before we came, the New World knew not the Old; but since we have begun to come, the Young World has taken the Old by the hand, and the two are learning to march side by side, seeking a common destiny."[48]

The images and narrative forms produced by Jews on the popular stages of the 1920s and early 1930s likewise rejected racialism and promoted an assimilationist ideology by stressing the importance of performance as a means of gaining acceptance into the stage community. Jews created idealized American communities on the musical comedy stage, which often promoted an inclusive assimilatory ideology for immigrant characters. Learned behaviors, such as language, accent, gesture, dancing and singing styles, and disguises made up of ingenious costumes, makeup, settings, and stage names, ensured access to the world defined onstage. The better one performed one's role, the surer one could be of acceptance by the other characters and by the audience. In their plots and characters, musical comedy writers revised the inner/outer split of Jewish modernity for the American context. Rather than demonstrating an identity split between an "outer" performed self and an "inner" true self, they rejected the notion of the core self and instead celebrated the freedom of performed identity.

This emphasis on visible performance virtuosity, rather than innate biological characteristics, was particularly strong on the vaudeville and musical theater stages in the early decades of the century, where performers often shifted ethnicity numerous times over the course of an evening. Irving Berlin was considered an ethnic chameleon because he could write songs in Italian, Irish, Jewish, and black dialects.[49] Chico Marx, a Jewish immigrant, played an Italian throughout his entire stage and film career. Weber and Fields, Jewish vaudeville headliners, became famous for their "Dutch" act. Douglas Gilbert in *American Vaudeville* describes the extraordinary quick-changes practiced by vaudeville comedian Frank Bush:

In his original act he opened in grotesque Jew make-up: tall, rusty plug hat, long black coat, shabby pants, long beard which ran to a point, and large spectacles. . . . Next he impersonated a German entering a saloon; then a Yankee farmer; and they were remarkable. They had no continuity or meaning in relation to story; they were pure characterizations. As the German he made up with a mop of iron-gray hair, a walrus mustache to match, a straw hat, and a long linen duster.[50]

Story was often irrelevant. Racial characterization itself, and the fascination of watching a performer transform himself from one race to another, formed the substance of the entertainment. Adopting a different nose, a new accent, a particular pair of pants, or a black face was sufficient suggestion that the performer had become the type indicated by the disguise. Who the performer "really" was, underneath the makeup, was largely unimportant. Vaudeville performers visibly subverted the basic assumptions of eugenics by demonstrating how easy it was to shift from one race to another. By changing races as quickly as they changed hats, these performers called into question the alleged immutability of racial bloodlines.

One major exception to this rule, however, was the identity of black performers. Whereas white performers in vaudeville could (and often did) "play black" (as well as Dutch, Irish, Italian, and Jewish), black performers could not "play white." Sophie Tucker, a famous Jewish "coon-shouter" (blackface performer) would end her act by removing a single black glove to reveal her white skin.[51] Her Jewish identity became unimportant, while her white identity was reinforced. Black performers (those who were "really"—that is, racially— black underneath the makeup) faced restrictions based on their racial as opposed to their stage identities. They were often prevented from performing on the same stage with white performers, and even on the rare occasion when a mixed-race company would perform (albeit in different acts), the black performers had to stay in different hotels and ride in different train cars.[52] This black/white exception in vaudeville inscribed a distinction between types of racial difference which eventually made its way into the structure of the middle-brow musical theater.

With the onset of the Great Depression, nativist sentiments and accompanying Jewish anxiety intensified. As the Nazi Party gained power in Germany, the antisemitic rhetoric that it popularized took hold in the already deeply racialized United States.[53] Aryan and white-supremacist groups such as the German American Bund (the American branch of the Nazi Party) and the Ku Klux Klan assaulted Jews with racist rhetoric and on occasion with physical violence. Nazi aggression in Europe escalated into war, but the U.S. immigration quotas established in the 1920s severely limited the number of Jews who could be rescued from war-torn Europe, and isolationism delayed intervention against Nazi atrocities. Partly in response to the liabilities of being characterized as a race, Jews began to resist the label and to insist on being redefined as a cultural or religious group. On the Broadway stage, Jewish writers, directors, and performers carefully erased stereotypical Jewish characters from their plays.

In the sophisticated musicals of the late 1930s, Jews, if they appeared at all, could be identified only by subtle gestures, offhand Yiddish phrases, or references to New York—cues that were meant to be understood only by Jewish audience members who were already in the know.

By the late 1930s, Jews had disappeared from view onstage because they had become white. As Matthew Jacobson has shown, during the 1930s and 1940s, in response to the German and Italian racialist codes and later the revelation of the death camps, "the academic community on both sides of the Atlantic produced feverish reevaluations of the race concept and its applications."[54] This revision of race had profound consequences for Jews and other recent immigrants, who suddenly found themselves grouped together with those of British descent as Caucasians, and granted many of the privileges accorded whiteness in America. Jacobson details the major developments this transformation brought about in the 1940s:

> First, *ethnicity* was adopted to describe a new brand of "difference" whose basis was cultural. . . . The faultlines dividing color from whiteness ("colored races" from "white ethnics") deepened. Second, ethnicity itself provided a paradigm for assimilation which erased race as a category of historical experience for European and some Near Eastern immigrants. Not only did these groups now belong to a unified Caucasian race, but race was deemed so irrelevant to who they were that it became something possessed only by "other" peoples. . . . Finally, the Cold War period witnessed a celebration of ethnic diversity as universalism in which conflations of "difference" and self-congratulation over the superior system of capitalist democracy were closely enmeshed, and the logic of this entire scheme was proved by a single anomaly: "the Negro." . . . The "ethnic" experience of European immigrant assimilation and mobility, meanwhile, became the standard against which blacks were measured—and found wanting.[55]

The postwar musicals *Oklahoma!, Annie Get Your Gun, South Pacific,* and *The King and I* offer a step-by-step illustration of the developments described by Jacobson. Rodgers and Hammerstein's stage communities in particular promoted an inclusive assimilatory ideology for ethnic immigrant characters. Unlike race, ethnicity was presented as a set of transient qualities that were nonthreatening because they could easily be performed away. As long as the characters could learn to speak, dress, and sing or dance in the American style, they were fully accepted into the stage community. To be labeled "ethnic" on the stage was an important step toward becoming a full-fledged member of the white community. Beneath the various accents and clothing, according to these plays, lay essentially similar white people with common values and beliefs. This emphasis on ethnic inclusiveness did not preclude the perpetuation of racial stereotypes about blacks. Racial imagery was often used in plots as a deflecting tool, highlighting the ability of ethnic Americans to become white and distancing ethnic immigrant characters from the dangerous tar of the racial brush. Ethnicity thus became a protection from black-ness.[56]

The interplay of race and ethnicity in the midcentury musical theater reveals a great deal not only about how Jewish artists assimilated into American culture, but also about how the notion of difference informs the construction of American community. The requirements for acceptance were detailed in the plots and numbers on the musical stage. But another drama, also involving the distinction between race and ethnicity, played itself out backstage. Jews' overt sympathy for blacks suffering under oppression—as illustrated, for example, in the significant role played by Jews in the founding of the NAACP—was combined with their covert fear of being perceived as black themselves.[57] Jewish fears about their own racialized history likewise influenced the way Jewish artists interacted with black artists and artistic forms. The relationship was both fruitful and uneasy. Jewish actors such as Al Jolson, Sophie Tucker, and Eddie Cantor "played black" when they performed in blackface, and Jewish composers such as Irving Berlin and George Gershwin adapted black musical forms. These Jewish artists seemed to be closely aligned with the black artists who developed ragtime, jazz, swing, and tap dancing. Yet the structure and content of the plays they wrote and performed reveal their ambivalence toward racial issues. While at times Jewish artists aligned themselves with "black" causes on the stage (as in *Babes in Arms*), they just as often used American racist attitudes to achieve "white" status by distancing themselves from the black artists whose musical and dance styles they so successfully popularized.[58] An investigation into the roots of the American musical theater thus leads to a discussion of relations between African Americans and Jews in America.[59] This fraught relationship, with its episodes of cooperation, compassion, suspicion, and betrayal, forms a significant and turbulent backdrop to the story of American Jews in the theater.

For the Jews of the Broadway stage, the twenty-five years covered in this book trace a crucial development not only in their communal ethnic identities but also in their personal relationships to the power centers of American culture. While many children of Jewish immigrants went to college, learned professions, and moved into the middle and upper classes, they often found non-Jewish social circles difficult to penetrate. During the 1920s, 1930s, and 1940s, Ivy League universities, as well as medical and law schools, established quotas for admitting Jews. Corporations, law firms, and hospitals quietly but firmly limited or prevented Jews from entering their halls. Country clubs, business clubs, and neighborhoods maintained restrictive covenants in order to preserve homogeneity. Assimilating Jews moved rapidly up the economic ladder in the 1930s and 1940s, yet were deeply aware of the social forces that never let them forget they were Jews.[60]

The Jews of the Broadway theater were among those who challenged the social limitations set by the genteel antisemites of the American upper classes. As they achieved financial success, they moved from urban Jewish neighborhoods to exclusive (and often restricted) addresses in Manhattan, Long Island, Connecticut, and rural Pennsylvania.[61] During the Depression and war years, they largely distanced themselves from Jewish organizational and religious life. In the late 1940s and early 1950s, however, writers like Irving Berlin, Richard Rodgers, and Oscar Hammerstein tentatively began to associate with Jewish fundraising organizations and to join congregations. The musicals they wrote vividly illustrate this shift from second- to third-generation attitudes and behaviors.[62] Margaret Mead described the stereotypical characteristics of the second-generation American:

> When that son leaves home, he throws himself with an intensity which his children will not know into the American way of life; he eats American, talks American, dresses American, he will be American or nothing. In making his way of life consistent, he inevitably makes it thin; the overtones of the family meal on which strange, delicious, rejected European dishes were set, and about which low words in a foreign tongue wove the atmosphere of home, must all be dropped out. His speech has a certain emptiness; he rejects the roots of words—roots lead back, and he is going forward—and comes to handle language in terms of surfaces and clichés.[63]

The Jewish characters of *The Jazz Singer* (1925), *Whoopee* (1928), and *Girl Crazy* (1930) emerged directly out of the conflicts experienced by the immigrant generation. *Babes in Arms* (1937) marked the second-generation rejection of ethnic specificity: Jewish characters were subsumed within an all-American cast, a trend that culminated with *Oklahoma!* in 1943. By the later 1940s, with *Annie Get Your Gun, South Pacific,* and *The King and I,* the immigrant resurfaced, but he or she was no longer Jewish. Rather, the immigrant represented the beginning of a nostalgic reimagining of the American Jewish past as an example for other, newer immigrant groups.

In revisiting the immigrant story, Rodgers and Hammerstein, Irving Berlin, and Dorothy and Herb Fields artistically represented not an actual generational role, but a mythical one. In 1938 Marcus Lee Hansen wrote of the third generation: "What the son wishes to forget the grandson wishes to remember."[64] Margaret Mead revised this claim. She argued that it was not the rejected Old World way of life that the grandson wished to remember but the process by which the Old World became the new: "We are all third generation, our European ancestry tucked away and half forgotten, the recent steps in our wanderings over America immortalized and over-emphasized."[65] Third-generation American Jews express a passion for their "American" ancestors—those who came to Ellis Island, lived on the Lower East Side, attended the Yiddish theater—not for the generations of relatives who never left Europe. In returning to the immigrant story in *Oklahoma!* and *The King and I,* Rodgers and

Hammerstein indicated that they had completed the process begun in the Yiddish theater and on the vaudeville stage. They had become Americans.

⋆ ⋆ ⋆ ⋆ ⋆

The mid-twentieth century saw a massive reorienting of American popular culture that began with the introduction of sound films and ended with the advent of television. The development of the Broadway musical during these years must be understood in the context of these changes. The earliest play examined in this book, *The Jazz Singer,* became famous when it was adapted to film as the first "talking picture"; and the last play, *The King and I* (1951), was produced in the year of the first commercial color television broadcast. The rise of sound films marked the death of the theatrical form that represents American success in *The Jazz Singer:* vaudeville. And the rise of television fundamentally altered both Hollywood films and the Broadway theater. Throughout the 1930s, as Hollywood musicals entertained Depression-era audiences across the country, the Broadway theater struggled to define itself as a unique and necessary medium. Performers such as Eddie Cantor and Willie Howard and musical writers such as the Gershwin brothers and Rodgers and Hart focused on the spontaneity of the live theater experience, allowing their characters a level of brash self-consciousness impossible in the carefully controlled products emerging from Hollywood. They developed an ideology of street-wise theatricality that favored skilled performers, pragmatic actors, and savvy operators, and skewered sentimentality. In these shows, ingenue lovers moved to the background while male comics, brassy female singers, and brilliantly athletic African American tap dancers took center stage.

In the first three decades of the century, the musical theater *was* popular culture. It flourished in two primary genres: the revue, exemplified in its most elaborate form by the Ziegfeld Follies (1907–1925, 1927, 1931) and the operetta, which reached its peak in *Show Boat* (1927). Revues were derived primarily from American sources—burlesque, minstrelsy, vaudeville—and were conceived as nonlinear spectacles of virtuoso performance. The audience went to hear a famous singer, to watch dancers, to laugh at comic sketches, and to admire the elaborate costumes and settings. While generally lacking plot, the shows were highly structured to elicit particular audience responses. Directors knew they had to open with a bevy of dancing girls, and they carefully planned the succession of songs and dances to generate a specific mood. Producers often independently purchased new ragtime songs from Tin Pan Alley songwriters and then interpolated them into a show wherever they would make a "hit."[66] The first act always closed with a number designed to bring the audience back for the second. Revues were thematic, rather than plot-driven. A show might be built around the season of spring, for example, or current headlines in the news, or weddings, or images of the future. The type of musical number in which an actor performed indicated the character he or she played. A love song called for an ingenue; a torch song might signal the entrance of a vamp; a comic number generally implied a racial characterization; and a large chorus number usually set the stage for the entrance of a star.

The other early twentieth-century form of popular musical theater—operetta—was imported to North America from England, Germany, and France. Initially popularized in the United States by the British team of Gilbert and Sullivan, operetta featured more elaborate plots incorporating comic and sentimental songs, recitative, and chorus numbers with lavish costumes and sets. Operettas were generally set in an exotic location or historical period and centered on romantic love stories about princesses, pirates, and gypsies. Jewish writers of German extraction, such as Sigmund Romberg and Jerome Kern, initially achieved popular success with operettas; and Oscar Hammerstein's early hits, including *Show Boat,* were considered to be the height of the American operetta form.

The *musical comedy* came of age in the late 1920s and had its heyday in the 1930s. More modern in both music and book, musical comedies of the 1930s featured ragtime and jazz and were generally set in the present, often in New York City. They drew on elements of both earlier forms, incorporating more complex plots while still relying on musical numbers and comedy bits to structure the performance. Thus, unlike revues or operettas, musical comedies always had a "book," a clever plot which played out in spoken dialogue and action and was usually dependent on a comic star, and which played with and against a set of "numbers"—songs and dances usually featuring stars and a large chorus. Whether they relied more on the vaudeville model or on operetta influences, the musical comedies of the 1920s and 1930s were united in privileging performance virtuosity and plot action over character development. From Fanny Brice's Yiddish shtick in the Ziegfeld Follies to Eddie Cantor's blackface waiter in *Whoopee,* "types" reigned supreme. *Characterizations,* not characters, provided the vehicles for performance on the musical stage of the 1920s and 1930s and allowed for the "assimilation effect." Characterization, stereotype, and genre formulas in these musicals allowed Jewish writers and performers to experiment with complex questions of racial identity.

An important element in the popularity of musical comedies was the nature of the community created onstage and with the audience. In order for a musical comedy to be successful, audiences had to leave the theater feeling as if they had been included in a celebratory, even religious experience. The chorus of the early musical comedies, generally composed of identically dressed leggy girls and tuxedoed boys, defined the contours of this experience. This strikingly nonindividualistic, homogeneous community, always dancing in step, might conceivably have intimidated audience members, who came from a wide variety of socioethnic backgrounds, especially in a period when fascist dictators were staging massive, tightly choreographed military demonstrations. Yet in fact the chorus was not seen as threatening by newly minted Americans because the stage community of chorus and stars embraced new members on the basis of merit. Performance ability was the only real criterion for admittance. Even the most individualistic performers on the stage were accepted into the theatrical community as long as they could contribute to the musical numbers. Comic stars such as Fanny Brice and Jimmy Durante, whose racial characterizations clearly did not fit the notion of beauty typified by the chorus girl or boy, could gain entry to the musical community not by their looks but by sheer force of talent. And stars, while always carefully distinguished from the chorus by their costumes, were not excluded from it. Stars controlled the chorus and understood it, often because, in true democratic fashion, they themselves had emerged from it. During the 1930s, in fact, the popularity of backstage musicals, in which a chorus girl replaces a star, grew enormously.[67] By the late 1930s, however, Rodgers and Hart had reimagined the chorus. While still a friendly meritocracy, the chorus of their 1937 musical comedy *Babes in Arms* was no longer homogeneous. Instead, the cast was a diverse group designed to loosely resemble American society itself.

As the realism of the movies became more popular and realism onstage began to win critical acclaim, theater artists scrambled to reposition self-conscious theatricality in the cultural marketplace. The musical comedy of the 1930s began, in the early 1940s, to develop a more "integrated" style—known in those days as a "book" musical style—which was distinguished by more realistic plots, the use of extended ballet sequences, and the integration of story and musical numbers. The plays were generally adapted from literary works, and while most of these works were hardly canonical, they were considered far more sophisticated than the formulaic books of the 1930s musical comedies.[68] In integrating formerly separate elements, these new musicals were able to sustain characters with more psychological depth. Their songs served not only to place them within a framework of set vocal or comic "types," but also to reveal motivations, beliefs, and personal history.[69] Rodgers and Hammerstein are considered to have inaugurated this new style with the opening of *Oklahoma!* in 1943.[70]

The claim that Rodgers and Hammerstein introduced a more mature, advanced, and sophisticated era in the musical theater is largely undisputed by historians of theater.[71] Yet a closer examination of the development of the form from "immature" musical comedy to "mature" realistic integration, within its broader American and Jewish historical context, reveals a far more complex story. Any artistic production that is so widely accepted as part of mainstream American culture must be examined not only in terms of its own formal creative agenda, but also in light of changing national ideals. The "ma-

ture" musical—site of two competing forms—is likewise the site of two ways
of understanding American identity: the performative and the psychological.
The theatrical characters, comfortable with performance, have control over
their self-definition. Their singing and dancing styles, their costumes, and
their modes of behavior determine both who they are and to which community they belong. They are self-conscious about performance, acknowledging that they are on stage and gleefully making full use of the conventions the
stage allots them for self-invention. Theatrical characters can perpetually redefine themselves by breaking into song. They become members of a stage
community simply by learning to sing and dance in step with the rest of the
company. They are practitioners of the assimilation effect.

The psychologically defined characters, while more detailed and realistically drawn, have much less control over their identity. These characters have
a consistent costume, accent, and gestural style that are fundamentally based
on *who they are*. They do not play self-consciously with their exterior appearance; it is a reflection of some truth within them. These characters do not
redefine themselves each time they sing; rather, the songs form a natural extension of the dialogue. Often these characters are excluded from group musical numbers, since they have difficulty learning new steps. They are not performing; they simply *are*.[72]

Historians' insistence on the term "maturity," with all of its progressive connotations, to describe this development of the form is clearly ideological. The
implication is that the integration of psychological realism and the collapsing
of the distinction between song and story on the musical stage represent a
positive and necessary new feature of the art form.[73] Yet, paradoxically, in fa-
voring integration of the elements over separation, with its self-conscious
emphasis on role-playing, celebrants of the integrated musical reinforced an
already deeply problematic mode of understanding American identity. Musical theater writers themselves adopted the integrated mode with some hesi-
tation. By juxtaposing characters whose songs were realistically embedded
in the plot with characters who used numbers more theatrically and self-
consciously, writers clearly expressed ambivalence about the transformation
they were depicting. And their ambivalence was well founded. Not only was
the assimilable/unassimilable divide created by this new form deeply troubling, but the increasing dependence on realism in the musical theater ultimately undermined the theatrical form itself. By adopting—however hesi-
tantly—the standards of film, television, and realist stage dramas, writers of
musicals ventured into an arena in which the musical form simply could not
compete. And so, after a brief heyday that lasted into the 1960s, musicals
quickly declined as the popular American cultural form.

★ Cantors' Sons, Jazz Singers, and Indian Chiefs ★

★ The Invention of Ethnicity on the Musical Comedy Stage ★

★ ★

> The singer of jazz is what Matthew Arnold said of the Jew,
> "lost between two worlds, one dead, the other powerless to be born."
>
> —Samson Raphaelson, Preface to *The Jazz Singer* (1925)

THE modern musical comedy began in the late 1920s as vaudeville and minstrelsy waned and the movies began to talk. The first sound film, *The Jazz Singer* (1927), nostalgically depicted the end of an entertainment era that featured the Jewish blackface star. As Jeffrey Melnick has observed, the "holy trinity" of blackface entertainers of the 1920s were all Jews: Al Jolson, Sophie Tucker, and Eddie Cantor.[1] As a singer who rarely performed in musicals, Sophie Tucker unfortunately will not figure in this study.[2] Jolson's career was largely over by the time *The Jazz Singer* was produced. His brand of racialized Jewish entertainment was rooted in forms from the past—minstrelsy, ragtime, and melodrama. Eddie Cantor, on the other hand, was able to transform himself into a modern jazz entertainer. Abandoning the role of blackface minstrel, he became instead a quick-change artist, riffing on ethnic stereotypes the way a jazz trumpeter might improvise a solo. Early musical comedy performers like Eddie Cantor and Willie Howard (as well as writers like George and Ira Gershwin) reimagined ethnic stage stereotypes as a radically modern theatrical mode. Samson Raphaelson's 1925 play *The Jazz Singer* offers an excellent illustration of the performance conventions against which modern musical comedy artists like the Gershwins and Cantor were reacting.

A Hebrew in Blackface

Raphaelson's play, like the 1927 movie of the same name, focuses on the struggle of the protagonist to figure out who he really is.[3] At home on the Lower East Side, he is Jakie Rabinowitz, a cantor's son who is expected to follow in his father's footsteps. After leaving home to escape his father's repressive Old

World attitudes, Jakie becomes Jack Robin, a blackface performer with a "cry" in his voice. Just as he is about to get his big break in vaudeville, he confronts a most difficult decision: his ailing father requests that Jakie replace him in the synagogue on the eve of Yom Kippur, the holiest day of the Jewish year, a time for fasting and repentance. Jack's opening night conflicts with the holiday, and so to fulfill his father's dying wish, he must give up his shot at stardom. As Jack struggles with his decision, he applies blackface makeup and rehearses his act. By the end of the rehearsal, he has decided, for one night at least, to return home and step into his father's shoes. The play ends ambiguously, as the producer and costar of Jack's show overhear his chanting in the synagogue and express great admiration for his talent and the hope that he will return to the stage. The movie is more definite: after Jakie's performance in the synagogue, he appears in a theater singing an awe-inspiring rendition of "My Mammy" to the cheers of the audience and his devoted mother.

Many critics have written about *The Jazz Singer* as a tale of assimilation, with blackface serving as the transformative process by which Jakie, the Jewish child of immigrants, becomes Jack, the American performer. They often disagree, however, about the way in which blackface actually effects this transformation. Some, like Irving Howe, have claimed that blackface is an act of identification that allows the Jewish performer to express solidarity with another oppressed American group. Others see blackface as a mask that hides Jewishness, or, more provocatively, as a way of proving that Jews are white Americans. Because the black can be removed, argues Michael Rogin, it establishes a safe distance between the white (Jewish) performer and the black character he or she portrays. Matthew Frye Jacobson qualifies Rogin's argument, claiming that blackface transforms the Hebrew Jakie Rabinowitz into the Caucasian Jack Robin. In other words, it empties Jewishness of all racial implications and makes it a marker of cultural, not racial, difference. W. T. Lhamon sees the adoption of blackface as simultaneously an act of assimilation and an act of defiance. Minstrel performers, he argues, used racial stereotypes both to assimilate to mainstream white culture and to express their class-based aversion to many of the values (racist and economic) of the very culture they wanted to join.[4]

While all of these arguments are persuasive in part, they miss two crucial aspects of the blackface question. First, we must look more closely at the assumption that it is specifically *blackface*, rather than the theater in general, which serves as the agent of assimilation in *The Jazz Singer*. In both the play and the film, "blacking up" prompts Jack/Jakie's crisis of identity—a crisis which inspires him to reflect on his own racial background and ultimately to return home to the Lower East Side in order to fulfill what he sees as his racial destiny. The power that will draw him back to the stage in the end is likewise figured in biological (specifically familial) terms. This racialized language throws the topic of assimilation into question. What does it mean to assimilate to an identity that is already, as Jack says, "in the blood"? Second, critics have tended to use *The Jazz Singer* to extrapolate to the whole arena of Jewish blackface entertainment, making the mistaken assumption that all blackface performances by Jews were essentially the same, with Al Jolson's performance in *The Jazz Singer* as the epitome. I argue instead that performers used blackface in diverse ways and for different purposes. Raphaelson's version, based loosely on the model of (and later played by) Al Jolson, emerged from a specific set of circumstances and must be considered a unique, not a representative, case. Musical comedy performers of the late 1920s and early 1930s, such as Eddie Cantor and Willie Howard, used blackface as well as other racial and gendered disguises to quite different theatrical and assimilatory ends.

The protagonist of Raphaelson's play *The Jazz Singer* struggles to reconcile two equally demanding families, both competing to claim him as their own. One consists of his Old World Jewish family: his cantor father, his nurturing *yiddishe* mother, and the other Jewish characters who populate the Lower East Side. The second consists of his New World theatrical family, which includes Mary Dale (his mentor and love interest), Harry Lee (his producer), and the other cast members in the vaudeville show. They are modern, ambitious, and fully acclimated to the New World American scene. The first act introduces Jakie's Jewish family on the Lower East Side. It is the cantor's birthday, and his wife Sara is discussing a particular birthday gift with Yudelson, a family friend:

> YUDELSON: It says on the sign: "Five Generations of Great Cantors, and the Fifth Is the Best."
> SARA: [*Slowly*] Five generations of great Cantors . . . That will make him think of Jakie.[5]

Jakie's life choices, according to the Old World, are biologically determined. Five generations of Rabinowitzes have been cantors, and it is expected that Jakie will follow in this tradition. When Jakie (now Jack) decides to appease his parents and chant the Kol Nidre service at the end, his appearance confirms his biological link to the cantorial tradition. The stage directions read: "JACK sits in silence for a moment; then, head in his hands, he begins humming to himself the plaintive, majestic cadences of Kol Nidre. He might be his own great grandfather in the Russian Ghetto hidden in some dark cellar praying to a forbidden God, as he sits there, weary, determined, humming a tune thousands of years old" (132).

But Jack's theatrical community is also represented as a family: his costar Mary Dale serves as both mother and girlfriend, and the producer Harry Lee stands in as a strict but caring father. When the theater "parents" follow Jack downtown to his Jewish parents' home to try to convince him not to abandon them, they confront Sara and try to persuade her of their exclusive claim.

> MARY: I love Jack, too, Mrs. Rabinowitz—and that's why I want him to go to the theatre tonight. . . . It's his one great opportunity. [*A pause.*] You know, I found him.
> SARA: You found him?
> MARY: I recognized his ability—I helped him to realize his own powers.
> (143)

Like the Egyptian princess who drew the infant Moses from the bulrushes, Mary has discovered Jack and made him her own. When Harry confronts Jack about his decision, Jack casts Harry in a paternal role, repeatedly comparing him to his cantor father. When Harry suggests that Jack try explaining once more to the cantor why he can't sing in the synagogue, Jack replies, "He couldn't understand any more than you can understand" (133). As Harry raises the stakes, Jack realizes that whichever choice he makes, he will be guilty of either metaphorical or actual patricide:

> LEE: I hate to bring in the personal element, Jack, but you have it in your hands either to make or break me.
> JACK: [*Head sunk in his hands.*] It's your money against my father's life, Mr. Lee. (135)

In despair over his situation, Jack again compares the two men: "My father's religion is a stone wall, and so is your business" (137). Harry refuses to give Jack up, and decides to speak with Sara one more time, to "convince her that he belongs to us, and not down here" (141).

While the theatrical family is presumably an adoptive family, both families turn out to have a biological claim on Jack. As he begins to black his face for the dress rehearsal, he reflects on his identity. Torn by a desire to please *both* families, and to fulfill both sides of his destiny, Jack agonizes over his dilemma. First, he reveals to Mary the conversations he has with God: "Sometimes when I'm alone—and I'm alone a lot more than you think—the old songs from the synagogue start wailing in my ears . . . and I—I cry. . . . In that hall bedroom in Chicago, I used to get down on my knees in the dark and talk to God in Hebrew. I—bawled him out . . . because he made me only half a Cantor—half a Cantor, and half a bum" (107). While his guilt about his father leads him to resent the demands of the theatrical side of his soul ("half a bum"), he never doubts that the theater is a fundamental part of his biological self. As he continues to apply the blackface makeup, he declares, "I've got Broadway in my blood" (107).

Ultimately, it is impossible for Jack to separate the pieces of his soul. While the blackface makeup serves as his entrée into the world of theatrical success (and symbolically marks his arrival as an American), his performance in this world is effective only when it is inspired by the deep emotions of his "Hebrew" side. Jack's mother enters his dressing room to beg him to come home, arriving only moments before his number. He rushes from her side to the stage and sings a heart-rending nostalgic song about home, parents, and deep regrets:

> I—want—you—to—understand . . .
> That—it's—my—mammy . . .
> And—my—daddy . . .
> I'm—going—back—down—South—. . .
> . . . . .
> I've had my fling,
> And it don't mean a thing—

> [*His voice breaks. He repeats in intensely personal agony, "It don't mean a thing . . . it don't mean a thing—my God!—it don't mean a . . .*] (116)

Jack's powerful performance stuns the other members of the cast. He generates electricity not by rejecting his past, but by joining the two pieces of his agonized soul. From this point on, the playwright repeatedly refers to Jack as "a Cantor in blackface."

In the last scene of the play, Mary and Harry struggle with Sara for Jack's soul. All of them claim that they just want Jack to be true to himself. Mary begs Jack, "Tell me that you are true to yourself, and I'll go" (146), and Harry claims, "I want that boy to be true to himself" (144). Sara implores her son, "I want you to do only what is in your heart" (146). At first, Jack admits that he didn't really want to come home, and doesn't understand the words of the prayers. But when he learns that his father has died, his Jewish blood rises within him: "He told me God would punish me! I thought I could get away from Cantors! Well, God showed me. . . . Mama! I'm going with you! I'm going to the synagogue! . . . I'm your son. I'm the son of my father. Mama, I'm a Cantor, see? I'm Cantor Rabinowitz! God's going to hear me sing Kol Nidre tonight!" (150). Jack dons his kittel (white sacramental robe) and his yarmulke and rushes off to the synagogue with his mother. But the play does not end here. Mary and Lee listen to Jack sing through the window:

MARY: You are going to hear a blackface comedian singing to his God. . . .
[*Now the choir can be heard in the noble strains of Kol Nidre. LEE and MARY stand motionless. JACK's voice rises, pouring forth in a flood of prayer; it subsides; rises again. Here is something of the same quality that he put, earlier that afternoon, into his cheap Mammy song.*] Don't you see, Harry, it's in his blood. . . . He'll *have* to come back. (152)

3. George Jessel (right) as Jack Robin in Samson Raphaelson's play *The Jazz Singer* (1925). The other two characters are Jack's mother, Sara (played by Dorothy Raymond), and the family friend Yudelson (played by Sam Jaffe). Photo by the White Studio. Courtesy of the Billy Rose Theatre Collection, New York Public Library for the Performing Arts; Astor, Lenox and Tilden Foundations.

4. George Jessel as Jakie Rabinowitz in Samson Raphaelson's play *The Jazz Singer* (1925). Photo courtesy of the Billy Rose Theatre Collection, New York Public Library for the Performing Arts; Astor, Lenox and Tilden Foundations.

Which is the true Jack? At the end, it turns out that both identities are true: he is both a Jew and an American, a cantor and a jazz singer.

Significantly, however, neither identity is *chosen*. In the terms of Werner Sollors' framework for understanding American ethnicity, both are figured as identities of *descent,* not *consent*.[6] Jack's Jewish and theatrical identities are both racial; they already exist within him. So he does not, as others have claimed, use blackface to assimilate to American culture. He uses it as a medium through which he can recognize and acknowledge the divisive, racially determined impulses that motivate him. The play implies that the only way he can achieve success in modern America is to embrace both of his racial identities: the American and the Jewish. Only by effectively combining them in either a jazz song or a cantorial dirge does Jack/Jakie become a powerful theatrical presence. While blackface performance certainly carries the historical and ideological weight other critics have attributed to it, in Raphaelson's play it serves as a marker not of blackness but of race itself.[7] When Jack adopts the blackface mask, he confronts the question of his own racial identity, but not in black and white terms. In the play, the mask does not free Jack to live a carefree and privileged white American life; rather, it reminds him, forcefully and visually, that his sense of self is ultimately racially determined. Despite the fact that Jack is a performer, he has little control over his own self-representation. Racial identity is immutable; it is written on the body and in the blood. Jack's task is simply to discover the "truth" about himself and live it as fully as possible.

Blackface in *The Jazz Singer,* then, is not a marker of modernity. In fact, Raphaelson's play can more easily be read as a nostalgic dramatization of a set of issues, tropes, and ideologies that were quickly fading in 1925. Blackface minstrelsy itself was no longer a popular form by the late 1920s. While minstrel costumes, music, dance styles, and characters still cropped up in revues and occasionally in musical comedy, blackface performance was more often used as a sentimental reference to times gone by. Similarly, the immigrant issues dramatized in the play were also coming to be viewed nostalgically by 1925. Stern, religious Old World fathers and nurturing supportive Old World mothers were recognizable, even clichéd figures by the time the play opened. But most significantly, Jewish comedians in the emerging musical comedy of the late 1920s were contesting the connection between race and performance promoted in *The Jazz Singer,* and were beginning to use blackface—in fact, all sorts of racial caricatures—less as symbols of racial essence than as a celebration of the powerful tool of theatrical self-invention.[8]

Ethnic Theatricality in the Wild West

The sophisticated musical comedy emerging in the late 1920s featured savvy Jewish comedians whose self-consciously theatrical characters had enormous

5. Eddie Cantor's multiple identities in *Whoopee,* as imagined by Alfred Frueh in *The New Yorker.* Copyright © The New Yorker Collection 1929 Alfred Frueh, from Cartoonbank.com. All rights reserved.

freedom to determine their place within the social and cultural framework of the stage community. Unlike Jakie Rabinowitz, who was locked into a racially defined role, these performers could adopt numerous characters in the course of a single play, altering their outward appearance, language, and gestures to suit the moment and thus becoming especially powerful in the world of the musical. They established a special relationship with the ultimate arbiters of theatrical success: the audience beyond the footlights. The performer let the audience members in on his secret, addressed them directly, or often just winked. The audience could share with the performer the pleasure of watching the rest of the cast—the straight men—become increasingly confused.

To American Jews of the 1920s and 1930s this ability to transform oneself was essential both on and off the stage. After the passage of the Johnson-Reed immigration act of 1924, Jews of eastern European descent in particular were shunted into an out-of-favor racial category. The danger of being essentialized, locked into an unwanted racial definition was clear: without control over his or her identity, an American Jew was subject to the illogical and dangerous whims of racial science and public persecution. For this reason many Jews resisted racial definitions and clung tenaciously to the notion that one could become an American simply by adopting American culture, language, and appearance. The musicals of the 1920s and '30s, many of them written and performed by Jews from immigrant backgrounds, suggest a strong opposition to rigid racial categorizations, advocating instead a more fluid conception of identity. Emerging from immigrant families and desperate to become Americans, Jewish performers understood the crucial importance of being able to adopt whatever personae they chose. Their ability to become someone else with a simple change of costume helped them to negotiate the perilous landscape of American racial ideology both onstage and off.

The Wild West was a particularly popular backdrop for musicals of the late 1920s and early 1930s, in part because it highlighted the importance of theatrical role playing in an environment in which identity was inherently unstable. While the West may seem an unlikely setting for such an urban form as the Broadway musical, there are actually striking similarities between the mythical West of the nineteenth century and the mythical city of the early twentieth. According to Daniel Boorstin, "the modern American city [was] to be a twenti-

6. Cartoon by Al Hirschfeld caricaturing performers in *Girl Crazy* (1930). From left to right: William Kent, Ethel Merman, Willie Howard, Ginger Rogers, and Allen Kearns. Hirschfeld's rendering of Howard as Gieber Goldfarb conforms closely to racial stereotypes. Copyright © by Al Hirschfeld. Reproduced by special arrangement with Hirschfeld's exclusive representative, the Margo Feiden Galleries Ltd., New York, www.alhirschfeld.com.

eth-century American West, with its own special vagueness, its own mysteries, its own false promises and booster hopes."[9] Like the streets of New York City, the mythical nineteenth-century American West promised anonymity and freedom from conventional social hierarchies. The newcomer in a Wild West town was like an immigrant—he started fresh. No one knew who he was or where he came from, and so his chances of success depended on how well he inhabited the role he chose.[10] As in the theater, success in the mythical Wild West was largely dependent on the ability to perform. The best shot or the best horseman quickly earned the respect of the local community.

But although both settings called for capable role playing, the specific skills required for success in the West differed significantly from those needed in the immigrant neighborhoods of New York. The mythical West was populated by the mythical Western man: the cowboy. Dubbed by Boorstin "the first American athletic idol," the hero of the Western housed "a strong character in a sturdy physique." His skills included "the agility to dodge Indian arrows, the stamina to ride for days, and the boldness to match fists with all comers."[11] The mythical immigrant in the city, however, was likely to depend more on wit and linguistic facility than on physical talents to become a successful urban American. The two most successful Wild West comedies of the period, Walter Donaldson and Gus Kahn's Ziegfeld extravaganza *Whoopee* (1929) and George and Ira Gershwin's musical comedy *Girl Crazy* (1930), create their humor by placing characters equipped with one set of skills (wit) into situations where the other set (brawn) is required. Both musicals feature specifically Jewish comic characters who depend on their wit to ensure their survival.[12] They are always putting on costumes—Indian headdresses, blackface makeup, women's dresses—to get out of trouble and outwit pursuers. Using these performance techniques, the self-conscious and highly theatrical Jewish characters not only evade their would-be captors but triumph over them.

Underlying the basic comic structure of wit versus brawn is a politics of gender and racial identity. Those who fight to win the West (cowboys) are white, male, and heterosexual. Those who must gain admittance through wit and role playing (Jews) are of dubious sexuality and often appear in nonwhite disguises. Yet because the musicals themselves are urban phenomena, originating on Broadway and not in Arizona or Texas, sympathy always remains with the misplaced (and nonwhite) urbanite, not with the all-American cowboy. The unlikely presence of an urban Jewish immigrant in the Wild West is funny precisely because the Jew, with his superior theatrical skills, is capable of outwitting the cowboys. While the Jewish characters in *Whoopee* and *Girl Crazy* may be threatened by the circumstances in which the plot and setting place them (indeed, they are usually running for their lives), they are never in real danger, because they, and only they, control the boundaries of the performance. And though the cowboy may be able to shoot a gun in the course of the play, the Jewish comic can (and often does) stop the show.[13] Unlike the cowboy, the comic is aware that there is an audience just beyond the boundaries of his story, a plot that must be resolved, and a curtain that must eventually come down.[14]

The musical comedy of the 1920s and 1930s privileged this self-conscious style of performance. Characters in *Whoopee* and *Girl Crazy* have little psychological depth; their boundaries are determined by their role in the plot, the type of songs they sing, and the way they look. Little motivation (if any) is necessary for a number to begin, and numbers are as much about the celebration of the performers' skills as about plot or character development. The musical comedy of the 1920s and 1930s was, in fact, a meritocracy, and Jewish performers (and the characters they played) worked hard to come out ahead.

Based on the Owen Davis play *The Nervous Wreck* (1923), *Whoopee* was created as a musical vehicle for Jewish performer Eddie Cantor, who played Henry Williams, a hypochondriac sent to California to improve his health. The thin fabric of the plot concerns Sally Morgan, daughter of a ranch owner, who is unhappily engaged to marry Sheriff Bob. She has been forbidden by her father to marry her true love, Wanenis, because he is half-Indian. The curtain rises on the wedding scene, with hundreds of chorus girls and cowboys preparing for the big event. At the last minute Sally convinces Henry to help her escape, and they drive away with the sheriff's entire posse hot on their trail. The rest of the play involves Henry and Sally's adventures in outwitting their pursuers. Henry hides from the cowboys by posing as a cook, a blackface minstrel, and an Indian. The pair finally end up in safety on the Indian reservation, where Sally and Wanenis are united after Chief Black Eagle reveals that Wanenis is actually white. Henry likewise finds himself engaged—to his nurse (Miss Custer), a dominatrix with a penchant for weak men—and both couples live happily ever after, "making whoopee." Florenz Ziegfeld presented the highly successful production on Broadway in 1928 and 1929. Among the hit songs from the musical were "Making Whoopee," "Love Me or Leave Me," and "I'm Bringing a Red, Red Rose." MGM produced a film version in 1930 with the same cast, which closely approximates the Broadway style, and added the popular Cantor hit "My Baby Just Cares for Me."[15]

Girl Crazy also enjoyed enormous success in 1930. Originally written for the Jewish comic star Bert Lahr, it ended up starring the Jewish vaudevillian Willie Howard. Both Ginger Rogers and Ethel Merman had their first Broadway hits in the production, Merman alone stopping the show seven times. The orchestra was comprised of an extraordinary ensemble of future jazz greats, including Benny Goodman, Gene Krupa, Glenn Miller, and Jimmy Dorsey. And the score included numerous unforgettable Gershwin tunes, such as "Embraceable You," "Sam and Delilah," "But Not for Me," and "I Got Rhythm."

Like *Whoopee*, *Girl Crazy* covers familiar musical comedy ground. The central character, Danny Churchill, wealthy New York playboy, is sent out West by his father so that he will stop chasing girls. Upon arrival, however, he meets Molly (played by Ginger Rogers), the postmistress and the only girl in the area. He decides to liven up the scene by turning his father's cattle farm into a dude ranch for city folks, complete with a gambling hall and nightclub acts. He imports all of his friends from New York to work on the ranch, and enough women arrive to provide the requisite leggy chorus. He also hires Slick, a gambler, and his wife, Frisco Kate (played by Ethel Merman), to run the nightclub. Various complications ensue in his romance with Molly, who does not think Danny has the right stuff to be a cowboy. But while the whole gang is in Mexico on an evening's romp, the love story falls into place. By the end, Molly is ready to move to New York as Danny's wife and all is well with the world.

Woven into this straightforward plot is another story, that of Gieber Goldfarb. Gieber is the Jewish taxi driver who drives Danny all the way from Broadway and 48th Street to Custerville, Arizona. Finding that he is out of gas, Gieber has to stay in the West with Danny. His encounter with the Wild West is not quite as smooth as Danny's, however. In fact, for most of the play he is running for his life. In a few short hours Gieber appears not only as a taxi driver but also as an Indian, a sheriff, a woman, and a variety of famous performers. Like Eddie Cantor's Henry Williams, Willie Howard's Gieber is a master of disguise and of theatricality. In contrast to the other characters in the play, Gieber (like Henry) perpetually breaks the stage illusion, reminding the audience that they are in a theater and that he is simply an actor playing a role.

Moreover, Gieber assumes that those around him are also performers. In the first scene the cowboys prepare to lynch Gieber, who insists that they are just actors and that he has stumbled onto the set of a Hollywood Western.[16] So self-conscious is Gieber about his position as an actor in a theater that he refuses to acknowledge the reality of danger: "Say, you fellers can't kid *me*. That shootin' wasn't on the level. I know you're just a bunch of movie actors out on location. The west ain't like this really. . . . Yeah . . . I'll bet there ain't one of you'se hams that knows which end a gun shoots from." The cowboys become even more menacing and try to tie Gieber's hands. Gieber still refuses to believe they are for real, and also throws in a joke about his Jewishness: "You can't tie my hands. . . . Ain't this gonna be a talking picture? How can I work in it?" Gieber's (supposed) inability to talk without his hands sets him apart from the reticent cowboys, and the fact that they do not get the joke sets up an important device that operates throughout the play. Gieber's humor is for the audience; the cowboys (who never get the jokes) serve as straight men. Despite the fact that they hold Gieber at gunpoint, it is Gieber who has the ear of the audience and hence the upper hand on the stage.

Both Gieber and Henry establish their Jewishness through self-conscious comic asides to the audience. When Wanenis, explaining the effort he has made to assimilate to white culture, tells Henry that he has "studied the ways" of Henry's "race" and attended its schools, Henry exclaims, "An Indian in a Hebrew School!" Wanenis does not respond, but we can assume that the audience did.[17] When in Act 2 Henry is invited to smoke a peace pipe with Chief Black Eagle, he sings (to the tune of "Old Man River") "Old Black Eagle and old man Siegal," and later, when the chief offers to make him an Indian, Henry exclaims, "Big Chief Izzy Horowitz!"[18] Dressed as an Indian and bargaining with a tourist over the price of a blanket, Henry begins haggling in Yiddish and ends by dancing and singing an "Indian melody" which sounds more like a Hasidic niggun. Neither Black Eagle nor the tourist remarks on Henry's antics; indeed, it seems unlikely they would recognize a Jew, much less a Jewish joke. His Jewishness is a "private" joke for the audience. Ironically, Henry is more intimate with the two thousand members of the general public who have purchased tickets for the show than with the only other person on stage, with whom he is having an apparently private conversation.

Gieber, likewise, plays his Jewishness for laughs from the audience. He complains about a (clearly) non-Jewish girl who is following him around, claiming "his family would never allow it," and when Danny says "See you in church," Gieber responds, "We two will never meet in the same church!" Later in Act 1, as he is racing away from some cowboys who want to kill him, Gieber pauses long enough for the following interchange with Slick, the gambler:

GIEBER: I'm near starved.
SLICK: You want something to eat? Here's a ham sandwich.
GIEBER: [*grabbing sandwich from* SLICK *and starting to eat*] I can't stand the sight of ham.
SLICK: What are you eating it for, then?
GIEBER: I want to get it out of my sight.

These comic references to Hebrew school, intermarriage, different churches, Yiddish language and music, and Jewish dietary laws leave no doubt about the Jewish identity of the characters and also indicate that Broadway audiences of the late 1920s and early 1930s were comfortable and familiar with Jewish ethnic humor and Jewish characters on the stage.[19]

Gieber's and Henry's Jewishness sets them apart from the other characters and determines their courses of action in the plays. The only Jews in a world of cowboys and Indians, Henry and Gieber are always running for their lives, although they have committed no crime. In *Whoopee*, Sally dupes Henry Williams into helping her escape her impending marriage. She tells him that Sheriff Bob has decided on an elopement and asks Henry to drive her to the station, leaving a note for the sheriff saying that she has eloped with Henry. The sheriff, of course, takes off in hot pursuit. Similarly, in *Girl Crazy*, even before Gieber's first entrance, shots are heard offstage. Gieber races on, pursued by

an angry pack of cowboys who falsely accuse him of killing the sheriff. Even when he convinces them that he did no such thing, they soon manufacture other reasons for chasing him. When Gieber accidentally is elected sheriff himself, he unwittingly makes enemies of the meanest thugs in the county. The anarchy and wide-open spaces of the mythical West are supposed to offer freedom from the constrictions of the city, but for these Jewish characters, the West is a place of danger while the city represents safety. Gieber asks the cowboys, as they prepare to lynch him in the first scene, "So *this* is God's country?" Clearly, it is not *Gieber's* God's country.

From the moment they arrive in the West, Gieber and Henry find themselves at odds with the locals. They do not speak the same language or observe the same customs. They are constantly getting into trouble with those who are bigger and stronger, and who are better shots. But Gieber and Henry do not follow the expected path of assimilation by trying to blend into this powerful white majority of cowboys and ranchers. Rather, Gieber and Henry escape their pursuers—ironically, brilliantly—by becoming women, blacks, and Indians: members of the disempowered groups inhabiting the Western landscape.[20] They adopt disguises that in the world of the play render them powerless, and hence unworthy of notice. But those same disguises also make them distinctly *noticeable* to the audience, which is in on the joke.

Omitted from historical narratives of the West or simplified using stereotypical representations, these groups exist only as types, not as individuals. Gieber and Henry use the very invisibility of individuals within these groups as a refuge.[21] In dressing as women, for example, Gieber and Henry (temporarily) lose their specificity as Jewish characters and become anonymous sexualized objects. On the musical stage, the function of a Jew was to connote difference: there was always only one Jew, almost always a man, and he was funny because he was so different from the others on stage. In contrast, the function of a woman on the Broadway stage, particularly in Ziegfeld productions, was to connote sex. The chorus line of women in *Whoopee, Girl Crazy,* and a host of other musicals promoted the sexiness of scores of identical legs, arms, breasts, and faces moving in synchronized rhythm.[22] In adopting the appearance of a black or an Indian, Gieber and Henry hide behind the sameness of racial typing, invoking the prejudiced canard of racial otherness: "They all look the same." In *The Jazz Singer* blackness allows Jack to acknowledge and use his Jewishness, but in these plays, once the Jew dons the costume of the black minstrel or Indian chief, he is indistinguishable from other blacks or Indians. Paradoxically, in *Whoopee* and *Girl Crazy* a Jew can fade into the scenery if he "becomes" black. Jewish difference is erased in this case (albeit temporarily) by performing the sameness of difference. By disguising himself as an Indian or a black minstrel, then, the Jew joins an American group that, although oppressed, at least belongs in the West. The blackface mask or Indian headdress offers invisibility, and hence momentary security—a condition marginally preferable to that of the foreigner: the (one and only) Jew.

Jewish male comics regularly appeared in drag on the musical comedy stage. This association of Jewish men with femininity must be read in the context of the complex history of European antisemitic and racialist rhetoric. "Historically," Daniel Boyarin writes, "the Jewish male is, from the point of view of dominant European culture, a sort of woman." By "woman" he does not mean "a set of characteristics, traits, behaviors that are essentially female" but rather "a set of performances that are culturally read as non-male within a given historical culture."[23] Maleness according to these terms is constituted by physical strength, assertiveness, courage, and directness. By contrast, physical weakness, illness, and passive forms of gaining power—dissimulation, intrigues, tricks, and lying—constitute the feminine.[24] Boyarin traces this gendered understanding of Jewishness as far back as the Roman era, when, he claims, the rabbis defined *themselves* as feminized as a way of resisting a hypermasculine and oppressive Roman state. Sander Gilman shows how connections between Jewishness and femininity which had been developing over the centuries coalesced in the rabidly antisemitic Germany of the late nineteenth century. Infected by the racialist (and sexist) thinking of the times, both Jews and non-Jews accepted the assumption that Jewish men (or, more specifically, eastern European Jewish men) were closely linked to the feminine and that this linkage was necessarily negative. A highly precise German scientific and medical discourse explained Jewish difference in terms of sexuality. Circumcision, in fact, became the biological marker of the Jewish man's feminized state.[25] Otto Weininger, a deeply self-hating baptized Jew, directly articulated connections between Jewishness and the feminine. In his treatise *Geschlecht und Charakter* (Sex and Character; 1903), he established a psychological model that took the Aryan/masculine psyche as one of its two poles and the Jewish/feminine psyche as the other.[26] According to this discourse, the Jewish male inhabits a liminal state, not quite a woman but also not fully male. "Jewish males are 'gender-benders,'" Gilman writes. "They exist between the conventional categories of 'normal' (and normative) sexuality, just as they exist between the categories of European national identity and ethnopsychology."[27]

In *Whoopee,* Cantor's portrayal of Henry Williams provides a surprisingly literal illustration of the feminized Jewish man. He is weak, cowardly, and afraid of guns. When Sally explains to Henry why she has run away, Henry cannot understand why she has chosen him as her escort:

SALLY: I did it because I thought you would help me. I thought you were brave.
HENRY: I'm not brave. I can't even help myself.

And when Sally produces a gun, Henry exclaims: "Put it away! I can't stand the sight of guns. I hate guns. Put it away. I don't like guns. Even when somebody says, 'son of a gun,' I almost faint."

Henry is always taking his temperature, popping pills, and explaining that he has come to California for his health. Yet his illnesses are vague, and his nurse insists repeatedly that he is a hypochondriac:

> HENRY: Miss Custer, I don't think I'll be troubling you much longer.
> NURSE: Oh, don't talk like that Henry. When you came West a year ago,
>   you may have been sick then, but now you're as healthy as I am.
> HENRY: Is that good?
> NURSE: There's really nothing the matter with you.
> HENRY: Nothing the matt— . . . What about the pain around my heart?
> NURSE: Oh, that'll go away!
> HENRY: Yeah, and I'll go with it.

Henry's ailment is largely psychological. A man who worries incessantly about his health and always needs someone to take care of him is, in the Western landscape, hardly a man at all. In fact, worrying about one's health (to the point of hysteria) is even more feminizing than poor health itself. As Gilman points out, in the late nineteenth century, hysteria and other neuroses were often attributed not only to women but also to Jewish men. "While it is clear that women still are the predominant sufferers from the disease, it is evident . . . that there is a clear 'feminization' of the male Jew in the context of the occurrence of hysteria."[28] Furthermore, conditions in the United States supposedly made the male Jew particularly susceptible to neurosis. According to Freud's teacher, Moriz Benedikt, the struggle for life in American capitalist cities led to Jewish male hysteria: "Mental anxiety and worry are the most frequent causes of mental breakdown [among Jews]. They are all excitable and live excitable lives, being constantly under the high pressure of business in town."[29] The excessively excitable Henry Williams has heeded Dr. Benedikt's diagnosis, going West to escape the pressures of the city and be cured of his feminizing ailments.

Henry's illness also seems to be directly related to his sexual organs, although again he is vague on the subject. To prove his ill health, he makes many references to his "operation":

> NURSE: Henry, you're just a hypochondriac!
> HENRY: Yeah, am I? How would you like to see my operation? [HENRY
>   rises, lifts shirt and begins to unbutton pants]
> NURSE: No! No! Sit down.

Nurse Custer's shock seems to indicate that the nature of Henry's "operation" is best not revealed, to her or anyone. Henry never specifies what type of operation he has had, but it clearly is related to something in his pants. He later gets involved in an altercation with a wealthy ranch owner named Underwood, and they begin comparing ailments in a sexually charged game of one-upmanship. When Underwood mentions the scar from his operation, Henry replies: "You think you've got a scar? I'm going to show you something, my dear man, that will amaze you. . . . Now look down here [*pulling open his pants*]. [*Underwood looks in amazement.*] Now let me take a look at yours [*Henry looks down Underwood's pants*]." As the play progresses, references to Henry's operation become increasingly bawdy. At the conclusion, when Henry and Nurse Custer are finally engaged, Henry sings joyfully of the pleasure his "operation" will give to his intended:

> My baby don't care for shows
> My baby don't care for clothes
> My baby just cares for me!
> My baby just loves those consultations,
> And how she enjoys my operation!

What sort of operation might affect Henry's sexuality and be evident from a glance inside his pants? Clearly, it was a circumcision.

Gilman writes at length on the questionable gender identity of the circumcised male, according to nineteenth-century medical discourse: "There is an anatomical (read: sexual) distinction which sets the male Jew apart from other 'males.' It is the practice of circumcision which defines the body of the male Jew, at least within the discourse of science. . . . The act of circumcision sets the Jewish male apart (in that he is no longer fully a male)."[30] In having an operation on his penis, Henry (as a male Jew) has become less of a man. He goes West to be "cured" of his problem, but he also brings the problem with him. In the opening number, for example, he has convinced the sheriff's friends to dress in tuxedos for the wedding. They look ridiculous and uncomfortable, and the other cowboys laugh at the deputies for dressing like dandies. The deputies upbraid Henry for embarrassing them:

DEPUTY: You dressed us up like this, didn't you?
HENRY: Yes, well, I hope you appreciate it.
DEPUTY: To show you how much we 'preciate it, we gonna dress you up.
HENRY: But I don't want to be dressed up! [*They carry* HENRY *away*]

When Henry next appears, he is dressed in a pair of Nurse Custer's bloomers which have prickly cacti hanging all over them. The deputies have taken their revenge by exposing Henry's feminized state quite literally (and distancing themselves from it at the same time). They have dressed him in women's underwear and then adorned him with that which he supposedly lacks: large *prick*ly phalluses.

Henry remains in this costume throughout the next scene, in which he and Wanenis discuss Wanenis' problems with Sally. Every time Henry tries to sit down, a cactus pricks him in the rear end and he springs up again. This apparently silly joke of *being pricked in the rear* evokes a third characteristic of the nineteenth-century medicalized Jewish male described by Gilman: Jewish men were considered not only feminized but also more likely to be homosexual. German physician Moses Julius Gutmann observed: "Most frequently they [Jews] are sexual neurasthenics. Above all, the number of Jewish homosexuals is extraordinarily high."[31] Allusions to homosexual sex in *Whoopee* are blatant and pervasive. In Henry's interchange with Wanenis, which is ostensibly about Wanenis' heterosexual obsession with Sally, Henry continually interjects comic bits about the cacti on his pants. He says to Wanenis, "You think you have problems. . . . [*turning around*] Look where cactus is growing! [*tries to sit and jumps up*] Oh!" When Henry makes a joke at Wanenis' expense, he then turns to him to hug him. Just before they touch, Henry shouts "Ow!" and springs up. He has been pricked once again.

The rest of the play is rife with allusions to Henry's implied homosexuality. When Henry and Underwood first meet, Henry is holding him at gunpoint. Henry directs Underwood to start his car, but the language is full of double entendre:

HENRY: Crank my flivver!
UNDERWOOD: What? Me crank a flivver?
HENRY: Go on, you old crank.
UNDERWOOD: I'm a sick man!
HENRY: *You're* sick! I'd love to show you my operation! [*begins to undo his pants, then stops*] Go ahead, crank it!

References to sickness become clear allusions to homosexuality. In the later scene with Underwood their mutual comparison of "operations" leads to a long, involved bit in which the two of them roll around together on the floor, looking into each other's pants. When they finally end up seated on the bench again, where they began, Underwood says, panting and out of breath, "Yes, sir, my boy, that is some operation!"

Henry's "illness" prevents him from engaging in heterosexual sex. Two women propose to him in the course of the first act. In response to Nurse Custer's amorous approaches, Henry replies, "Why do you make overtures to me when I need intermission so badly? Miss Custer, I couldn't marry you. I'm too delicate." Trapped on a mountainside in a broken-down car, Sally also proposes to Henry:

SALLY: Why don't you marry me and take me East?
HENRY: It's impossible!

SALLY: You know, we wouldn't really have to be man and wife. Secretly, we could be just good friends. (1–36)

Sally accuses Henry of never having been in love, and he replies with a song. The song tells of an old flame who left him because "she turned out to be the girlfriend of a boyfriend of mine."

Henry's relationship with Nurse Custer is apparently heterosexual. Yet the gender identity of both characters is unstable. In Nurse Custer's big production number with the cowboys her demeanor is that of an alluring woman, but whenever she appears with Henry she plays the butch to his femme. Claiming she "has a positive passion for a weak man," she makes an aggressive pass at him:

NURSE: Oh, look in my eyes Henry. Don't you know I love you?
HENRY: Oh, Miss Custer.
NURSE: [*climbing on top of him on the bench*] Do you know that I'm sure you love me?
HENRY: Oh please, Miss Custer.
NURSE: Oh, Henry don't you know how I feel? [*He stands on bench to get away. She picks him up*] Henry, marry me!
HENRY: Put me down! Put me down!

If Henry is feminized, Nurse Custer is clearly masculinized. In addition to being named after the brutal army general and Indian slayer, she likewise cross-dresses. For reasons that are never made clear, in Act 2 Nurse Custer appears in a cowboy outfit, with chaps, a Stetson, and a mustache. Angry with Henry for running away with Sally, she has eagerly joined the posse that is out to catch him. She wanders into the inn where Henry has been employed as a cook and nails up a "Wanted" poster of Henry:

HENRY: [*examining poster*] $500 reward . . . [*pretending to be Greek, singing*] O solo mio! O solo mio!
NURSE: [*immediately recognizing him*] Hey, who are you?
HENRY: Me work here. Me Greek. You put that sign up?
NURSE: Yeah, and I'm hungry to get that guy.
HENRY: You hungry? I'll fix you up one roast beef, one buttered toast, one strawberry pie.

Once again, Henry and Nurse Custer's gender roles are reversed, this time literally. The nurse is dressed as a cowboy. Henry is dressed as a cook, and offers to make dinner for the "cowboy." He momentarily poses as a "Greek," a barely coded homosexual reference. While a cook is not necessarily a woman's role, in this play the gender of the role is specifically noted. In the scene just before Henry's arrival at the inn, two farmhands are lamenting the disappearance of the cook and are trying to prepare breakfast:

MORT: [*removing blackened pan from oven*] Boy, that's terrible.
ANDY: Well, I told you I ain't no cook. Say, why don't *you* try it?
MORT: There ain't nothin' female about *me*.

There is obviously something female about Henry. Nurse Custer desperately wants to find out if Henry loves Sally. When Henry insists that he does not, she is overjoyed:

NURSE: Oh, I could kiss you for that [*throws arms around him*].
HENRY: [*still pretending he doesn't recognize her*] What do you want to
    kiss me for? What kind of a cowboy are you?
NURSE: [*removing hat*] Don't you know me?

Though she removes her hat, Nurse remains in her cowboy clothes for most of the rest of the play.[32] Henry eventually accepts her as his mate only after he has come to view her as a cowboy.

Gieber's drag scene in *Girl Crazy* also aptly illustrates the feminized Jewish male, although Gieber never takes his feminization as far as Henry does. While waiting for a train out of town, Gieber sees the bad guys Lank and Pete approach, hot on his trail. Gieber decides to hide in the bathroom. The script reads: "He rushes to door R. marked 'Men.' This door is locked, so he is compelled to hide in door marked 'Ladies.'" Gieber is literally "locked out" of the "right" door—the one to the men's room. Yet unlike Henry, who relishes his feminized state, Gieber wants access to traditional male identity, but it is unavailable to him. Pursued by figures who are models of the very manhood he cannot acquire, he must hide in the inner sanctum of femininity: the ladies' room. Quickly assessing his situation, Gieber steals a woman's clothes and reappears in dress and veil. By appearing in drag he loses his identity as *the* Jew Gieber Goldfarb (who is "wanted" by the usurping sheriff, Lank) and acquires the status of *a* woman, *any* woman (who is wanted by all men). Pete and Lank are still suspicious, though, so Gieber must complicate and develop his new role. In order to divert the men, Gieber simpers, flirts, and implies that he is a prostitute. As the scene heats up, Gieber gets increasingly nervous that he will either be found out or forced into a homosexual encounter. Finally, attempting to escape, he is literally exposed: he loses his dress and runs off in his undershorts.

For both Henry and Gieber, feminization is a means of escaping from trouble. Henry uses his "sickness" to excuse himself for not having the appropriate characteristics of a Western male: a love of guns and a yen for women. Gieber dresses in drag in order to fool his would-be captors. This choice seemingly disempowers them. Why would a man choose to adopt the mask of a woman in a world in which men clearly hold the reins? Or do they hold the reins? While the Western may privilege the man, the musical privileges the woman. As D. A. Miller has argued, the "feminine gender" guarantees "easy, almost automatic access to the musical stage."[33] The unwritten law of the musical theater ordains that "though male and female alike may and indeed must appear on the musical stage, they are not equally welcome there: the female performer will always enjoy the advantage of also being thought to *represent* this stage, as its sign, its celebrant, its essence, and its glory; while the male tends to be suffered on condition that, by the inferiority or subjection of his own talents, he assist the enhancement of hers."[34] The star of a musical, as we have come to understand her, is therefore almost always female, as Miller catalogues them: "(Ethel) Merman, (Mary) Martin, (Carol) Channing, (Angela) Lansbury, (Julie) Andrews, (Gwen) Verdon, (Elaine) Stritch, (Patti) LuPone, (Bernadette) Peters."[35]

While the stories of *Girl Crazy* and *Whoopee* use all of the cues and clichés of traditional Westerns, the fact that they are musicals (as opposed to action films or dime novels) alters the power relations within the genre. Miller, writing about Louise in *Gypsy,* notes that despite the fact that she dresses as a boy, she does not gain the advantages of doing so which accrue to other cross-dressers of the drama, like Portia and Viola: "What good are, say, all a boy's advantages at school if she doesn't go to school? Or the catcher's mitt she is stupidly encumbered with on her birthday when her world gives out status according to how well one plays the boards of a stage?"[36] Supporting Miller's argument is the fact that the production numbers in *Girl Crazy* were built around the talents of two female stars: Ethel Merman and Ginger Rogers. And the musical numbers in *Whoopee,* as in all Ziegfeld musicals, were constructed to showcase the main attraction of the evening: the Ziegfeld girls. But both plays were also written specifically for Jewish male comics (Eddie Cantor, Bert Lahr, and Willie Howard), whom Miller does not explicitly discuss in his argument. As Miller points out, the leading male parts in most musicals are throwaways: "Every female who enters the star spot is paired with a less brightly lit male figure, ridiculous or pathetic."[37] Any number of competent actors could play Wanenis or Danny Churchill in *Girl Crazy,* but the female leads required powerhouses like Merman and Rogers. Yet what Miller does not notice is that the comic also plays the "female" star role, both metaphorically and sometimes literally, and that he too is paired with less brightly lit figures—the *straight* men against whom his popularity is defined.[38] Henry's star shines brighter as he ridicules Underwood and Sheriff Bob. Gieber uses the stupid and pathetic Lank and Pete as the objects of his humor.

So taking on the role of a woman is, for Henry and Gieber, not necessarily disempowering in this context. In fact, it is the only way truly to gain the power accorded to center stage. The gendered power dynamics of the musical are particularly relevant in a Ziegfeld production like *Whoopee,* for, as Miller writes,

> This is a regime that promulgates a spectacle performed by Beautiful Girls and be-held by an Invisible Man whose desire (and whose power to have a theatre devoted to arousing it) they objectify. In other words, however, this is a regime in which the same man who enjoys the right to orient the spectacle also incurs the duty, if not quite to disappear from it (absolute renunciation being incompatible with plot), at any rate to forgo, in favor of secondary roles, that pride of place which he may freely take in almost every other sphere.[39]

How, then, can Eddie Cantor, clearly a man, hold the star's place in a Ziegfeld musical? By feminizing himself. And Willie Howard, the creator of Gieber Goldfarb, who had the unenviable task of sharing the boards with Ethel Merman, was always jockeying for center stage, at times by actually dressing in drag. In creating their characters, Cantor and Howard had to contend with the stereotype of the feminized Jewish man, which was often attached to them by the antisemitism of the era. Because they were actors in musicals, however, they did not have to allow the stereotype to disempower them; instead, they manipulated it to their own benefit. Like the rabbis of ancient Rome whom Boyarin writes about, Cantor and Howard reject the macho image of the cowboy (which would force them to disappear into the unenviable role of straight man) and instead adopt a feminized persona that allows them literally to dance circles around the "real" cowboys with whom they share the stage.

Dressing in drag (or playing the feminized man) offers its advantages to those eager to escape trouble and capture center stage. Adopting the identi-ties of disempowered racial groups similarly offers Henry and Gieber unlikely empowering safe havens. Like Gieber, who had to choose between bathrooms, Henry is also forced into a hiding spot that suggests a seemingly undesirable disguise. As Sheriff Bob enters the inn where Henry has been hired as a cook, Henry jumps into the stove. A few moments later the stove explodes and Henry pops out, in full blackface. Like Lank and Pete, the sheriff smells a rat, and like Gieber, Henry goes into his act in order to divert them. He plays a shuffling minstrel stereotype, singing and tapping his way through "My Baby Just Cares for Me." So impressed are the cowboys that Henry offers an encore. But he is discovered when a piece of his body is exposed: forgetting about his disguise for a moment while washing his hands, he reveals his white skin and once again has to race off in search of a new identity. The blackface makeup is empowering in this context for two reasons. First, because the blackface is re-moved during the course of the play, the disguise reinforces the fact that the wearer is white. Second, blackface allows the wearer to perform the ragtime or jazz songs that are the central idiom of the musical stage of the period, and thus gives the comedian the opportunity to dominate center stage.

7. Eddie Cantor and his shadow in *Whoopee,* ca. 1929. Photo by the Vandamm Studio. Courtesy of the Billy Rose Theatre Collection, New York Public Library for the Performing Arts.

★ ★

The most effective and extended racial disguises Gieber and Henry adopt, though, are those of Indians. When Gieber's erstwhile girlfriend Patsy offers him an old Indian outfit, he jumps at the opportunity to escape discovery by the bad guys and adopts the role of "Big Chief Push-in-the-Face."[40] Henry likewise hides out on the Indian reservation in a red union suit (to indicate his "red" skin) and a full headdress and manages to thoroughly fool Underwood,

8. Eddie Cantor as Henry Williams in Indian disguise, with Jeanette Reade as Nurse Custer. Museum of the City of New York.

★ ★

who unwittingly bargains with Henry for souvenirs for his daughter. Throughout both musicals, the association between Jews and Indians is direct and self-conscious. In *Whoopee,* Indians become Jews and Jews become Indians. As Henry and Sally drive into the reservation, an Indian stops them, saying "Hoy!" Henry comments, "A Jewish traffic cop!" Chief Black Eagle decides to adopt Henry into the tribe. Henry becomes Chief Izzy Horowitz by smoking a peace pipe and dressing in Indian clothes. His disguise is apparently convincing— Underwood does not recognize him even when Henry begins bargaining in Yiddish. The only one who does recognize him is Nurse Custer, who asks him why he is wearing red underwear and feathers. Henry replies that he is a fireman, and then, indicating that his Jewishness has been exposed, explains, "Here is my hook [pointing to his nose] and ladder."

In *Girl Crazy,* the movement between Jews and Indians is also self-consciously fluid. While Gieber is upstairs changing into his costume, Chief Eagle Rock appears. The playwrights make an effort to distinguish between Eagle Rock and the soon-to-appear Gieber by remarking in the stage directions: "Producers, please note, Eagle Rock must be a *real* Indian." Eagle Rock is simply dressed, speaks perfect English, and has just returned from college. When Gieber enters he assumes the pose not of a "real" Indian but of a stage Indian who wears a full headdress, whoops loudly, and speaks a strange gibberish

9. Gieber Goldfarb (Willie Howard) with Chief Eagle Rock, the "real" Indian, played by Chief Rivers. Photo by the White Studio. Courtesy of the Billy Rose Theatre Collection, New York Public Library for the Performing Arts; Astor, Lenox and Tilden Foundations.

that confuses Eagle Rock thoroughly. The two "Indians" try a number of languages before Gieber finally introduces himself in Yiddish. This works, Eagle Rock responds, and the two exit speaking animatedly.

Both the real Indian and the disguised Indian turn out to be Jews, or at least to be intimately knowledgeable about Jews. This joke reveals the close connection between Jewish and Indian characters on the American stage in the early twentieth century. It also points satirically to the use of Jews in Hollywood Westerns: more often than not, one would find Jewish actors underneath the feathers and warpaint (this joke has reappeared on a regular basis, perhaps most famously in Mel Brooks's *Blazing Saddles*). Connections between the two groups extend even further: Jews not only dressed up as Indians in stage and film Westerns, but they also served similar functions within the plot.

In the early and middle nineteenth century, plays featuring Indian characters were popular entertainment on America's stages. A central figure was an older Indian chief who generally died by the end of the play. Before expiring, he often gave his blessing to a young white couple who wanted to be married in opposition to their parents' wishes. In this way the Indian was responsible for ensuring that the romantic match succeeded and that the play reached its necessary resolution.[41] Later in the century the Indian character became humorous rather than melancholy, and, as Werner Sollors notes, the stereotype was urbanized to appeal to multiethnic immigrant audiences.[42] But the basic function of the Indian remained: to act as a protector of the romantic young couple and ensure their marriage before the end of the play. In *Whoopee* and *Girl Crazy,* this function is picked up by the Jewish comic dressed as an Indian.

Henry Williams is at first duped into helping Sally. But as the play proceeds, he increasingly takes responsibility for her happiness. Sally's father, Mr. Morgan, has forbidden her to marry her true love, Wanenis, because he is part Indian. He has instead promised her to Sheriff Bob, a decidedly unpleasant alternative. Sally decides to run away and engages Henry's services as driver. Henry does not know at first what he is getting into, and is quite angry with Sally when he realizes the situation in which she has placed him. But by the end of the first act he willingly accepts full responsibility for Sally's happiness. Escaping from Underwood's ranch and pursued by a posse, Henry takes Sally with him. They drive to the Indian reservation, where both will be safe and where Sally will be able to marry Wanenis. Though it is the revelation that Wanenis is actually white which finally clinches the match, Henry's assistance has created the conditions in which the revelation can occur.

In *Girl Crazy* the obstacle between Molly and Danny is not specifically parental disapproval but rather regional differences: she cannot believe he will ever be a cowboy, and he wants ultimately to return to New York City. To spite Danny, Molly takes off for Mexico with his old rival, Sam Mason. Gieber intervenes, and though he is no longer dressed as an Indian at this point, he fulfills the "Indian" function, serving as the theatrical linchpin who ensures that the main characters end up in each other's arms. While running for his own life, Gieber still takes the time to attend to the troubles of Molly and Danny's love affair:

MOLLY: I'm so depressed.
GIEBER: Ah, you're crazy. Hoover said the depression was over.
MOLLY: I can't help it. I've found out I'm in love and it's too late.
GIEBER: It's never too late—look at that Turk 156 years old.
MOLLY: I mean it's too late because Danny—oh, what's the use.
GIEBER: So now you're cryin' because you think he might like you better with a red nose.
MOLLY: I s'pose I look awful.
GIEBER: Terrible. . . . Can't you smile a little? Come on—try.

Gieber tries to cheer her up with humor, but she responds by singing tearfully:

> They're writing songs of love,
>   But not for me;
> A lucky star's above,
>   But not for me.
> With love to lead the way
>   I've found more skies of gray
> Than any Russian play
>   Could guarantee.

Unwilling to give in to Molly's melancholy, Gieber appropriates her words, launching into one of the most extraordinary theatrical moments in the play. At first he simply repeats one verse of Molly's song back to her, but she only cries harder. So he marshals all of his resources:

GIEBER: Come on, Molly, cheer up. Pretend I'm Maurice Chevalier, that soldier moving picture actor, and he was singing the same song to you, like this.
[*He sings one chorus to her as Chevalier would sing it.*]
[MOLLY *smiles, brightens up—at finish they both exit stage L.* GIEBER *and* MOLLY *return for encore*]
Well, Molly, if you don't like Maurice Chevalier singing, it may be if I sing it the way Jolson would sing it, you'd like it better.
[*Sings a chorus as Jolson would sing it*]
They exit at finish. They return again. GIEBER *repeats same business— singing as Eddie Cantor would sing it. They exit at finish.*

Enter KATE *and* SLICK. *If necessary,* GIEBER *and* MOLLY *return*—GIEBER *sings one chorus as Georgie Jessel would sing it.*

The levels of role playing in this scene are dizzying. At one point, Jewish vaudevillian Willie Howard is playing Jewish cab driver Gieber Goldfarb playing Jewish performer Al Jolson playing a black jazz singer. But Gieber does not stop there—he utterly destroys the integrity of the *Girl Crazy* world in favor of an orgy of self-invention, performing one impression after another.[43] Needless to say, his ploy is successful and Molly finally "brightens up."[44] Only moments later, Danny is suspected of assaulting Sam Mason, and Gieber and Molly plot to get him safely out of Mexico. Gieber then enables Molly and Danny to share a freight train back to Custerville together. As the last act draws to a close, Danny finally asks Molly to marry him and Gieber seconds the motion.

For the Jews writing and performing in Broadway musicals in the 1920s and 1930s, the choice to align themselves with Indian stereotypes seems a curious one. These Jewish artists (or their parents) had left Europe in order to escape the sort of ghettoization and subjugation to which Native Americans in the United States fell victim. In these decades, Jews were eager to acculturate to the ways of white Americans. Why associate themselves with such a marginalized group? It turns out that, contrary to what one might expect, association with Indians had hidden advantages in early twentieth-century America. Just as male Jewish performers twisted the feminization stereotype to meet their needs, so they manipulated racial otherness as a way of gaining not marginality but centrality.[45]

In the 1920s and 1930s, Indians were increasingly perceived not as aliens but as the first Americans and were being claimed as the "forefathers" of true Americans. Zane Grey, author of countless Western novels, wrote that the Indian "by every right and law and heritage" was "the first and best blood of America."[46] Why was it that Indians could become Americans, but eastern and southern Europeans could not? In much the same way that Jack Robin was already a Hebrew and a jazz singer, Indians did not need to assimilate—they simply *were* Americans already.[47] Both the Johnson Act of 1924, which limited immigration, and the Citizenship Act of 1924, which declared all Indians citizens, were, according to Walter Benn Michaels, designed "to keep people from *becoming* citizens":

> The Johnson Act guaranteed that aliens would not become citizens by putting a halt to mass immigration; the Citizenship Act guaranteed that Indians would not become citizens by declaring that they already were citizens. Both acts, that is, participated in a recasting of American citizenship, changing it from a status that could be achieved through one's own actions (immigrating, becoming "civilized," getting "naturalized") to a status that could better be understood as inherited.[48]

10. Willie Howard as Gieber (center) with the romantic leads John McGowan as Danny and Ginger Rogers as Molly, in *Girl Crazy.* Image from Elks Magazine, 1930. Museum of the City of New York.

Jews were (for obvious reasons) unwilling to forgo the possibility of "becoming" American by assimilation—indeed, they continued to celebrate the freedoms associated with performing identity on the musical stage throughout this period. Yet they also had to confront an increasingly racialist culture that had defined them as biologically (and hence immutably) alien. As one method of countering this prejudice, Jews strove to associate themselves with the founding myths of America—to prove that they, like the Indians, were *already* American and that America was *already* Jewish.[49] They supported historians and societies that argued that Columbus was a Jew, that the Puritans were actually a Hebraic sect, and that the Indians were the Ten Lost Tribes of Israel.[50] Oscar Straus, American diplomat and founder of the American Jewish Historical Society, undertook research in the 1890s to show that Jews accompanied Columbus on his voyage to America. He hoped that if he could prove the presence of Jews on Columbus' ships, "this fact would be an answer for all time to come to antisemitic tendencies in this country."[51] By the 1930s, as Jonathan Sarna has pointed out, belief in the theory that Columbus *himself* was a closeted Jew was widespread, clearly intended as an antidote to rising nativism in America.[52]

The idea that the Indians were the Ten Lost Tribes also has a long history.[53]

In 1651 Menasseh ben Israel put forth the theory in his pamphlet "Mikveh Yisrael" (The Hope of Israel). In 1837 the American Jewish public figure Mordecai Manuel Noah delivered an important lecture on the topic, alluding to common customs and common aspects of language. As Sarna points out, Noah "understood that if the Jews and Indians were one people, the Jews were then both 'the first people in the old world'—the ancestors of Christianity—and 'the rightful inheritors of the new.' Jews could claim proudly, 'we were here first.'"[54] Regarding links between the ancient Hebrews and Puritans, Sarna notes: "Later generations of Jews, following the Puritans themselves, placed heavier emphasis on this alleged Hebraic character. One motivation for the extraordinary number of these uncritical comparisons, I think, was the unconscious premise that whoever rejected the Jews, rejected the Puritan Fathers who made this country great."[55] By becoming Indians (or having Columbus, the Puritans, and the Indians become Jews), Jews could claim to be original "native" Americans, with all of the privileges accorded this position.

In adopting the identity of the Indian on the musical stage, the Jewish comic not only takes on the Indian's "first American" status, but fulfills an essential function in the comic plot: he ensures that romantic (New World) love triumphs. This role further enmeshes the Jewish character in a profoundly American system—indeed, it makes the Jew the keeper and protector of that system. As Werner Sollors argues, representation of romantic matches on the American stage is closely intertwined with the belief in a freely elected democratic government. Just as government by descent (aristocracy, royalty) is abandoned in the New World in favor of a government of consent (of the people, by the people, for the people), so Old World family-arranged marriages are abandoned in the New World in favor of romantic matches freely chosen: "American allegiance, the very concept of citizenship developed in the revolutionary period, was—like love—based on consent, not on descent, which further blended the rhetoric of America with the language of love and the concept of romantic love with American identity."[56] In the nineteenth century, Indian characters in the drama legitimated the idea of democracy by standing in as parental figures for the young couple in love and bestowing their blessings (or curses). If the Indian blessed a romantic union between two young white people, these white people became his chosen successors and he became their adoptive ancestor. "Indian plays" serve, in Sollors' reading, as a national allegory: the young lovers "received a 'legitimate' blessing for their decision to break out of the arranged marriage with old-world aristocracy and rank in order to wed the 'natural' republican system of America they so dearly loved. The romance conflict thus supported the argument for independence, autonomy, and a fresh start in the name of supposedly ancient Indian traditions."[57] By taking on the role of the Indian, the Jewish characters in these mu-

sicals also became the agents of democracy, ensuring that American democratic values were accepted and perpetuated in the mythical Wild West.

Yet although these musicals are structurally related to the nineteenth-century Indian plays, they are the products of a different era with different concerns. Both genres confront the problem of what it means to be American, but
in the Indian plays the concern is to differentiate the American from the British *political* systems. The early twentieth-century musicals, in contrast, explore the problems of defining an American *cultural* and *racial* identity. While
the Jewish characters, like the Indians before them, support romantic love as
a symbol for American democracy, they emphasize different elements of the
democratic system. In the early and mid-nineteenth century, the Indian plays
sought to justify the American consent-based *system of government* as opposed to a descent-based (aristocratic) European system. In the twentieth
century, the musicals are more concerned with justifying a consent-based
community as opposed to a descent-based one. A character's entry into the
musical community depends solely on his desire and ability to *become* part of
the world of the stage. In ensuring the success of romance in the musical,
then, the Jewish comic supports a distinctly American set of ideals: democracy, meritocracy, and equality. Playing the Indian, he ensures his own American identity by both acceding to nativist ideology (associating himself with
"native" Americans) and by resisting it (insisting on a community of consent).

While Jewish and Indian characters intermingle in these musicals, it is important to note that Jews do not become *actual* Indians, but simply *perform
the role* of the Indian stereotype in order to reap the benefits of the mythic as-
sociations without suffering the stigma faced by real Indians on reservations.
Henry becomes a show-biz Indian by donning a headdress and smoking a
peace pipe. Wanenis, in stark contrast to Henry, seems to be a *real* Indian. Interestingly, Wanenis' experience follows the nativist model described by Michaels quite closely. He cannot become white, despite the fact that he wears
modern clothing, speaks perfect English, and has studied to be a mining engi-
neer. Wanenis cannot marry Sally so long as he is an Indian (the Indian's role is
to bring a white couple together, not to marry a white woman). Likewise, he
cannot *choose* to stop being an Indian and play another role. Only when Black
Eagle reveals that Wanenis was born to white parents does Wanenis "become"
white. Years of living as an Indian instantly drop away. Wanenis becomes white
only because he is *already* white.

In *Girl Crazy* the fact that both Gieber (the "performed" Indian) and Eagle
Rock (the "real" Indian) speak Yiddish is a sly satire on the being/becoming dichotomy. The joke sheds light on the tension in the 1930s between the two notions of self-definition: racial identity, which is biological and hence immutable, and assimilative (later called ethnic) identity, in which one can adopt the

dress, language, and customs of a culture and become a part of that culture. The Indian/Yiddish joke sets up a tension between a "real" character, whose identity is determined not by language or dress but by racial background, and a "fake" or theatrical character whose identity is determined wholly by performed behavior. Gieber fears that when compared with Eagle Rock, a real Indian, his disguise will not hold up and he will be exposed. He therefore makes a concerted effort to establish a connection with the Indian through language. But the very connection that they finally establish undercuts the racial/assimilable (or being/performing) dichotomy by revealing *both* characters to be performers. Neither the racially "real" Indian character nor the pretend Indian character has a fixed identity. Both are capable of dramatically reinventing themselves, Eagle Rock using language and Gieber using costume. In the world of *Girl Crazy,* at least, reality *is* performance, and an effective (i.e., self-conscious) performance is the only reality that matters.

Gieber and Henry's brand of theatricality triumphs on the musical stage. Not only do Gieber and Henry unite Molly with Danny and Sally with Wanenis, but they also outwit the bad guys and win their audiences' unequivocal affection. When, in *Whoopee,* Underwood's son Chester offers to conduct a "psychological investigation" in order to determine who robbed them on the highway, Henry (still in blackface) cleverly sidesteps the plan and shows up both Chester and Sheriff Bob. Gieber, likewise, not only outwits the bad guys who were trying to kill him but also administers what he calls "Goldfarb justice." Having become the county sheriff, Gieber is the hero of the tale. As he makes his entrance in the last scene, the cowboys and ensemble shout, "Three cheers for Gieber Goldfarb!" and strains of Goldfarb's campaign song, aptly titled "Goldfarb, That's I'm" (a spoof of George M. Cohan's "Harrigan, That's Me"), can be heard in the background. Because of Gieber's and Henry's various machinations, the comic plot lines are neatly sewn up, the bad guys have been punished, and the various couples are back together again. In the final exchange of *Girl Crazy,* Danny asks Molly to marry him. Before Molly can respond, Gieber breaks in with the last line of the play: "Go on—marry him, Molly. It's 11:15 already." Reminding the audience at the very last moment that they are witnessing not reality but a show that must end by 11:15 so folks can go home, Gieber remains an unfailingly self-conscious performer. From his first entrance, when he thinks he is on a movie set, to his final line, when he reminds us all that we are in a theater, he controls and manipulates the theatrical illusion with ease.

The characters of Gieber and Henry reveal the reciprocal nature of the Jewish-created musical theater experience. Not only do they find refuge within the American community onstage by adopting various roles and disguises, but they also turn the entire (non-Jewish) Wild West into a theatrical world in which performance determines identity. Theatricality demonstrates and celebrates the extraordinary American capacity for self-fashioning. Even in the face of increasingly threatening American antisemitism in the early 1930s, first and second generation American Jews knew that America offered them possibilities for self-determination they would never find in Europe. Gieber and Henry giddily dance from one racial or gender stereotype to another in a world in which identity is utilitarian, not confining. In *Whoopee* and *Girl Crazy,* notions of race and racial passing that held currency in the contemporary off-stage world were turned on their heads. Henry and Gieber have no interest in passing as cowboys (since cowboys have little power on the musical theater stage). Instead, they find racial and gender difference more effective in constructing disguises and more useful as a theatrical device. By moving rapidly among a set of minority and subaltern identities, they escape not only their cowboy pursuers, but also the supposedly immutable racial and gender categories used to determine political power in early twentieth-century America.

3

Babes in Arms

The Politics of Theatricality during the Great Depression

> They call us Babes in Arms
> But we are Babes in Armour.
> They laugh at Babes in Arms,
> But we'll be laughing far more.
> On city streets and farms
> They'll hear a rising war cry.
> Youth will arrive,
> Let them know you're alive,
> Make it your cry!
>
> —*Babes in Arms,* Act 1, scene 1

THE title song to the musical *Babes in Arms,* by Richard Rodgers and Lorenz Hart, opens with a militant call to arms. In a play best remembered for originating the clichéd story about a bunch of young performers putting on a show in a barn, the fierce determination of the song seems wildly overblown. The most famous version of the play is about apprentices at a summer stock theater who want to perform their own revue and the stingy theater owner who will not let them. With a rousing chorus of the song "Babes in Arms," they decide to take matters into their own hands. They find a barn, and the rest is history. Their situation may be challenging, but the plight of a few aspiring summer stock actors does not seem to merit quite the level of passionate rebellion described in the song. Neither "city streets" nor "farms" appear in the play. And being an apprentice may not be fun, but does it explain a "rising war-cry"? What are these kids so worked up about?

The disjunction between song and story is the result of a massive rewriting of the script in the late 1950s. The story described above is not the story written by Rodgers and Hart in 1937. The original script has never been published and is available only in archives and by special request from the Rodgers and Hammerstein Organization. The 1937 *Babes in Arms* tells the story of the youth of Seaport, Long Island, a small town originally founded as an actors' colony. The parents—all out-of-work vaudevillians—have gone on a tour sponsored by the Works Progress Administration (WPA). Their children have been left behind to work in the local New Deal youth project, dubbed a "work farm" by the kids. The kids do not want to go to the farm, and all of the young folks in town (not just the actors' children) get involved in plotting a way to stay off the farm. They are a varied bunch: the male leaders of the group include Val (an idealist intellectual), Marshall (a budding lawyer) and Gus (a streetwise kid always ready for a fight). Their nemesis is Lee Calhoun, the son of a rich southern colonel. The girls include Billie, a hobo who has just dropped into town, Dolores, the sheriff's nymphomaniac daughter, and Baby Rose, a former child star. Among the younger kids (of whom there are at least thirty) are Booker and Lincoln Vanderpool and Ivor and Irving de Quincy, hoofers described in the script as "small black clouds." The kids convince the sheriff of the town to give them two weeks to raise the money they need to stay off the farm; they hope to do this by producing a play. In the course of rehearsals, two couples come together, Gus and Dolores and Val and Billie. The show is a success, but Val offends their "backer," Lee Calhoun, by insisting that Ivor and Irving perform in the show over Lee's racist objections. Soon afterward, Lee's father goes bankrupt, and the young people are back where they started. Billie threatens to leave because she has no desire to end up at the work farm, and Val is distraught at their impending separation. At a send-off party for the kids, Val and the others turn on the radio to listen to the landing of a famous French aviator, René Flambeau.[1] By sheer luck, Flambeau loses his way in the clouds and ends up crash landing just outside Val's house. Val impersonates the unconscious aviator and convinces the radio audience that his father's field would make an excellent airport. The kids are saved from the work farm; Flambeau (when he comes to) agrees to back their show; Billie agrees to stay with Val, and all celebrate joyfully with a rousing chorus of "Babes in Arms" as the curtain comes down.[2]

Unlike the bland 1950s rewrite, the 1937 script is a rich and complex historical document. It offers a snapshot of attitudes of the era, and reveals a sensibility deeply informed by the cultural, political, and theatrical events of the decade.[3] The score is one of the most memorable in the American musical theater, including such jazz standards as "My Funny Valentine," "The Lady Is a Tramp," "Where or When," "Johnny One Note," and "I Wish I Were in Love Again." Richard Rodgers and Lorenz Hart had been writing together for years, but only in the late 1930s did they begin to reach their potential as theater artists. They produced a string of hits in those years that reshaped critical and commercial expectations for the Broadway musical.[4] Their combination of sophisticated, often cynical musical numbers and edgy New York–centered plots appealed to the jaded urban elites who could still afford theater tickets in the depths of the Depression.

Richard Rodgers and Lorenz Hart represented a new Broadway generation in more than just musical style. Rodgers and Hart are the first figures in this book who did not change their names. They did not have to. Unlike Irving Berlin (Israel Baline), George Gershwin (Jacob Gershowitz), Ira Gershwin (Israel Gershvin), Eddie Cantor (Edward "Izzy" Iskowitz), and Al Jolson (Asa Yoelson), Rodgers and Hart were both born in America to middle-class Jew-

11. Performing the number "Youth Will Arrive" in the 1937 Broadway production of *Babes in Arms*. Photo by Richard Tucker. Museum of the City of New York.

★ ★

ish families.[5] Hart's parents were immigrants who had arrived in America as teenagers and were eager to have Americanized children (they gave Lorenz a classical name, while naming his younger brother after Teddy Roosevelt). Hart was raised bilingually, speaking German and English in his home and attending English-language schools. Both of Rodgers' parents were born in the United States and his home was patriotically American. Rodgers and Hart both grew up in comfortable style on the Upper West Side and attended Reform synagogues (if they attended at all) and Columbia University.[6] Though they lived in Jewish circles—from their childhood neighborhoods, to their summer camp (both went to the Weingart Institute, a camp for Jewish boys in the Catskills), to their college drama fraternity, to the world of Broadway and Hollywood—they rarely acknowledged or discussed their Jewishness publicly.

Rodgers and Hart make evident, in their plays, the great distance that separates them from the writers who emerged directly from the world of the Lower East Side. Their works of the later 1930s differ from the musical comedies discussed in Chapter 2 in that they feature no openly Jewish characters. In the increasingly volatile political atmosphere of those years, many Jewish creators of popular entertainment felt compelled to obscure their own Jewishness and to tone down or eliminate ethnic characters. A dramatic rise in antisemitism in the United States and abroad created unease and instability for comfortably acculturated American Jews like Rodgers and Hart. Although as second- or third-generation Americans, such upper-middle-class Jews were relatively secure about their national status, the rising tide of antisemitic demagoguery forced Jews to consider their public commitments carefully. The popularity of outspoken antisemites like Gerald L. K. Smith (who inherited Huey Long's Share the Wealth movement) and Father Charles Coughlin, a radio personality who preached against Communism and the "International Jewish Conspiracy" and was reputed to be heard by 14 million Americans, meant that Jews were living in a state of perpetual fear and anxiety.[7] The horrifying experience of German Jews under Nazi rule, many of whom came from backgrounds similar to those of their American counterparts and who had long considered themselves Germans, was enough to unnerve even the most well-established Jews in the United States. Jews particularly feared being accused of warmongering for "personal" (that is, tribal) interest, and therefore few Jewish-created shows and films directly addressed the rise of Nazi antisemitism or called for explicit diplomatic or military action on the part of the U.S. government.[8] Jewish writers and producers feared that audiences outside urban areas would react negatively to Jewish characters, and they felt that the best way to combat antisemitism politically was to keep all matters relating to Jews as quiet as possible. Aside from a few offhand comments, then, Rodgers and Hart's *Babes in Arms,* while clearly engaging with the politics of the 1930s, avoids directly confronting Jewish political concerns (or dealing openly with Jews at all).

Yet in its formulation of a liberal political ideology, the play does articulate a palpable New York Jewish sensibility. *Babes in Arms* offers the observer of American Jewish culture a detailed document of the way secular, assimilated Jews constructed, through political affiliation, a new form of "socioethnic" Jewishness (as Rodgers calls it in his memoir). Much attention has been focused on those Jews who became radical political activists in the 1930s, but most assimilated Jews actually became not radicals but New Deal liberals. This play contains the elements of Jewish liberalism—including many of its contradictions—which were consolidated into a recognizable political trend during the 1930s and which became one of the most reliable examples of secular Jewish identification for the next fifty years. As Henry Feingold has argued, the "watershed" for Jewish involvement with American liberalism was the decade beginning in 1938, the year after *Babes in Arms* opened.[9] During these years, American Jews voted in record numbers for the Democratic Party, regardless of their economic class. They idolized President Franklin D. Roosevelt and voiced strong approval for his New Deal programs.[10] Many Jews worked in the Roosevelt administration, which led right-wing and antisemitic critics to dub the Democratic social agenda the "Jew Deal."[11] Rodgers and Hart were no exception to this trend. Both were stalwart liberals and supporters of the New Deal. In *Musical Stages,* Rodgers mentions that he and Hart were both "ardently pro-FDR."[12] Describing the creative process for *I'd Rather Be Right,* the affectionate New Deal satire produced in the same year as *Babes in Arms,* Rodgers says:

> Creating such a musical comedy at this time was in itself an affirmation of the freedom we had always enjoyed and had long taken for granted. Hitler, who had come to power in Germany the same year Roosevelt first took office, had already instituted repressive measures against non-Aryans and "enemies of the state." Abolition of all forms of dissent was also part of Mussolini's Fascist regime in Italy and of the aggressive military leaders in Japan. Spain was in the midst of a civil war led by Franco, with the blessing and backing of Hitler and Mussolini. In one country after another, one saw the extinction of human life and liberty. Suddenly all those who had been moaning about what had happened to us during the Depression were beginning to realize that ours was one of the few nations on earth where people weren't afraid of their leaders. We could talk against them, we could vote them out of office—and we could even put them up on a Broadway stage as the butt of ridicule in a song-and-dance show. (184)

Rodgers also notes that during the Boston tryout of *Carousel* in 1945, when he learned of Roosevelt's death, he canceled understudy auditions and called his wife immediately. "We could hardly speak," he recalls. "All we did was cry over the phone" (243).

Babes in Arms illustrates the basic features of American Jewish liberalism. The play presents an underprivileged group fighting for freedom and liberty. The optimistic leaders are intellectuals who rely on the open exchange of ideas to effect change. The group believes in equal opportunity, regardless of race, religion, or ethnicity, and in hard work as the ticket to success. They aim to create an inclusive, tolerant, and diverse community. The white leaders of the community specifically argue for black civil rights and against nativism. Less apparent, but also present, are a set of contradictory issues which have complicated Jewish liberalism over the decades. The way in which the white leaders support black civil rights in the play, for example, exposes the problematic power dynamics that repeatedly impeded the formation of a lasting black-Jewish alliance. And the unwillingness of the Jewish writers to include overtly ethnic characters calls the inclusiveness of the community into question. Similarly, the play illustrates the tension inherent in Jewish liberalism between a socialist and a democratic capitalist ethos. The play strongly emphasizes the group's power to effect social change, but represents that power as resistance, not revolution, despite the sentiments of the title song. The play also articulates the problems intellectual Jewish liberals have faced trying to unite high ideals with practical goals. The opportunistic outsider turns out to be wiser about how the world actually works than the intellectuals. Finally, the idea that hard work and talent will lead to success is undermined by the fact that the group's show actually fails. They end up achieving their goals instead through a stroke of miraculous good luck—a deus ex machina.[13]

Babes in Arms also demonstrates Rodgers and Hart's new approach to the musical theater itself. By the mid-1930s, the musical theater was floundering and both its creators and observers were unsure of the place it ought to hold in the American cultural landscape. Rodgers and Hart responded to this crisis by creating a piece of musical theater that conflates acting in the theater with acting in the political arena and thereby insists on the importance of the musical theater in an active democratic society. The play asserts the legitimacy of musicals in an era when they were threatened with extinction. As a commercial enterprise, musicals in the 1930s were risky at best. Broadway was in a deep slump, suffering both from the paralyzing effects of the Depression and from the increasing competition of Hollywood films. In 1937, fewer shows were produced on Broadway than in any of the previous thirty years.[14] Vaudeville houses both in New York and on the road, venues which for an earlier generation of performers had represented the heights of success, were rapidly closing or being transformed into movie theaters.[15] The decline of vaudeville is illustrated dramatically in *Babes in Arms:* the vaudevillian parents are absent and utterly ineffective. They cannot even take care of their own children.

Other forms of commercial mass entertainment, such as movies and radio, were cheaper to produce and easier to promote. In fact, Rodgers and Hart even tried Hollywood themselves in the mid-1930s. They had recently returned to Broadway, in 1936, after a disappointing stint at MGM. Deriding the California lifestyle as an "unpressured indolent existence," Rodgers could not wait to get back to New York: "What had happened inside us that could impel us to accept money without working for it, spend day after day on the tennis courts or in the local bars, and simply allow our talents to rot? How could we have let ourselves be caught in this trap? What *had* happened to us?"[16]

Likewise, Hollywood offers nothing to the kids in the play. Two of them have moved "back East." Billie has just come back from Hollywood, where, as she wryly notes in the first scene, everyone agreed that she "was no actress." Since it quickly becomes clear that Billie is actually a brilliant actress, the implication is that Broadway and Hollywood demand different types of talent. Baby Rose, the former child star, also declares in "Way Out West" that she has had enough of the West:

> I've roamed o'er the range with the herd,
> Where seldom is heard an intelligent word.

She is thrilled to be back in New York City:

> Git along, little taxi, you can keep the change
> I'm riding home to my kitchen range
> Way out west on West End Avenue.

Whatever success the movie industry may be having in producing musical films, it is clearly not, according to Rodgers and Hart, making effective use of Broadway talent.

If popular culture was edging out the musical theater from below, "high," nonprofit theater was pressing in from above. The Theatre Guild, founded in 1918 to produce theater of high artistic quality, had come into its own by the 1930s. Dedicated to realist, expressionist, and avant-garde playwrights like Bernard Shaw, Eugene O'Neill, and Maxwell Anderson, by the 1930s the Guild had ventured into musical theater as well, producing the Gershwin/Heyward folk opera *Porgy and Bess* (1935). The success of the Theatre Guild also inspired independent producers to search out works deemed artistically significant. In 1931, Harold Clurman, Cheryl Crawford, and Lee Strasberg founded an offshoot of the Theatre Guild, the Group Theatre, which was devoted to teaching the Stanislavsky acting method and to producing plays of social significance.

In that decade the federal government became a producer of politically engaged, aesthetically sophisticated theater, and this effort provided yet another challenge to the commercial Broadway musical. Responding to the crisis on Broadway, in 1935 the WPA established the Federal Theatre Project (FTP) to provide jobs for artists of the stage. Although it was a government organization, the FTP encouraged politically progressive, accessible productions and had as one of its major goals the establishment of a national theater. The FTP sponsored a number of works of musical theater, the most famous being *The Cradle Will Rock* (1937), by Marc Blitzstein; this radical musical, about laborers during a steel strike, was deeply influenced by the techniques of Bertolt Brecht and the music of Kurt Weill.[17] Labor culture was also making its presence felt on Broadway. *Pins and Needles* (1937), with songs by Harold

Rome, was a politically charged revue performed entirely by union members and sponsored by the International Ladies Garment Workers Union. It opened at the Princess Theatre—renamed the Labor Stage for the occasion—in late 1937 and enjoyed a surprisingly long run.[18]

The Broadway musical theater needed to find its own niche in this new cultural landscape. As its acknowledged standard-bearers, Rodgers and Hart led the way. They clearly could not compete with the mass appeal of movies, so they began to nudge the musical comedy form closer to the world of legitimate "art" theater. With *Babes in Arms* and their next play *I'd Rather Be Right* (1937), they rejected the typical musical comedy subjects—young, rich playboys and debutantes in love—and chose to focus instead on themes of social significance.[19] Whereas shows like *The Cradle Will Rock* advocated radical revolution, workers' uprisings, and Communist ideology, however, Rodgers and Hart's plays reflected the more moderate liberal views of their creators and their mainstream audiences. The pair also devoted more attention to the quality of their scripts: it became increasingly important that the dialogue and plot of the play hold their own in terms of quality and coherence.[20] Instead of relying exclusively on popular dance forms, they began to include "dream ballets" in their musicals, choreographed by masters such as George Balanchine.[21] And they began to link the musical theater with opera, as in the song "Johnny One Note" in *Babes in Arms* and in the "rhymed dialogue" recitative of "At the Roxy Music Hall" in *I Married an Angel* (1938).

In attempting to establish cultural legitimacy for the musical theater, however, Rodgers and Hart moved beyond aligning their work with the world of high art. They recognized that live performance itself was losing its relevance in the face of film and radio technology. So they not only had to establish legitimacy for the musical theater as a cultural institution, but they also had to justify the significance of costly theater productions—which depended on live actors and audiences—in an increasingly technologized society. *Babes in Arms* is a play about the New York theater, and integral to its plot are the many tasks involved in mounting a theater production: securing backers, finding a venue, writing the script, casting and directing actors, performing numbers, and receiving reviews. These mundane processes of the theater business in turn become symbols of political action in *Babes in Arms*. By building their musical around an act of performance (putting on a play) which is an explicit act of resistance, Rodgers and Hart created a play that was fundamentally about the political and social purpose theater could serve in 1930s American culture. In their work, acting on the stage becomes not a substitute for but a version of acting in the political sphere. *Babes in Arms* thus marks a moment of transition in both American Jewish history and in the development of the musical theater.

Fighting for a Place in the Sun

My generation thirsted for another kind of action, and we took great pleasure in the sit-down strikes that burst loose in Flint and Detroit. . . . We saw a new world coming every third morning. . . . When I think of the library [at the University of Michigan in the mid-1930s], I think of the sound of a stump speaker on the lawn outside because so many times I looked up from what I was reading to try to hear what issue they were debating now. The place was full of speeches, meetings and leaflets. It was jumping with issues.

—Arthur Miller, "The University of Michigan," *Holiday Magazine,* December 1953

Play day is done,
We've a place in the sun
We must fight for.
So babes in arms to arms!

—Lorenz Hart, "Babes in Arms," 1937

Babes in Arms appeared at a volatile and desperate moment in American history. In 1936, 16.9 percent of the American population was unemployed. By early 1937, when the play opened, this figure had declined slightly and prospects appeared somewhat brighter. The recovery, however, was still years away, and by the end of 1937 the economy was in even worse shape than before.[22] Massive dust storms swept through the Midwest that year, wiping out the crops of thousands of farmers in Kansas, Oklahoma, Colorado, and Nebraska and increasing the flow of "Okies" heading west in search of work.[23] The situation in Europe was equally unnerving. In March 1936 Hitler sent troops into the Rhineland, a violation of the World War I peace accords. That same year, he also cemented alliances with fascists in Italy, Japan, and Spain. A steady flow of German émigrés, mostly Jewish artists and intellectuals bearing tales of Nazi persecution, poured into American cities during the late 1930s.

In the face of such widespread suffering, there was a popular perception among liberals that every citizen was responsible not only for alleviating his or her own financial woes, but also for helping to heal the rest of society. According to Democratic Party rhetoric, each citizen was called on to work for the betterment of the world. President Franklin D. Roosevelt took this as the mission of his second term, in his 1936 inaugural speech: "I see one-third of a nation ill-housed, ill-clad, ill-nourished. . . . The test of our progress is not whether we add more to the abundance of those who have much; it is whether we provide enough for those who have too little."[24] Promoting one brand of New Deal liberalism, Hollywood movies—such as *Mr. Deeds Goes to Town* (1936) and *Mr. Smith Goes to Washington* (1939)—tended to espouse a nostalgic image of the power of individual action. Frank Capra's popular films, for example, celebrated the common man who provides a beacon of sanity and sincerity in a corrupt, "wised-up" world. The problem with America, according to these movies, was not the system but the people within the system who were no longer living up to America's high ideals. With clear vision, hard work, and radical acts of courage, these movies implied, individuals could shock American society into remembering its democratic founding principles and prod those who had strayed to return to the high road.

The promise (or threat) of collective action also galvanized massive numbers of Americans during these years. Labor unrest at home, for example, led to a period of massive union organizing. By the summer of 1937, the Congress of Industrial Organizations (CIO) claimed to have more than 3.4 million members.[25] Strikes proliferated and working conditions improved slowly. Numerous political organizations, all claiming to hold the key to social reform, attracted thousands of new members. On the left, Communists, Socialists, Marxists, Trotskyists, and liberals of all stripes wrote manifestos, formed movements, went to meetings, organized protests, and agitated for social reform. Students on college campuses, protesting what they called the "Great Betrayal of 1917," went on peace strikes, insisting that they would not fight in another war in Europe.[26] Left-wing organizations supported plays like *The Cradle Will Rock* and *Pins and Needles,* which popularized their ideals. Jews were a strong presence in all phases of the left-wing movements, from union organizing to theater productions, although most did not ultimately become devoted radical activists.[27] On the right, leaders like Huey Long, Charles Coughlin, and Gerald L. K. Smith used rallies, radio speeches, graphic art, and newspaper diatribes to arouse disaffected Americans with nativist, populist, antisemitic, and sometimes fascist leanings.

In *Babes in Arms,* the youthful characters must figure out how to act in this unstable political situation. Threatened with the loss of their liberty, they contemplate the range of possibilities for political action available to them. After exhausting a wide variety of political stances, they decide that the best way to act is to "act"—in other words, to put on a show. In the first scene, the vaudevillian parents living in the actors' colony of Seaport depart on tour, and their children discover that they are to be transplanted to a work farm for the duration of their parents' absence. The kids are ambivalent about the farm, which is run by the Civilian Conservation Corps (CCC). Val, the lead, believes that the farm will compromise his "personal liberty." Marshall is more practical and recognizes that the kids can't survive without basics like books and food:

MARSHALL: I suppose you know they've got a swell library on that farm.
VAL: Shut up!

MARSHALL: It's only till the folks come back. And they have a ball team.
And listen, Val, you don't mind eating once in a while, do you?
VAL: We could eat here.
MARSHALL: On what?

Marshall, studying to be a lawyer, uses the inducement of a "swell library" to try to sway Val, who fancies himself a philosopher. Budding intellectuals, Val and Marshall would have fit comfortably into the New York Jewish scene of the 1930s, where, during the Depression, ambitious Jewish boys were expected to work their way up via higher education at one of the city's free colleges. Val is almost ready to give in when Billie, a beautiful hobo who has just drifted into town, protests. The personification of American grit, self-reliance, and determination, Billie is scornful of those who would take handouts from the government:

BILLIE: You'll make a very nice pair of public charges.
VAL: That settles it. I'm not going.
BILLIE: Great! I'm glad you're willing to stand on your own.
VAL: I'll find a way. I'm a pragmatist.
BILLIE: That'll help. I don't know what you can do, but you can do something. The idea of a bunch of healthy kids being fed like down and out bums!
VAL: Marshall, let's stick it out!
MARSHALL: But how?
VAL: With guts!

This brief passage expresses the complex attitudes of Americans to the Depression and the New Deal. On the one hand, the work farm, like other New Deal programs, is a beneficial and necessary enterprise. It provides indigent children with a place to live, food to eat, books to educate their minds, and useful labor for their hands. It keeps potentially delinquent kids out of trouble. Yet for the kids, it represents a loss of independence. They want to be self-sufficient; they do not want to have to depend on the government (or their parents) for their basic needs. Billie sets up a moral hierarchy with "healthy kids" at the top and "down and out bums" at the bottom. She neglects to acknowledge that these healthy kids may quickly become "down and out" if they do not eat. Instead of government programs, Billie advocates individual action—of whatever sort—and refuses to blame external systems for personal failure. "I don't know what you can do, but you can do something," she says to Val as she taunts him for even entertaining the idea of becoming what she derisively calls a "public charge."

Billie advocates taking responsibility for one's position even if, as in the case of Val and the others, they have little or no apparent control over their situation. Billie articulates a trend during the Depression that Lawrence Levine believes explains why the United States in the 1930s did *not* experience a revolution akin to those that erupted in other countries:

> Despite all of the objective evidence that the American people were victims of external circumstances largely beyond their control, substantial numbers of them had so internalized the traditional sense of personal responsibility for such conditions as unemployment and poverty, that while on the one hand they might reject Herbert Hoover for not giving them adequate help, on the other they felt a deep sense of shame for being in such a dependent position.[28]

Alan Brinkley likewise argues that Americans needed to "reconcile their beliefs in individualism, material success, opportunity, consumerism with a world in which those beliefs no longer found material support." One way in which they did so was to adopt the perspective that Billie represents in the play. They "lay the blame for their problems not on their society, not on the economy, not on the culture, but on themselves."[29]

Billie, who has traveled "three thousand miles with some pretty tough characters," refuses to acknowledge that she or Val or the rest of the kids have anything to be afraid of in rejecting adult protection; the only thing they should fear is the shame of depending on others. She conveniently ignores the fact that the kids have access neither to jobs nor to money, and she is openly scornful of Marshall's initial concern that he and Val will have nothing to eat. Refusing to believe in the irrational disintegration of society during the Depression, Billie adopts the sentimental stance of her contemporaries Scarlett O'Hara and Ma Joad—a stance which Lawrence Levine articulates as that of "the individual who refuses to give in, . . . [who] rise[s] above disaster in pursuit of redemption."[30] Billie embodies the essence of the famous aphorism from Roosevelt's first inaugural address: "The only thing we have to fear is fear itself."

Like other Americans, Jews reacted to government aid with contradictory impulses. While they overwhelmingly supported the formation of a welfare system, they were rarely willing to make use of it themselves, even when they were in great need. As Beth Wenger has described, the organized Jewish community still referred to the three-hundred-year-old "Stuyvesant Promise" when making decisions about Jewish charity:

> In 1654, when the first Jews arrived in New Amsterdam, Governor Peter Stuyvesant petitioned his superiors at the Dutch West India Company to forbid their settlement. The company, however, admitted Jews to the colony on the condition that "the poor among them shall not become a burden to the company or to the community, but be supported by their own nation." Successive generations of Jews

fulfilled the pledge to Peter Stuyvesant by building Jewish philanthropic organizations and consistently opposing government intervention in private charities.[31]

By the later years of the Depression, however, Jewish organizations simply could not keep up with the demands for assistance and had to rely on public sources to supplement the communal charities. In addition to feeling ashamed about taking charity, then, Jews on relief also worried about the effects of accepting charity from government sources. Always concerned with the public image of the Jewish community, they were anxious that Jews not be perceived as a further drain on the economy.

Inspired by Billie's optimism and energy, Val and Marshall decide to take control of their own fates—to act. Despite Billie's influence, however, they do not choose to do so through acts of individual courage. They do not run away with Billie to become tramps, for example. They feel a responsibility not only to themselves but also to the other kids in the town. Their brand of self-reliance bears more relationship to that of the Jewish philanthropies than to Billie's individualism. They decide to organize the community to fight against the oppression of the work farm:

VAL: We'll call a meeting! I'll organize the bunch.
MARSHALL: They think we can't take care of ourselves!
VAL: We'll show 'em!

The excitement of organizing prompts them to burst into song. Fired up by a sense of right and a sense of what they deserve as free Americans, they sing:

> Play day is done,
> We've a place in the sun
> We must fight for.
> So babes in arms to arms!

Marching down the streets of Seaport, heading for the American Legion hall, an enormous chorus of young performers joins Val, Marshall, and Billie in their rousing "battle song" (as it is called in the script). The insistence that they have their own "place in the sun" transforms the youth of Seaport into a movement. They become a symbol of liberal purpose: a marginalized group fighting hard for their piece of American prosperity during the Depression.[32]

The image of youth taking action was a familiar one in 1937. In the late 1930s, young people did indeed "arise" and take up arms. Whether connected with campus protests, strike demonstrations, civil rights agitation, or actual fighting in Spain, youth movements were sweeping the country. High school and college students joined the Young Communist League, the Young People's Socialist League, the Student League for Industrial Democracy, the National Student Federation, the National Student League, the American Student Union, and a host of other activist groups. Overshadowed in the popular memory to-day by the many other political events of the volatile 1930s and by the New Left student movements of the 1960s, these student movements are not well known. But in the late 1930s, historian Robert Cohen notes, the student dem-onstrations involved hundreds of thousands across the country. Some com-mentators claim that half of the undergraduate population was involved at one point or another.[33] Many of the leaders of these organizations were Jewish students.[34] College campuses with significant Jewish populations, such as Co-lumbia University and City College of New York, were rocked by debates over free speech on campus, student autonomy, and antiwar demonstrations. In 1932, the New York Board of Education threatened to raise fees for the munici-pal colleges. Students from City, Brooklyn, and Hunter colleges, nearly 90 per-cent of them Jewish, marched on City Hall in protest and succeeded in having the plan revoked.[35] Columbia University, the alma mater of both Rodgers and Hart, was the site of some of the most decisive debates over free speech on campus. In 1932, more than 75 percent of the student body boycotted classes to protest the expulsion of the editor of the student newspaper, who had writ-ten articles that offended the university administration. The editor was rein-stated. In 1936, three thousand Columbia and Barnard students marched in a nationwide student antiwar strike.[36] Even younger students, attending New York City high schools, protested unfair practices. When New Utrecht High School, located in the largely Jewish neighborhood of Borough Park in Brook-lyn, announced an increase in the price of milk in the cafeteria, the working-class student body, whose families generally suffered greatly during the De-pression, feared they would be unable to afford the higher price. Members of the Young Communist League at the school organized a successful milk boy-cott, and the school administration rescinded the increase. So impressed was the press by this action that the New York *Daily News* dubbed the school "the cradle of the American revolution."[37]

Determined to start their own revolution, in Act 1, Scene 3, the kids of Sea-port eagerly assemble in the American Legion hall. Their meeting begins with a debate over the best course of action. Val asks the kids to clarify the issue at hand: "On our side we have youth, truth and the love of liberty. What's the other side got?" Lee, the right-wing, rich southerner who is opposed to orga-nizing and who has little sympathy for the plight of the theater folk, replies, "The sheriff!" Lee insists that in the face of the powerful town government, the young people are incapable of acting: "Let me make a motion that you all have nothing, you all can do nothing, and you all amount to nothing." Deter-mined to resist, the group shouts Lee down. Marshall, the prospective lawyer, then suggests that they should draft a set of resolutions and present them to the sheriff. This leads to a debate about the type of action the kids should take. Peter speaks first: "I think nobody should own anything. We should place everything we have into a communal fund." But Peter's desire for Communist-style revolution does not hold up in the face of questioning.

LEE: What have you got?

PETER: Nothing. But we'll all get jobs. Then we put everything we have into one fund.

GUS: How are we going to get along? Suppose you haven't got a pair of socks to your name?

PETER: Suppose I haven't. You got a pair of socks, Sam has a pair, Val has a pair. The four of us divide them up and we have three quarters of a pair—apiece. [*He sits down puzzled and whistles in bewilderment*]

Val calls Peter's ideas "a little radical," but insists that the group must be open-minded.

By contrast, Lee proposes a social-Darwinist approach to the kids' problems. He insists that he should lead because he is rich: "The man who makes more deserves more because he's superior. You've got to have superior men just as you have superior races." Gus rejects Lee's claim to superiority on the basis of money, but insists that *he* can act because he is physically strong and brave. "There's only one kind of government," Gus insists, "F-O-R-C-E. Force! The big shots around here got to run the little shots. And the biggest shot of all dictates to everybody." A girl tries to bring Gus back to the question at hand, asking how his proposal would keep them off the work farm. Gus replies with a hotheaded and impractical plan:

Well, for instance—suppose I'm walking down Albee Avenue minding my own business. Up comes the Sheriff. He says, "What are you doing?" I says, "Walking down Albee Avenue." He says, "No you ain't. You're going to the Work Farm." Thereupon I presents him with a set of resolutions—two of them—one to the basket and one to the chin—And when he turns around to run, I present him with the third resolution complete with knee action. If all you guys would do that, we'd have a government that is a government.

Val, enjoying the discussion and acting as moderator, tries to make the best of the fact that they do not seem to be able to agree on a solution to their problem: "It may appear on the surface that all our ideas are a little different, but when we put them all together I think we ought to get something very interesting." Billie is unimpressed:

BILLIE: Yes, a new bunch of farmers. I move the meeting be adjourned.

VAL: But we've just started.

MARSHALL: Billie is right. Let's stop talking and do something.

VAL: All in favor?

ALL: Aye!

VAL: The meeting is adjourned.

Val's eagerness to "organize," even if the resulting dialogue does not lead to action, critiques the processes of liberal and radical political groups of the time. Factional arguments, splinter groups, and consensus-building logjams were all features of the organizing meetings of 1930s activists.[38]

Billie, on the other hand, resists deliberating and dreaming. Like Roosevelt in the first hundred days of his term, she wants to see immediate results. When the meeting finally breaks up, Val asks, "Wasn't it wonderful?" Billie responds with skeptical sarcasm:

> BILLIE: Marvelous! A great meeting! Spirit! Youth! Determination!
> VAL: Do you think we've accomplished anything?
> BILLIE: What's the difference?

Billie recognizes what Val, Marshall, Peter, and the others do not: they are acting in the wrong way. Her characterization of the meeting sounds like a trailer for countless Hollywood films about kids who fight the system. She is the only one who realizes that this sort of sentimental play-acting will never lead to real change. These young people are playing the roles of political activists, modeling themselves on romantic characters from books and movies. But they are doing so _in earnest,_ without self-consciousness: despite the fact that they are theater children, they do not recognize that they are acting. Billie, who has seen the world, knows that this type of acting will not solve their problems.

Val is demoralized by Billie's sarcasm, the meeting falls apart, and the kids are frustrated. They are fired up but have no project toward which to direct their energy. They begin to argue, and the gathering soon devolves into a brawl. The sheriff appears and, in a flash, the kids instinctively hit on the natural solution to their problem. As the sheriff enters, the kids disguise their fights by pretending they are dancing. As Val tries to explain to the sheriff why they have gathered for a meeting, an idea hits him:

> VAL: We're rehearsing.
> SHERIFF: What are you rehearsing for?
> VAL: What are we rehearsing for?—Why—
> MARSHALL: [_getting the idea_] Why, for our show!
> SHERIFF: What show?
> VAL: The Follies—The Follies. Our own Follies.
> GUS: Yeah, we're going to put on a show and make a lot of money.

The kids begin to sing the opening lines of "Babes in Arms" and the sheriff is carried away as well—literally. The kids raise the sheriff up on their shoulders as they all sing the rousing final lines of the verse: "So babes in arms to arms!"

The inclusion of the sheriff in the reprise of the number demands explanation. How can the very figure of authority in the town be incorporated in a revolution? Despite Billie's spirited individualist model, the young people have realized that they cannot achieve real change on their own. They need group action. In the initial, militant rendition of "Babes in Arms," the kids mimicked political radicals and threatened to undertake their own revolution. But they were stymied by their inability to agree on a plan. Each speaker offered an inherently un-American political model—whether communism, socialism, or fascism—whose implementation would require overturning the current system. Yet these kids are, at heart, not radicals but good Americans. The sheriff can be included in the second rendition of "Babes in Arms" because the kids have found a way to reach their goals without revolution. They redirect their activism away from overt political revolution and toward effective action *within* the system. As Billie recognized earlier, in order to act (politically), the group must act (theatrically). Through the performance of a play, the group can both take responsibility for themselves *and* achieve a real change in their status. Acting in the theater becomes the way in which these kids can act in the political arena.

★ ★ ★ ★ ★

The most significant political action the young performers take in planning their show is to insist on a racially and ethnically diverse cast. Their choice to racially integrate the show-within-a-show reflects Rodgers and Hart's innovative casting choices for the play as a whole. The cast of *Babes in Arms* represents a dramatic departure from earlier musicals. As indicated in the title, the group itself is the star of the show. Radically and deliberately democratic, the diversity of the show's cast represents Rodgers and Hart's liberal vision of American community on the musical theater stage. Although certain characters are featured and some have more songs than others, the effect is of an ensemble show. Billie—the apparent star—sings only two solos.[39] Love stories fade into the background in the face of the higher drama of the kids' fight for freedom. Earlier musicals like *Whoopee* and *Girl Crazy* tended to follow vaudeville's lead in featuring a few headliner stars backed up by a chorus of homogeneously beautiful women (or identically dressed young men). In a nontraditional and risky move, especially in the depressed Broadway business of the late 1930s, Rodgers and Hart avoided using stars in *Babes in Arms* and instead cast their musical almost entirely with unknown young actors.[40] Alfred Drake, Mitzi Green, and Wynn Murray (who played Marshall, Billie, and Baby Rose respectively), all of whom later became familiar faces on the Broadway stage, were just beginning their theatrical careers in 1937. Green had had some brief success as a child star with Paramount in the early 1930s, but her career in Hollywood had come to an end a few years before she starred in *Babes in Arms*. The only big-name performers Rodgers and Hart cast were the Nicholas

Brothers—a pair of black tap dancers who headlined with Cab Calloway at the Cotton Club in Harlem and had just begun to break into movies.

Rejecting the homogeneous choruses of traditional Broadway musicals, Rodgers and Hart turned the characters in the play—both major roles and chorus parts—into a diverse community composed of members with a wide array of ideological concerns and racial and ethnic backgrounds. The reviewer for the New York *American* was delighted by this unusual development: "There is not a chorus girl in the lot. Nor a chorus boy, and what a relief that is."[41] Members of a variety of socioeconomic classes join the actors' children: the rich southern boys, the sheriff's daughter, a former Hollywood star, and Billie, the wandering hobo. All of them hold a broad range of political opinions, yet they are able to unite to fight for independence. The entire first act of the play celebrates the diversity of the group and illustrates the struggles and satisfactions inherent in trying to mold a heterogeneous group into a well-oiled production company.

It is notable that the community of "babes" extends beyond the children of the actors. People of different classes and backgrounds come together to find a solution to the theater kids' problem. In this way, the play also reflects the ethos of the youth movements of the 1930s. The American Student Union (ASU), which represented the youth arm of the Popular Front, was formed in December 1935 in a historic meeting in Columbus, Ohio. Four hundred delegates attended the meeting from colleges, high schools, and student councils representing a total of 200,000 students. The delegates included Communist, Socialist, and unaffiliated liberal young people from every region of the United States and from all socioeconomic classes. At the meeting a platform was established for the organization: the ASU committed itself to the "right to Education and Security" for all young Americans. In particular, the platform declared that "a society which cannot find places for its young people *except in work camps and on battlefields* stands condemned."[42] Although in *Babes in Arms* the kids demand the right to perform onstage, not the right to attend school, the play's plot clearly echoes the rhetoric of the student movement. As Cohen notes, the ASU movement represented not just a cause, but a community united by a shared egalitarian ethic.

The cooperative strategy of *Babes in Arms* seems also to be an implicit evocation of (and perhaps argument for) the left-wing Popular Front, the larger movement under whose auspices the ASU was organized, which achieved its greatest successes during the years of *Babes in Arms*'s run. In 1935, Stalin directed Communists around the world to adopt the Popular Front strategy by joining with all parties on the left in the fight against fascism. The Popular Front was best described as "American social democracy," historian Michael Denning argues: neither a revolutionary movement nor a simple extension of New Deal liberalism, it was an alliance between the American Communist

Party and the New Deal and all those who fell in between.[43] The young people of *Babes in Arms* adopt the strategy of the Popular Front in the creation of their diverse community, but, like most liberal Americans of the time, they never stray too far to the left in their political ideology. Their goal, after all, is to *avoid* the socialized institution of the work farm, to act independently—to save themselves by using the capitalist system more effectively, not by overturning it. Like the Jewish philanthropic organizations determined to take care of their own, the kids' theater performance illustrates how American self-reliance can operate at the level of community without necessarily progressing to revolution. To resist becoming "down and out bums" who rely on "handouts" from the government, the enterprising kids intend to produce a financially successful play and to achieve independence within the capitalist system.

The cast of *Babes in Arms* makes a political statement not only in its ideological positions, but also in its representation of ethnic and racial issues. In the first confrontation with the sheriff, Billie obliquely acknowledges and justifies the diversity of the group of kids: "Look at these one hundred percent descendants [*Gus covers the nose of the boy just in front of him*] of one hundred percent parents." By adopting the rhetoric of the "One Hundred Percent American" movement, which was nativist, anti-immigration, and isolationist, but then substituting "parents" for "Americans," Billie ridicules notions of ethnic purity. But by having Gus cover the nose of a boy in the crowd, the writers wink at the audience. Of course there are Jews in this crowd, they imply, they just have their noses (and names and other specifying characteristics) covered to fool the dumb hicks (like the sheriff) who want to believe that America should be homogeneous.

But the wink is subtle and easy to miss. While the play endorses an accepting and inclusive community, the very real nativism and prejudice of the 1930s forced Rodgers and Hart to exclude overtly ethnic characters even from settings—such as a town made up of New York theater people—which would obviously comprise a large number of Jewish and Irish ethnics. For a play to make money on tour around the country, producers assumed it must not "offend"—that is, offer ethnically identifiable characters. Ethnic markers are therefore carefully removed from the names of the "white" characters. While Val and Marshall seem to have been drawn from the halls of City College or New Utrecht High School, their names (Val LaMar and Marshall Blackstone) reflect none of this ethnic particularity. A reviewer noted that Mitzi Green played the part of Billie with a manner that "recalled . . . Fannie Brice," one of the most overtly Jewish comedians of the previous decade.[44] Yet her name, Billie Smith, gives no clue that she might be played with ethnic inflections. Dolores, the daughter of a policeman, and her boyfriend, Gus, a boxer, in an earlier decade would have been Irish, but in this play they are given the almost absurdly British surnames Reynolds and Fielding.[45]

While the play covers the noses (and names) of the Jews and other ethnic characters, it makes open statements about black civil rights. Like the ASU, which declared its commitment to eliminating racism, intolerance, and segregation as they applied to "Negro, Jewish, Chinese, Indian and other minority groups," the community of *Babes in Arms* is defined most overtly by its respect for diversity and tolerance of difference.[46] In casting the show, the producer (Lee) and the director (Val) lock horns over the question of racial integration. The struggle in the theater between business and art is translated here into an overtly political struggle over race relations in which Lee, the southerner, is clearly morally culpable. A central element of the plot revolves around whether two of the black dancers—Ivor and Irving de Quincy—will be allowed to perform in the show. Lee, the producer (supported by his father's money) is opposed:

LEE: Who else is in the show?
MARSHALL: Oh, the little colored boys, Ivor and Irving.
LEE: That's out! Not if I'm going to have anything to do with it.

Lee is a staunch segregationist. But his little brother, Beauregarde, is a close friend of Ivor's and does not understand Lee's racism. In the first scene, when Val discovers Ivor and Beauregarde shooting craps, he asks why they are playing in Ivor's cramped little boxcar (which is also his home):

BEAUREGARDE: Aw, he won't come to my house.
IVOR: You see, Mr. Val, his brother Lee don't fancy us nohow.
VAL: Why not?
IVOR: We is a little too brunette for his taste.

Val's naive question and Ivor's self-conscious answer indicate that Lee's behavior is out of the ordinary for the Seaport kids. Beauregarde uses the stage convention of a comic "bit" to expose Lee's irrational insistence on his southern heritage and its accompanying attitudes. Lee plays the straight man without even realizing it:

LEE: Come on! You ought to be ashamed hanging around those little black tramps. I don't know what's gotten into your Southern blood.
BEAUREGARDE: I thought the Civil War was over.
LEE: Not for Southerners. Have you forgotten General Lee?
BEAUREGARDE: Of course not. That's the guy that was licked by General Grant.
LEE: Fine Southern spirit!
BEAUREGARDE: I don't feel as Southern as you do.
LEE: You got the same ancestors.
BEAUREGARDE: Yeah. One Great Grandfather born in South Dakota.

By exposing Lee's supposedly aristocratic southern "ancestry" as a fantasy, the writers undermine the claims of nativism. Although Lee and Beauregarde have the same ancestors (and they are not even really southern), they disagree on the importance ancestry plays in one's approach to racial difference.

While Marshall easily agrees to Lee's request that the black kids not perform, Val is unwilling to give in. He tells Billie in Act 1, Scene 6, that he has "a good spot for the two little colored boys," but Billie responds:

> BILLIE: You can't use them!
> VAL: Who says I can't?
> BILLIE: Lee, and you can't antagonize him now.

Val is deeply troubled by this news, and particularly by the fact that Billie seems unconcerned:

> VAL: It's not fair that those kids can't be in the show.
> BILLIE: Maybe not, but there are times when you have to compromise.
> VAL: For what?
> BILLIE: For everybody's good. You kids want to keep off the Work Farm, don't you? You've got to play politics once in a while.
> VAL: You're an opportunist! . . . I've had enough of this.
> BILLIE: What's the matter?
> VAL: I don't want to be corrupted.

The conversation reinforces the distinctly different ways in which Val and Billie act in the political arena. Val is an idealist, unwilling to compromise his beliefs for the sake of larger goals. Billie is a pragmatist, who is happy to use political diplomacy if it will help her to achieve her ends.

Val and Billie's conversation also evokes a particularly difficult and problematic dilemma in New Deal racial politics. In order to pass sweeping New Deal legislation which included major initiatives like Social Security, unemployment insurance, and the formation of the WPA, Roosevelt appeased the Southern Democrats whose votes could determine the fate of his legislation. In 1934 Roosevelt decided not to support a federal anti-lynching bill, because, as he explained to NAACP secretary Walter White: "If I come out for the anti-lynching bill now, they [southerners] will block every bill I ask Congress to pass to keep America from collapsing. I just can't take that risk."[47] Roosevelt therefore advocated patience on the race issue. When members of the American Youth Congress met with Eleanor Roosevelt in 1936, she too counseled patience. Louis Burnham, a black student leader in the ASU, offered his simple answer: "We are tired of waiting, Mrs. Roosevelt."[48]

Many Jews also felt that compromise on the issue of civil rights was inappropriate. In supporting civil rights for all Americans, Jews fought not only for blacks, but for their own security in troubled times. Jewish philanthropists such as Julius Rosenwald were instrumental in the founding of the NAACP. Jewish lawyers such as Arthur Spingarn and Jack Greenberg helped to found the Legal Defense Fund, which mounted the first legal challenge to segregation. The Jewish lawyer Samuel Leibowitz helped to reverse the Scottsboro Boys' rape conviction before the Supreme Court in 1932, and Louis Marshall was a strong proponent of the anti-lynching law in New York State in the 1920s. Jewish labor leaders were stalwart allies of activist Philip Randolph, head of the largely black Sleeping Car Porters Union.[49] While Rodgers and Hart were not actively involved in these organizations in the 1930s, they certainly knew and respected people who were. Rodgers' colleague and later partner Oscar Hammerstein, for example, served as a vice president of the NAACP.

Val, like the ASU leaders and many Jewish activists, rejects the "political" solution offered by Billie. A few scenes later, with the show in progress, Val, Billie, and Lee have a confrontation over the issue. Ivor is ready to go on and Val wants to let him. Billie intercedes, covering for Lee's prejudice by telling Ivor that Lee thinks he is too young to perform. Val, the director, says to Lee, the producer:

VAL: I want him to go on.

LEE: You want him? Who cares? Let me tell you something: *I'm* running this show.

VAL: Well, I've done all the work, and I won't let you interfere; you with your nasty prejudices.

LEE: You won't, eh? [*To Ivor*] They told you you're not going on because you're too young, hey? I'll tell you the truth. You're not going on because you're too *black!*

VAL: Lee, what you've just said may be perfectly right from your point of view, but—on the other hand— [*He socks Lee on the jaw. Billie tries to stop him but is too late. Lee falls and slowly gets up rubbing his chin*]

LEE: That settles you. I'm out of it for good. Now you can go to the Work Farm!

VAL: Go on, Ivor, and make good.

Val fights powerfully for the integration of his cast—an argument that was much needed in the 1930s, in the theater world as well as in the larger society. As Allen Woll relates, while the occasional musical of the 1920s, like *Show Boat* (1927), featured a mixed cast, by the mid-1930s, segregation had returned to Broadway: "On the whole, the existing but often limited notion of theatrical integration disappeared during the early years of the Great Depression, as black employment opportunities remained relegated to the black musicals of the decade."[50] The Federal Theatre Project, unlike commercial Broadway ventures, encouraged integration and insisted on interracial casting; in addition to reflecting the general Jewish liberal sensibility of the time, Rodgers and

Hart may have been specifically reacting to this change in the theatrical environment in writing this scene.[51]

At the end of Act 1, Val asserts himself as the director, pushing Ivor on stage. Ivor gives an emotional and electrifying performance: *"He dances like mad, crying enormous tears as autos offstage and back of the auditorium honk their wild approval. The cheering and clapping make Ivor hoof and cry all the more as the curtain falls to* END ACT ONE. *"*[52] The scene, as described in the stage directions, is a compelling example of the conflation of the theatrical and the political. Angered by Lee's racism and also racked with guilt that he (not Lee) has destroyed the kids' chance to stay off the work farm, Ivor weeps as he dances. His anger, his guilt, and his confusion make him dance even more beautifully. The better he dances, the more the audience cheers, and the more he weeps. Harold Nicholas, who played Ivor, was an extraordinary dancer whose athletic grace and intricate footwork were legendary. Yet this scene evokes the complex and disturbing power dynamic between the black performer and white audience—a dynamic that, no matter how benignly presented, invokes the history of slave auctions and minstrel shows.[53] The honking horns are a violent means of expressing approval: the white audience members sit wrapped safely in their automobiles, voicing their pleasure via a machine, while the young black boy dances alone, exposed and vulnerable on the stage.[54] This unseen stage audience, with its honking horns, clearly represents and eventually becomes the actual audience, which stopped the show with their cheering at the end of the dance sequence.[55] In fact, the scene also unravels the neat integrationist message of the fight between Val and Lee explicitly as well as implicitly. Val and Lee are both white and their dispute is not just over theater or politics but also over a white girl—Billie—whom Val suspects of having kissed Lee. Ivor becomes a pawn in their struggle, and when Val pushes him onstage, Val "liberates" Ivor to perform with the white cast but also forces him to do so in order to prove his own (Val's) moral superiority over Lee.

Despite Val's integrationist politics, then, the black characters are set apart in significant ways. While Val, Lee, Billie, Gus, and Marshall make choices about the type of theatrical and political action they want to take, the black characters are given little opportunity to make choices. The white characters decide whether or not the black dancers can perform, and the white audience decides whether or not the performance is acceptable. Race defines Ivor and Irving from the beginning. In the cast list on the second page of the script, Lincoln, Booker, Irving, and Ivor are called "black clouds." Nearly every reviewer identified the Nicholas Brothers by their race. John Mason Brown of the New York *Post* called them "admirable sepia steppers"; Richard Lockridge of the New York *Sun* called them "little Negro boys"; the New York *American* dubbed them "a pair of dusky youngsters"; others labeled them "colored lads," "brown dancing imps," and "Mad Zulus out of Harlem."[56] Blackness is their defining

12. The Nicholas Brothers dancing in the finale of *Babes in Arms* (1937). Photo by Lucas-Pritchard. Museum of the City of New York; Lucas-Pritchard Collection.

characteristic—they are limited to playing black stereotypes. Their primary political function in the play is to give the white people a chance to argue over racism.

None of the black kids actively participates in the discussions about plans for resistance and revolution. Irving and Ivor actually show up so late that they miss the planning meeting entirely:

IRVING: When's the meetin' startin'?
BOOKER: It's over!
IVOR: You mean we is late?
BOOKER: Ivor, if you was any later, you wouldn't even know about it.

Those who apparently have the most to fight for have the least amount of theatrical and political agency in the play. Val and Marshall proudly declare that adults will not control them, but they treat Ivor like a child incapable of fighting his own battles. Harold Nicholas played Ivor when he was sixteen years old—and although he was short, he was hardly a tiny child and was not much younger than the principals. When Val tells Ivor to go on, Ivor replies, "No, I didn't mean to hurt you and Miss Billie. I don't want to go on." Ivor's desire to please his white elders and his deferring to Billie (a tramp, no less!) as "Miss" (which none of the other kids do) have an uncomfortably subservient ring. In this aspect of their representation of the activist community, Rodgers and Hart depart from their contemporary youth movement models. The ASU leadership included a number of black students, many of whom bravely protested the Roosevelt administration's racial policies. Far from wanting to hold back so as not to hurt the larger white population—"you and Miss Billie," as Ivor configures it—these black students demanded an end to institutional racism. No white person spoke for Elizabeth Scott when she demanded of Eleanor Roosevelt during the 1936 march on Washington: "How do you think we should fight against Negro discrimination in this country and what are you going to do about it?"[57]

In promoting an egalitarian vision but neglecting to develop fully the agency of black characters, Rodgers and Hart create a subtly segregated theatrical community. The cast appears to be integrated—black and white appear onstage together. But the group is segregated by the ability of its various members to act in both the theatrical and political arenas. Rodgers and Hart begin to articulate an opposition here between ethnic and racial characters that Rodgers developed more overtly in his later work with Hammerstein. Despite their implied ethnic difference, the characters with big noses are all "white." By simultaneously arguing for racial equality on behalf of the black characters and insisting that the ethnic characters are white, Rodgers and Hart play it safe on both sides of the racial coin. Arguments for racial equality ensure that Jews as well as blacks will not suffer discrimination. And arguments that Jews are not a racial group at all but rather a division of white America protect Jewish interests in the eventuality that racial equality is not achieved.

In *Babes in Arms,* performance style determines political effectiveness. Ivor, Val, and Billie each illustrate the powers and limitations of their particular theatrical assignments. Ivor and the other black dancers, Irving, Booker, and Lincoln, appear as performers in stereotyped roles that are enclosed within the world of the stage. Unlike Henry Williams in *Whoopee,* Ivor and Irving cannot move outside or even within their stereotypes. Whereas the Jewish vaudeville performers were free to adopt a variety of ethnic and racial disguises on a whim, the black kids could only play black. Like Henry and Gieber, when Booker needs to hide from the sheriff, he does so by becoming even more "black." In a typical minstrel routine, Booker hides in bed along with Beauregarde and a stolen chicken as Lee and the sheriff walk in the door. Booker's trace of dialect becomes pronounced as he pretends to be sick: "Oh, I'se ill! I'se awful indisposed with palpitations!" And while the black characters often challenge racism, they always do so as *black* performers. For example,

13. The Nicholas Brothers and others in a typical minstrel routine with a chicken, from *Babes in Arms* (1937). Photo by Lucas-Pritchard. Museum of the City of New York; Lucas-Pritchard Collection.

★ ★

the racist producer Lee drags his little brother from the organizing meeting, chastising him for playing with the black kids: "Beauregarde Calhoun! And you were named for a great Southern general. Come on!" The black kids respond by taunting Lee with a minstrel song "Is it true what they say about Dixie?" Unlike Val, Peter, Lee, and Billie, who speak in the political language of the day (and also perform in musical numbers), the black characters can speak only from within the language of stereotypical black performance: minstrelsy and Dixie songs.

In a most obvious and distasteful example of the way in which the black characters are limited to performing blackness, Ivor and Irving sing and dance to their specialty song, entitled "All Dark People":

> And just the same as flowers get honey
> All God's chillun got buck-and-wings
> Paleface babies don't dance in the street,
> All dark people is light on their feet.

While the number itself was a high point of the original production, showcasing the talents of the Nicholas Brothers, the lyrics of the song undercut some of the political power the dancers might have drawn from their virtuosic performance. Through the stereotype of "natural" talent, Ivor and Irving are denied the mobility of the self-conscious performer—the performer who can change costume, ethnicity, and race at will. They have little power over the mechanics of the play-within-a-play and hence over the political action the performance represents. Val *pushes* Ivor onto the stage. Ivor does not go on his own.

Unlike the black kids, Val *can* shift from role to role. But despite the fact that he is the child of actors, Val is strikingly untheatrical and politically naive. He is earnest, romantic, idealistic, and unselfconscious. He perpetually redefines himself based on the philosopher he is reading that day: "I pick up a book like *Das Kapital* by Karl Marx and I think it's wonderful. Then I read a book on individualism by Nietzsche and I think Marx is crazy. Then I listen to Roosevelt on the radio and I think I'm crazy." When Val switches roles, however, he assumes that his indecisiveness is an aberration—that he (or someone) is crazy— rather than a simple convention of the theater. So although Val shifts roles, he is not aware that his mobility can be a theatrical device. Over the course of Act 1, while Val changes his ideological positions, he remains consistent in his earnestness. He struggles to do the right thing, to fight for liberty, to support the kids. But Val's idealism is shrugged off by more astute observers like Billie as romantic dreaming. Political orthodoxy of any sort, this play implies, is neither entertaining nor effective.

Val plays earnestness well; but because he is not *aware* that he is acting, his political agency is revealed to be as limited on the musical comedy stage as that of the black characters—perhaps even more so. Irving and Ivor at least demonstrate theatrical virtuosity. But Val (as Billie astutely observes) lacks self-consciousness onstage and is unaware of or unconcerned about his audience. After Val and Billie argue over the inclusion of Irving and Ivor in the play, Val storms off, afraid he will be "corrupted" by Billie's opportunism. Reflecting on Val's naiveté, Billie sings:

> Behold the way our fine-feathered friend
> His virtue doth parade.
> Thou knowest not, my dim-witted friend,
> The picture thou hast made.

Val is, as Billie recognizes, politically unsavvy. He is also, therefore, theatrically unsavvy. He can inhabit a role but he cannot *act*.

★   ★   ★   ★   ★

In *Babes in Arms,* Rodgers and Hart develop a complex system of theatricality as a *mode of acting* that sets their work apart from the contemporary political theater. This mode depends on the characters in the musical demonstrating self-consciousness as they perform. They must understand that the role they play is a *role,* and that they have the power to manipulate it at will. Most of the characters in *Babes in Arms,* with the exception of Val, achieve this.

The characters are aided in their self-conscious performances by the musical comedy structure that separates song from story, engaging in the Brechtian "radical separation of the elements." In 1930 Brecht wrote: "The great struggle for supremacy between words, music and production—which always brings up the question 'Which is the pretext for what?': is the music the pretext for the events on the stage, or are these the pretext for the music? etc.—can simply be by-passed by radically separating the elements."[58] *Babes in Arms* offers an excellent demonstration of the way the elements of the play work together but never blend together. This separation of the elements allows the performers to express their self-conscious acting style by openly transforming themselves as they shift from straight scene to musical number. All of the cast members in *Babes in Arms* play young kids, but they sing surprisingly sophisticated songs. Gus, the young hothead, and Dolores, his ex-girlfriend, are supposed to be sixteen or seventeen, at most. Yet in "I Wish I Were in Love Again," they sing of "the classic battle of a him and her" with remarkably adult cynicism. The effect of this juxtaposition is to remind the audience that there is a performer behind the character, and that this performer is capable of radical self-invention each time a musical number is introduced.

The combination of self-conscious performance and separation of the elements allows the musical itself to become a political statement. Again the comparison with Brechtian theater is instructive. The musical numbers achieve aspects of Brecht's epic theater, one of which was the alienation effect: "A technique of taking the human social incidents to be portrayed and labeling them as something striking, something that calls for explanation, is not to be taken for granted, not just natural." The object of the alienation effect is "to allow the spectator to criticize constructively from a social point of view."[59] It is never "natural" for people to break into song in the middle of a conversation. (They certainly never do it in the realist theater.) When the singers turn to the audience to perform a number, they are reminding the audience that the reality represented on stage is only a theatrical illusion. But in Rodgers and Hart musicals, the alienation effect of the musical numbers is transformed into the assimilation effect.[60]

Instead of a radical call for musical and political revolution, Rodgers and Hart created a uniquely American theatrical form which demands that the American musical, and implicitly America itself, live up to the ideals of liberal capitalism, the central one being that the United States is a meritocracy in which everyone has a chance to advance according to his or her talents and commitment, without reference to racial, ethnic, religious, or other hereditary characteristics. The linguistic acrobatics of the lyrics in *Babes In Arms* critique blind adherence to assumptions about identity and encourage experimentation and self-invention. For example, in the second act, two former lovers, Gus and Dolores, argue over Dolores' inability to remain faithful. Gus begins a verse of "You Are So Fair," a song that details not Dolores' virtues but the problems she causes for him. The first line—"You are so fair"—implies a standard romantic cliché: you are so blond and light-skinned, and, by extension, so beautiful. But the complex puns built into the song lyrics ask the audience to think about the implications of the word "fair":

> You are so fair—
> Like an Oriental vision,
> But you won't make that decision.
> You're not quite fair.

The song begins with one meaning of the word "fair" (physically attractive) and then shifts to another meaning: honest, impartial, conforming to the rules. The lyrics also undercut the assumed connection between beauty and light skin, surprising the listener by comparing fair Dolores to an "Oriental vision." In the next phrase Gus sings of how he would willingly marry Dolores if only she would stick by him:

> I'd pay your fare
> To Niag'ra Falls and back too,
> But you never will react to
> This love affair.

Now we have two more homophonic examples: "fare" (the price of a ticket) and the second syllable of the word "affair." The wordplay continues with references to "bill of fare" (menu), "how you'll fare" (get along, succeed), "you're only fair" (not so great), "hair ain't fair" (back to light-colored), and "savoir faire" (knowledge of how to behave). The song is, therefore, not only about the anxiety of not knowing if love is reciprocated, but also about the problems of establishing meaning through language, and, by extension, of establishing identity through stereotype. In subjecting the word "fair" to a dizzying array of interpretations, the song asks the audience to be aware of the ways language constructs identity.

This type of wordplay proliferates in the song lyrics. The title "Babes in Arms" is itself a puzzle—it could refer to babies held in their mothers' arms or children carrying guns. The posters for the original show featured sexy young girls in halter tops with bare arms—yet another meaning of "babes" in arms. Likewise, the line "All dark people is light on their feet" plays with the fixed (or fluid) implications of racial language. The line could mean that dark people are good dancers, but it also could mean that when they dance they become "light," or white. In "The Lady Is a Tramp," sung in Act 2, Billie calls into question the whole notion of being a tramp:

> I like the green grass under my shoes.
> What can I lose?
> I'm flat! That's that!
> I'm all alone when I lower my lamp.
> That's why the lady is a tramp.

What does Billie mean by "tramp"? Is she a hobo? A free spirit? Or a prostitute? By claiming that *because* she is "all alone when she lowers her lamp" she is a tramp, she turns societal injunctions about gender identity on their heads and asserts her right to redefine herself through performance. The music for the song is a celebratory anthem, not a moral harangue. Her independence and free-thinking, not her lack of virtue, earn her the title "tramp." The song forces the audience to question not only Billie's social standing, but the very nature of the moralizing labels applied to independent women. In drawing attention to the slipping and sliding of language, then, Hart's lyrics force us to examine assumptions about identity, and in particular to be suspicious of clichés which implicitly or explicitly constrain characters' ability to define themselves through their performance.

But while the songs expose the workings of language and convention, they do not call for those conventions to be discarded. Unlike Brecht, Rodgers and Hart believe in working within the system (both the theatrical one of the musical comedy and the national one of American liberal capitalism). So they affirm the necessity of theatrical convention as long as it is employed self-consciously, with full awareness of its formulaic purpose and mutable nature. Gus and Dolores' first song, "I Wish I Were in Love Again," sung in Act 1, captures this impulse. They nostalgically reminisce about their relationship, but instead of seeing it through rose-colored glasses, they remember

> The broken dates,
> The endless waits,
> The lovely loving and the hateful hates,
> The conversation with the flying plates—

Yet they are not deterred by the conflict they recall. The verse drives toward an affirmative refrain: "I wish I were in love again!" Gus and Dolores are deeply aware of the false claims of romantic love: "The furtive sigh, / The blackened eye, / The words, 'I'll love you till the day I die.'" They recall the painful juxtaposition of physical abuse and "I love yous," but still they do not reject the notion of being in love: "The self-deception that believes the lie— / I wish I were in love again." They deceive themselves, but they know they deceive themselves; indeed, they like (and need) the deception. And so, in great leaps of imagination, and at risk to life and limb, they optimistically long for more op-portunities to continue that same self-deception. Gus and Dolores know that the conventional romantic love plots they keep performing in are fraught with emotional dangers, but they also believe that these plots embody a worth-while ideal. So, with irrepressible American optimism, they keep trying for a happy ending. Brecht would have scorned their devotion to the love plot as false consciousness.[61] Rodgers and Hart see it as a uniquely American form of theatrical self-consciousness.

★ ★ ★ ★ ★

Although Val is the nominal leader of the group, the responsibility falls to Billie to teach the kids—and Val in particular—the elements of theatricality that will afford them the success (and freedom and independence) they desire. Billie understands the pitfalls of naive earnestness and appreciates the importance of skillful role playing in achieving political and theatrical goals. From the mo-ment she appears, Billie is playing a role. She stumbles into Val's kitchen pos-ing as a prep school girl:

> BILLIE: Oh, I don't know what to say—I—Oh, I just can't—
> VAL: Why, what's the matter?
> BILLIE: Oh, this is very embarrassing. You see, my car is stalled—
> VAL: Where?
> BILLIE: Oh, down the street. We were on our way back to school—Miss Finley's—
> VAL: You hit something?
> BILLIE: No—we ran out of gas.
> VAL: But you can get gas over at Tony's—
> BILLIE: Well, you see I had nothing smaller than a hundred-dollar bill. Oh, it's very embarrassing. We need a dollar.

When Billie learns that Val is the son of vaudeville actors, she settles for a cup of coffee and then admits to the gullible Val that she is *not* going to finishing school after all. (It is significant that Val, a child of vaudevillians, cannot see through her act. Stripped of its former glory, his vaudevillian heritage no longer affords him the skills necessary to negotiate the changing theatrical landscape.) Billie then concedes that her performance was not up to snuff be-cause she did not have the right costume: "I shouldn't have tried that finishing school gag in this little Schiaparelli number." In the organizing meeting, Billie, by playing the patriot, convinces the sheriff to give the kids two weeks to re-hearse their show. She convinces the guys that they do not need stars for their show, because she can *act* like a star:

BILLIE: I'll give you a star.

LEE: Who?

BILLIE: Luise Rainer.

LEE: What are you talking about?

BILLIE: [*Imitating Luise Rainer playing Anna Held in "The Great Ziegfeld"*] Hello—Hello, Flo? Yes, this is Anna. . . . I'm going to be in a revue. . . . I wish you were going to produce it. . . . Oh, that is nice. I'm so glad for you. Yes, Flo. Thank you. Goodbye, Flo. [*sobs*] Darling.[62]

She likewise uses her "feminine wiles" to persuade Lee to fund the show:

BILLIE: Well, of course, we'd see a lot of each other if we do the show.

LEE: Would we?

BILLIE: Of course we would. How could I come to any decision without consulting you? Oh, Lee, we've worked so hard to put this over and sometimes I get so tired and feel so weak and little. [*She looks up at him*] And then I realize that I'm only a woman.

LEE: You poor little girl.

BILLIE: Oh, Lee, I do need a big strong arm to lean on sometimes.

LEE: Billie, I'll put the show over for you.

BILLIE: Will you?

In play-acting the weak feminine role, Billie emphasizes the strength that she actually possesses as a woman. The fact that the only character who understands how to achieve political power in the play is a woman may be less a feminist statement than yet another example of D. A. Miller's claim that women enjoy an enormous theatrical advantage over men on the Broadway stage. Billie's strength can also be understood in relation to the upheaval in gender power dynamics many families experienced during the Depression. With so many men unemployed, many women could no longer comfortably rely on husbands and fathers to support them. They needed to adopt pragmatic and independent life plans. When husbands lost their jobs or suffered pay cutbacks, wives and daughters often went to work to help make ends meet. Many unemployed men suffered psychological crises, fearing that their joblessness had undermined their authority in the household. Despite the fact that only 25 percent of all wives worked during the Depression, the perception arose that women were gaining the upper hand in the workplace. Because jobs designated as "women's work" did not always suffer the same fluctuations as jobs reserved for men, women also seemed to be able to find work more easily. Those who did not work outside the home were forced to become extremely resourceful managers of household budgets, dictating to the last penny the ways in which the family's meager income was to be spent.[63] In Billie's signature song, "The Lady Is a Tramp," she demonstrates the power of her theatrical skills. Using self-conscious performance, a sophisticated musical number that clearly marks the distinction between performer and character, and a song that demands the audience listen closely to the meaning of her words, Billie combines all of the elements essential for a successful character in Rodgers and Hart's musical arena.

Billie's independence and pragmatism can be viewed as necessary skills for a woman in Depression America. But although her frank, independent style may mirror Scarlett O'Hara's, her theatrical approach to political action is far more closely related to that of Dale Carnegie. In his manual *How to Win Friends and Influence People,* a best-seller in 1937, Carnegie argued that success depended not on hard work or technical expertise, but on "personality and the ability to lead people."[64] Carnegie advised persuasion by subtle means. He counseled readers to bring people around to their way of thinking by "letting the other man think the idea is his."[65] Billie offers a step by step illustration of Carnegie's methods in her interaction with Lee. She may spout the rhetoric of nineteenth-century individualists, but she actually lives by theatrical techniques that, in the 1930s, were understood to be the secrets to success in corporate America. Her theatrical tactics also recall those of Roosevelt himself. In his political style, from his intimate fireside chats on the radio to his rousing campaign speeches, Roosevelt was a highly theatrical figure. His popularity depended in large part on his ability to play a wide variety of roles and to take his cues from whichever audience he needed to please at that moment.[66] Rodgers and Hart emphasized their own view of Roosevelt as a theatrical performer when they cast Broadway veteran George M. Cohan to play him in their next production, *I'd Rather Be Right.*

Just as Roosevelt understood the need to compromise in order to push through his New Deal legislation, Billie knows that offending Lee by insisting that Ivor perform will destroy the whole plan for keeping the kids off the work farm. And she is right. Despite all of the good intentions, hard work, and "spirit and determination" of the kids of Seaport, the director offends the producer, the producer loses his money, and the show fails to achieve its goal. In the second act, the kids, and Val in particular, faced with defeat, are finally ready to learn from Billie:

> VAL: I don't expect you to stick, but if you do, let me tell you one thing:
> I'm on to myself. I'm through with these half baked theories.
> BILLIE: Oh, there's nothing wrong with theories, if they're convenient.
> VAL: Don't you believe in anything?
> BILLIE: I believe in two things: luck and guts.

Billie exposes the way in which the Depression raised questions about the traditional Jewish—and American—belief in upward mobility. In addition to rejecting Val's theorizing, she also omits hard work, education, and talent in her recipe for success. These values have not, in her experience, proven terribly useful amid the chaotic economy of the Depression. Instead, she advocates luck. Life is a gamble, Billie argues. You cannot determine what surprises fate has in store for you. The real test is whether you have the guts to take the chances life offers and do something with them.

When luck does strike, in the form of a deus ex machina—an aviator falling out of the sky and into their laps—Val is finally ready to take charge, to *act* in both senses of the term:

BILLIE: Marshall, telephone the airport, they'll send help.
VAL: Not yet!
BILLIE: What?
MARSHALL: Why not?
VAL: Because I say so!

Val asserts himself and orders the kids to help him dress up in Flambeau's clothes. Billie does his makeup. Val demonstrates his French accent, then tells Marshall to tie Flambeau up. When the kids wonder if it would be right to do it, Val demonstrates that he grasps Billie's pragmatism, insisting: "This is the time for action, not ethics." As the crowds arrive to interview Flambeau, all of the kids must act as if Val is the real aviator. Val gives a "French" speech and the crowd is utterly fooled. Val is elated. In a private moment with Billie, he gloats: "Isn't it marvelous? I've done it at last."

In learning how to put on and take off a role, Val learns how to negotiate the real world. No political ideology, the play seems to say, will help him become an *actor* in the way theatricality will. By seizing his lucky break and *acting* persuasively, Val fulfills for himself and the rest of his community the liberal capitalist dream of upward mobility. The dream is fulfilled in two ways: the aviator uses his prize money to back the show, giving the kids a shot at Broadway success—an apt reward for Val's effective acting. But Flambeau also gives the kids the far more significant prize of a lucrative family business. He agrees to keep quiet about Val's impersonation of him, in which Val (as the aviator) endorses his own family's land as the site for a new airport. "Buster McCabe," claims Val as Flambeau, "he say ze landing was forced. I say so, too, in ze air, but eet was not. I look down here and see ze beautiful town of Seaport and zis most beautiful place for ze airport in ze world. My frands, I do not know why ze estimable citizens of la belle New York must go so far for airport as Newark. Seaport is bettaire—much bettaire—so near, so clear, so beautiful!" The endorsement of the "aviator" leads the airlines to begin bidding immediately on Val's land. The youth of Seaport will have not only fame, but also riches.

The aviator subplot seems an apparently irrelevant conclusion to a play about the theater. But the conclusion is not irrelevant to the story about Jewish liberalism. During the 1930s, the mayor of New York, Fiorello LaGuardia, insisted that New York needed its own airport. In 1934 he refused to disembark from his flight when the plane landed in Newark, claiming that his ticket said "New York" and Newark was in New Jersey.[67] The same year that *Babes in Arms* opened on Broadway, ground was broken in Queens (not far from the western edge of Long Island) for what would be named, in 1939, LaGuardia Airport. Ironically, the airport was built by WPA workers through a "work farm" project just like the one the youth of Seaport resist. So the finale of the play, which envisions prosperity deriving from an airport, offers a none-too-subtle gesture of support for New York's mayor, beloved by Jews in the late 1930s for his liberal social policies and commitment to political reform. He, like Roosevelt, gave many Jews their first chance for government jobs by overturning the corrupt Tammany political machine and implementing a merit system for selecting civil servants.[68] LaGuardia, like Roosevelt, was also known for his theatrical persona. Indeed, these two politicians are among the few to be honored as the central subjects of Broadway musicals, written, of course, by Jews.[69]

In *Babes in Arms,* then, Rodgers and Hart demonstrate how theatrical self-consciousness coincides neatly with a pragmatic and liberal political sensibility. The play connects Jewish liberalism with Jewish theatricality: the best tools for enacting liberal political beliefs are those with which Jews are already supplied by virtue of their historical experience. Via this circuitous route, Rodgers and Hart justify *both* Jewish secular identity and the new style of musical comedy they have created. Underneath the simple story of a group of all-American kids who just want to make good in hard times lies a story about the complicated path secular Jews took to define a political identity that allowed them access to the American mainstream. The kids are both exceptional and representative. Their performance resolves an old American paradox: how to reconcile individualism with union. In America, one *must* play a role; the moral crux is to be aware that one is performing and to consciously choose a good role. In this way, the personal becomes the political. Like another old performer, Walt Whitman, the babes in arms celebrate themselves, and in doing so they celebrate all Americans.

4

"We Know We Belong to the Land"

The Theatricality of Assimilation in *Oklahoma!*

IN 1943, Americans were fighting a war characterized by racial hatreds on all sides. The villain in Europe was the fanatically racist Nazi Germany, which demanded of its followers a hatred of all non-Aryans and particularly of Jews. The Allies viewed the war in the Pacific as a racial war against the "yellow menace" of the Japanese. Those of Japanese extraction, even American citizens, were perceived as suspect and many Japanese-Americans suffered both psychological and physical humiliation when they were forced from their West Coast homes into internment camps in the Midwest during the years 1942–1944.[1] Black Americans, eager to take their places beside all other Americans in the armed services, chafed against enforced segregation and exclusion from combat positions. Blacks also wanted to take part in the great economic recovery that accompanied the declaration of war, but found the doors of many industrial plants closed to them as a result of racist hiring practices.[2]

Despite the explosive racial climate, American popular culture of the war years celebrated diversity and heterogeneity as a foundational element of the American democratic system—indeed, as one of the primary reasons for which the war was being fought. In January 1943, the Office of War Information directed Hollywood producers to "depict democracy by showing persons of different race, religion and economic status mingling on even terms in factory or other war service and also in settings of everyday life."[3] Countless Hollywood films illustrated the wonders of melting-pot America by portraying diverse platoons of Anglo, Italian, Polish, Hispanic, Jewish, and Irish soldiers all fighting together to save American democracy. For the most part, these "inclusive" groups excluded black and Asian Americans.[4] Hollywood—and some Broadway shows as well, as we shall see—solved the contradiction inherent in celebrating diversity within a racially segregated society by creating two categories of difference: ethnic and racial. Ethnic difference was ultimately superficial—represented by a love of different foods, religious rituals, or modes of dress—and therefore ethnics could easily assimilate into the American mainstream. Racial difference, on the other hand, was written in the blood and was therefore impossible to change.

The Jewish creators of Hollywood films and Broadway musicals had a particular stake in both celebrating the Americanness of ethnic others and defining the distance between race and ethnicity. The "Americans All" rhetoric that infused wartime culture seemed to offer the chance to finally settle the question of whether or not Jews were "one hundred percent Americans." As movies and plays demonstrated, American Jews took their place in battle alongside Greek, Italian, and Polish Americans and proved their patriotism by risking and often giving their lives. At the same time, Nazi antisemitism forced European Jews into a despised racial class that bore some resemblance to the historical situation of American blacks. While the threat of Nazi-style antisemitism in America was limited, American Jews were shocked by the sudden transformation of respected assimilated German Jewish citizens into hated aliens and began actively to resist the categorization of Jews as a racial group.

★   ★   ★   ★   ★

The opening of *Oklahoma!*—arguably the most American (and least Jewish) of the Broadway musicals produced during the war years—in 1943 marked a transitional moment in both the history of the American musical and the career of Richard Rodgers. *Babes in Arms* and the other plays by Rodgers and Hart of the late 1930s and early 1940s featured strong books yet retained a highly theatrical separation of elements, with numbers and plot alternating during the course of the show. Now that realism had become the prevailing mode in drama and Hollywood films, Richard Rodgers, along with his new partner, Oscar Hammerstein II, began to reject musical numbers that called attention to themselves in favor of a more seamless dramatic illusion.[5] Relying more and more on adaptations of plays and novels, Rodgers and Hammerstein merged the older musical comedy form with the realist drama to create what was hailed as a new genre, the musical play, characterized by the integration of story and musical numbers.[6] This push toward the "total work of art" can be seen as having ideological as well as artistic implications.[7] Rodgers comments in his memoir: "When a show works perfectly, it's because all the individual parts complement each other and fit together. No single element overshadows any other. . . . That's what made *Oklahoma!* work. . . . There was nothing extraneous or foreign, nothing that pushed itself into the spotlight yelling 'Look at me!' It was a work created by many that gave the impression of having been created by one."[8] The drive to create the effect of *e pluribus unum* in a work of art required the elimination of "extraneous or foreign" elements. Likewise, the American community represented in *Oklahoma!* struggles with and ultimately eliminates its "alien" elements before the musical reaches its celebratory conclusion.

Rodgers and Hammerstein inaugurated this new form with *Oklahoma!* and followed this breakthrough with midcentury classics of the American musical stage such as *Carousel* (1945), *South Pacific* (1949), *The King and I* (1951), and *The Sound of Music* (1959).[9] They have been credited with "irreversibly changing the face of American musical comedy."[10] The opening of *Oklahoma!* initiated a sea change in critical expectations, and more schematic musicals like *Girl Crazy* and *Babes in Arms* were retrospectively viewed as "fluff," devoid of substance or purpose, because their plot and numbers were not fully integrated and not psychologically motivated. The unmotivated introduction of a song was increasingly seen as a sign of an immature musical, and more realistic musical plays slowly but surely replaced the earlier musicals in the hearts of the critics. The language with which today's theater historians dismiss the highly theatrical musicals of the 1920s and '30s in favor of the "revolution" of *Oklahoma!* is startling in its unselfconscious triumphalism and antitheatrical bias. Ethan Mordden, perhaps the most strenuous proponent of the maturity of *Oklahoma!* and the integrated musical, describes the typical 1930s-style musical as an outright failure: "The entire show was a bald contrivance. The story didn't matter, and the characters were types. . . . [The play] was not a thing-in-itself but a well-organized collection of things. . . . It was not penetrating art. . . . It isn't about anything but the desire to entertain."[11]

In his view, *Oklahoma!* "swept the world, and announced the revolution in the writing and staging of musicals." What made *Oklahoma!* so great? "The parts fitted together because the intentions behind the work were inspired and fearless. . . . Rodgers and Hammerstein pulled it off by rejecting Broadway's rules on the very nature of entertainment."[12] Timothy Donovan argues: "There is no question that it was the perfect integration of the music into the narrative that elevates *Oklahoma!* to something more than traditional musical comedy."[13] And Richard Goldstein's writing on *Oklahoma!* reveals the way in which this triumphal reporting has obscured the history of musicals before Rodgers and Hammerstein. Not only is Goldstein's tone reverential, but his observations are also historically inaccurate: "They [Rodgers and Hammerstein] pioneered the development of the integrated musical featuring the seamless joining of dialogue, music and lyrics. . . . They were among the first to employ the United States as a subject for serious consideration in the musical format, instead of as merely a background for the lighthearted romantic romps which were the staple of earlier musical entries. . . . They also pioneered the inclusion of social commentary within the musical's form."[14] The work of George and Ira Gershwin, Irving Berlin, Rodgers and Hart, and Oscar Hammerstein and Jerome Kern are erased in this telling. As my earlier chapters have made clear, the United States as context and object of criticism found its way onto the musical stage well before 1943.

Rodgers and Hammerstein's musicals are unquestionably innovative, but by using *Oklahoma!* to create such a sharp dividing line between "immature" and "mature" musical theater, critics have obscured the dynamics that make *Oklahoma!* such a powerful musical. While the play does adopt elements of the realist theater of its day, it also retains a residual reliance on the theatrical elements of earlier musicals: a sharp distinction between dialogue and numbers and a subtle self-consciousness about their theatricality. Numbers are still associated with particular types of characters and still serve more to showcase virtuosity than to reveal complex psychological information. Although the story struggles to subsume the musical numbers, the play ends with a rousing finale that celebrates community and asserts the primacy of the theatrical event. Audiences exit elated by the tunes rather than by a profound connection with a character's psyche.

Recognition of *Oklahoma!*'s two representational modes—the more realistic development of character through dialogue and plot and the celebratory energy of the musical numbers—offers insight into the way in which the play's subject, America, is constructed through a deceptively simple story of frontier romance and of Oklahoma's maturation from territory to state. One of the complex functions that the juxtaposition of dramatic realism and theatricality serves is to reveal the American tension between individual desire and communal cohesion. The story presents a set of characters with individual problems that demand resolution. On the surface, the story seems to be about the importance of choice and freedom in romantic love. The dialogue centers on questions such as: What does Laurey want? How can Curly get his girl? Will Ali free himself from Annie? Will Jud have his revenge? But the driving energy of the musical numbers contradicts the overt message of the plot: instead of privileging individual choices and dilemmas, this energy celebrates a wartime utopia. Differences meld into a unified loving American community. Access to this community is determined not by *character* but by *function:* anyone willing and able to perform the songs and dances can join.[15]

A utopian energy infuses the cowboy Will's first song in the play, which describes how "ev'rythin's up to date in Kansas City."[16] He draws those around him into the song and dance, teaching his chorus-community how to adapt to the modern world. First, he instructs the matriarchal Aunt Eller in the two-step while the cowboys look on, initially skeptical.[17] As Will's performance escalates into an impressive tap number, the cowboys slowly learn a few steps and join in the dance. When the number finishes, the full chorus of cowboys is tap-dancing together, the rhythmic sounds of their steps ringing out a happy, unified acceptance of modernity.

Most of the musical numbers in the show involve a similar communal vision. Only three songs are solos, and two of them—"Oh, What a Beautiful Mornin'" and "I Cain't Say No"—include an onstage audience. In the famous opening number, the hero, Curly, sings a paean to the land, to youth, and to the limitless opportunity of the frontier, as Aunt Eller and the heroine, Laurey, watch:

> Oh, what a beautiful mornin'
> Oh, what a beautiful day.
> I got a beautiful feelin'
> Ev'rythin's goin' my way.

The song's initially individualistic message is redefined when a large portion of the ensemble reprises the number twice in unison. In the first act, when wagons stop at Laurey's farm on the way to a "box social," a chorus of happy young couples sings the refrain and waltzes to its sweeping melody. And in the triumphant finale, as the happily married Curly and Laurey rush off to their honeymoon, the entire ensemble reprises the song "lustily," "gaily," and "loudly," according to the stage directions (84), so that the individualism of the line "Ev'rythin's goin' my way" becomes a communal celebration of "our way."

The flirtatious Ado Annie expresses individual desire in the solo "I Cain't Say No," but her bubbly rebelliousness in the first act is tempered and directed into more acceptable (and marriageable) channels in the second. She agrees to marry Will, settle down, and give him "All 'er Nuthin'" (66–67). Even Curly and Laurey's love song, "People Will Say We're in Love," a moment that seems the ultimate expression of personal desire, emphasizes how their love will appear to those around them:

> Don't throw bouquets at me,
> Don't please my folks too much,
> Don't laugh at my jokes too much—
> People will say we're in love!

Communal cohesiveness is equated in the play with maturity: Oklahoma cannot become a "grown-up state" and join the Union until the members of the community have learned to get along.[18] In "The Farmer and the Cowman," some members of the company at first side with the cowboys' interests and others with the farmers'. A fight ensues, until Aunt Eller, the disciplinarian, halts it with a gunshot. The chorus meekly returns to the refrain:

> Oh, the farmer and the cowman should be friends.
> One man likes to push a plough,
> The other likes to chase a cow,
> But that's no reason why they cain't be friends.

In the next verse, as the group looks ahead to the future, the merchant (the most likely representation of the Jew in the nineteenth-century American Midwest) is subtly slipped in next to the farmer and the cowman—an integral part of this emerging utopian community:

> And when this territory is a state,
> And jines the union jist like all the others,
> The farmer and the cowman and the merchant
> Must all behave theirsel's and act like brothers.

Finally, Aunt Eller voices the liberal sentiments that will allow all kinds of people to be assimilated into the community. The assimilation will occur through dance, romance, and intermarriage, she explains. The chorus cheers the notion and reprises Aunt Eller's verse:

> I don't say I'm no better than anybody else,
> But I'll be damned if I ain't just as good!
> Territory folks should stick together,
> Territory folks should all be pals.
> Cowboys dance with the farmer's daughters!
> Farmers, dance with the ranchers' gals!

At the end of the number, the stage directions call for a "gay, unrestrained dance" (54). Once the parameters of the community have been established, the members can celebrate their individual freedom within those bounds.

In Rodgers and Hammerstein's worldview, becoming a member of the Union is a process of sublimating individual needs to communal interest. Cowboys must settle down and become farmers; the frontier must be "tamed" into a useful agricultural resource; young people must marry and bring up new Americans. As Curly says once Laurey agrees to marry him: "Oh, I got to learn to be a farmer, I see that! Quit a-thinkin' about th'owin' the rope, and start in to git my hands blistered a new way! Oh, things is changin' right and left! Buy up mowin' machines, cut down the prairies! Shoe yer horses, drag them plows under the sod! They gonna make a state outa this, they gonna put it in the Union! Country a-changin', got to change with it! Bring up a pair of boys, new stock, to keep up 'th the way things is goin' in this here crazy country!" (71). Marriage becomes the metaphor not only for the maturation of the play's characters, but also for the relationship between a state and the Union. The political maturation outlined in "The Farmer and the Cowman" is realized toward the end of the second act, in the title song, "Oklahoma." The song begins when Curly and Laurey emerge from the farmhouse as husband and wife:

AUNT ELLER: They couldn't pick a better time to start in life!
IKE: It ain't too early and it ain't too late.
CURLY: Startin' as a farmer with a brand-new wife—
LAUREY: Soon be livin' in a brand-new state!
ALL: Brand-new state! (75)

The song and the dance that follow convey infectious feelings of exaltation and possibility. In 1943 this celebration of American statehood and American democratic values tapped into wartime nationalism.[19] Yet audiences have continued to adore this moment in the play, for the number celebrates the communion of the audience with the players. The joyous applause that inevitably follows the number joins audience members and performers in the communal utopian vision of Rodgers's and Hammerstein's America.[20]

In this vision of social unity, everyone shares the same homeland: immigrant (Ali) and native-born (Curly and Laurey) alike sing "We know we belong to the land" (76).[21] This insistence that the merchant belongs to the land as much as the farmer and the cowman was particularly important for American Jews, since centuries of persecution had been based on Jewish homelessness. Rodgers and Hammerstein also seem to have been influenced by the potent Zionist imagery of the 1940s, which promoted a utopian socialist vision of a homeland where Jews could return to the soil, become farmers, and claim the land as their own.[22] The show's poignant and nostalgic rendering of the Oklahoma land mirrored a long-awaited Jewish dream of homecoming. The story represented not just a sentimental rewriting of a time in American history when everyone "behaved like brothers" but also a plea for greater inclusiveness in the present. By creating a mythic time when nobody "was better than anybody else," when the health of the nation depended on the people's acceptance of one another, Rodgers and Hammerstein constructed a new idea of what America should be—an idea that entailed openness to ethnic outsiders.

* * * * *

In *Oklahoma!* "otherness" is defined the way America is defined: through the juxtaposition of realistic exposition and theatrical numbers. There are two opposing representations of the other in the play: Ali Hakim, a theatrical, assimilable ethnic ("white") immigrant, and Jud, a realistic, unassimilable, and racially characterized ("dark") man. The tension between the two is exposed in a set of parallel love triangles. In the central love story, Laurey, an innocent farm girl, and Curly, a cowhand, are clearly meant to be together, but they

tease each other throughout the first act and Laurey finally agrees to attend a box social with a farmhand, Jud, rather than with Curly. Jud ends up threatening both Laurey's sexual innocence and Curly's safety. After disrupting Curly and Laurey's wedding, Jud dies in a fight with Curly. The secondary love story is a comic one. It concerns Ado Annie; Will Parker, her faithful but slightly daft cowboy admirer; and Ali Hakim, an unmarried Persian peddler, happy in his bachelor state. Annie flirts with Ali, who gladly returns her attentions until her father insists on a wedding. Ali cleverly extracts himself from the union, but in the second act, Ali's flirtation with another farmer's daughter lands him in marriage after all. As the story ends, he is preparing, rather unwillingly, to settle down in town and run a store.

Jud and Ali have parallel roles in the love stories, but their otherness is radically different. Ali, a comic figure who sings, dances, and performs "bits," is a product of the theatrical side of *Oklahoma!* Jud is portrayed realistically and psychologically, and does not cross over into the communal realm of the musical numbers. The play is loaded with cues that connect Ali's and Jud's otherness to submerged ethnic and racial motifs in American cultural mythology. Ali serves as a thinly veiled stand-in for the Jewish immigrant. Jews, particularly Jews of German descent, formed a majority of the peddlers on the American frontier; the number of Persian peddlers was negligible, to say the least.[23] Groucho Marx was the first actor considered for the role on Broadway, but Joseph Buloff, a veteran of the Yiddish theater, ultimately took the part and played it with such a pronounced "Jewish inflection" that the character was generally assumed to be Jewish despite his "Persian" alibi.[24]

Jud, in contrast, is dark and evil. Described in the stage directions as a "burly, scowling man," "bullet-colored," and "growly" (17), he lives in a smokehouse with the rats. His sexuality, like that of the stereotypical male racial other, is threatening. He keeps postcards of naked women on the walls of his room, and these decorations make Laurey suspicious:

> LAUREY: He makes me shivver ever' time he gits clost to me. . . . Ever go
>   down to that ole smokehouse where he's at?
> AUNT ELLER: Plen'y times. Why?
> LAUREY: Did you see them pitchers he's got tacked onto the walls? (19)

Laurey flirts with Jud, but she fears the barely restrained sexuality that she senses in him: "Sumpin wrong inside him, Aunt Eller. I hook my door at night and fasten my winders agin' it. Agin' *it*—and the sound of feet a-walkin' up and down out there under that tree outside my room. . . . Mornin's he comes to his breakfast and looks at me out from under his eyebrows like sumpin' back in the bresh som'eres. I know whut I'm talkin' about" (19).

Laurey fears the racial "other"—Jud is something outside civilized society, barely human (she fastens her doors against *it,* not him)—that threatens to in-

14. Joseph Buloff and Celeste Holm as Ali Hakim and Ado Annie, in the 1943 production of *Oklahoma!* Museum of the City of New York; gift of the Burns Mantle Estate.

vade the white woman's private space and steal her virginity. Laurey uses racist imagery when she compares Jud to an animal, "sumpin back in the bresh som'eres."

In the "Dream Ballet" sequence, Laurey's fears of Jud's sexuality become more explicit. Wondering which man should take her to the dance, Laurey falls asleep and dreams an answer in ballet form. A joyous dance between Laurey and Curly is about to culminate in a wedding when "the ballet counterpart of Jud walks slowly forward and takes off 'Laurey's' veil. Expecting to see her lover, Curly, she looks up and finds 'Jud.' Horrified, she backs away. . . . She is alone with 'Jud'" (50). He drags her into a seamy world of can-can girls and bawdy dance halls and leaves her to watch the women perform a sexual and satiric dance. "Curly" arrives to save Laurey, and "Jud" kills him. As "Jud" carries her off triumphantly, the real Laurey awakens and decides to ride with Jud to avoid risking Curly's life.

On the way to the dance, Jud makes his move, an encounter only hinted at in the script: Laurey races onstage, frightened, and pursued by Jud. In the movie version, which in other respects follows the play closely, the scene has heightened sexual intensity and racial undertones. The film Laurey is played by Shirley Jones, an actress with golden hair, lily-white skin, and an attractive naiveté. Jud, played by Rod Steiger, is perpetually unshaven and smeared with dirt. As the wagons head to the Skidmore farm for the dance, Jud holds his cart back to be alone with Laurey, and then grabs her roughly and tries to kiss her. Laurey snatches the reins from his hands and sends the horses off in a frenzy, losing control of the wagon as it rushes headlong toward an oncoming train. The horses halt just before colliding with the train, and Laurey jumps out of the wagon and runs away.

Curly's interactions with Jud similarly evoke images of racial strife. Angered by Jud's apparent sexual power over Laurey, Curly tells her he is going to "see whut's so elegant about him, makes girls wanta go to parties 'th him" (38). Curly discovers that Jud lives in a dirty little smokehouse, "where the meat was once kept" (39). Jud's surroundings recall late nineteenth- and early twentieth-century derisive references to African Americans as "smokies"— "smoked Irishmen" in the North and "smoked Yankees" in the South—terms derived from the darkened color of smoked meat.[25] In a tense confrontation, Curly suggests that Jud might hang himself from a "good strong hook" in the rafters (40), a notion that evokes images of black men lynched for supposedly assaulting white women.[26] This scene spins into a song, "Pore Jud is Daid," in which Curly imagines his rival's funeral, where the townspeople will show Jud the respect they never expressed while he was alive. Jud, a lonely and miserable man, is drawn into this utopian vision of a world that lovingly accepts him, and he begins to respond to some of Curly's lyrics, which urge him to imagine the preacher's eulogy:

CURLY: Nen he'd say, "Jud was the most misunderstood man in the terri-
tory. People useter think he was a mean, ugly feller. [*Jud looks up*] . . .
But—the folks 'at really knowed him, knowed 'at beneath them two
dirty shirts he alw'ys wore, there beat a heart as big as all outdoors.
JUD: As big as all outdoors.
CURLY: Jud Fry loved his fellow man.
JUD: He loved his fellow man. (41)

Jud attempts to sing along with Curly, repeating his words reverently—according to the stage directions, *"like a Negro at a revivalist meeting"* (42).

As the confrontation between the two men intensifies, Curly invokes the image of America as a new Eden, and accuses Jud of being the hidden snake that
threatens to spoil paradise for those who enjoy the natural landscape: "In this
country, they's two things you c'n do if you're a man. Live out of doors is one.
Live in a hole is the other. I've set by my horse in the bresh som'eres and
heared a rattlesnake many a time. Rattle, rattle, rattle!—he'd go, skeered to
death. Somebody comin' close to his hole! Somebody gonna step on him! Git
his old fangs ready, full of pizen! Curl up and wait!" (44).[27] Jud's poverty, mean-
ness, and loneliness are his own fault, in Curly's view: "How'd you git to be the
way you air, anyway—settin' here in this filthy hole—and thinkin' the way
you're thinkin'? Why don't you do sumpin healthy onct in a while, 'stid of
stayin' shet up here—a-crawlin' and festerin'!" (44). Jud's surroundings reflect
the deep darkness within him. This fiercely individualistic, primitively sexual,
and lawless presence is an obstacle to the white utopian vision of love, marriage, and statehood which *Oklahoma!* promotes. Jud will never be able to assimilate into the community, and he must die in order to allow the musical to
reach its celebratory conclusion.

At Curly and Laurey's wedding party, Jud grabs the bride roughly, the groom
rushes to her rescue, and Jud pulls a knife. In the ensuing scuffle, Curly throws
Jud onto the knife, killing him as the crowd of wedding guests looks on. Curly's
role in the death is accepted by his community—he acted to defend his wife
against a dangerous outsider. The trial is peremptory and its outcome prede-
termined. Curly is tried by a court of insiders, in the living room of his wife's
home. The judge is a member of the wedding party. Although some in the community suspect that the proceeding is not fair, Aunt Eller's comic pragmatism
convinces them they need not worry about legal formalities:

CORD ELAM: Best thing is fer Curly to go of his own accord and tell the
Judge.
AUNT ELLER: Why, you're the Judge, ain't you Andrew?
CARNES: Yes, but—
LAUREY: Well, tell him now and git it over with.
CORD ELAM: 'T wouldn't be proper. You have to do it in court.

15. Jud Fry (Richard H. Gordon, left) and Curly (James Alexander) almost come to blows in Jud's smokehouse, in the 1943 production of *Oklahoma!* Photo by Fay Photo Service, Inc. Museum of the City of New York; gift of Harold Friedlander.

★ ★

AUNT ELLER: Oh, fiddlesticks. Le's do it here and say we did it in court.
CORD ELAM: We can't do that. That's breaking the law.
AUNT ELLER: Well, le's not break the law. Le's just bend it a little. (82)

Although light-hearted, this banter is a reminder of the times in American history when a white man (or mob) could kill a black man or an Indian with impunity. No one speaks for Jud at the trial, and he is forgotten moments after the "not-guilty" verdict is proclaimed. The chorus bursts into a rousing "Oh, What a Beautiful Mornin'" as the play draws to its close.[28]

Unlike Jud, Ali Hakim retains the sympathy of the audience throughout the play. Whereas Jud desperately wants Laurey, Ali is playful with women. He flirts harmlessly with Annie, ultimately ensuring that Will wins her hand. One of the most clever characters in the play, Ali makes money off the gullible and adroitly evades marriage to Annie. In fact, his name is probably derived from the Yiddish and Hebrew word *hacham*—a popular term that, as both Rodgers and Hammerstein would have known, means "clever man."[29]

Ali is assimilable because he is theatrical. He can persuade a chorus to perform with him and can create theater for those around him. His sexuality, unlike Jud's, is largely performance, on the surface and nonthreatening. His famous Valentino-style "Persian good-byes," kisses that leave Annie gasping for breath, seem as much for the audience's benefit as for hers. In contrast, Jud broods on his pornographic pictures in his lonely room. His sexuality smolders in private.

"Hoodblinked" into marrying Annie, Ali fumes about his situation in his comic number, "It's a Scandal! It's a Outrage!"—a tirade against the "marriage trap." A group of men gather around him and burst into song, addressing him as "friend" and asking, "Whut's on yer mind?" (33). Ali explains in song the scandal of shotgun marriages, and the men commiserate:

> It's a scandal! It's a outrage!
> When her fambly surround you and say:
> "You gotta take an make a honest womern outa Nell!"

Always aware of the shifting relationship between "acting" and reality, Ali replies, "To make you make her honest, she will lie like hell!" As Ali and the cowboys join together to plan a "revolution," the girls undercut their efforts, singing, "All right, boys! Revolve!" (35). The number ends with an upbeat dance in which the boys are each caught by a different girl. Ali has gained power and sympathy by theatrically establishing his distance from Jud, and by aligning himself with the musical community: the chorus.

Ali's Jewish identity is most clearly established by the authorial role he plays throughout the show. A seller of stories, fantasies, and myths, Ali seems the logical representation of his real-life creators. Indeed, on the invitation to a first-anniversary party for the show, Hammerstein billed himself "Mister Ali Hakimstein."[30] When Ali first enters, he is selling not only ribbons, notions, and eggbeaters, but also dreams and magic: "Don't anybody want to buy something? How about you, Miss Laurey? Must be wanting something—a pretty young girl like you" (24). As Laurey engages in a reverie of consumption, her desires become more fanciful, shifting from objects to the experiences that advertisements promise: "Course I want sumpin. [*Working up to a kind of abstracted ecstasy*] Want a buckle made outa shiny silver to fasten onto my shoes! Want a dress with lace. Want perfume, wanta be purty, wanta smell like a honeysuckle vine! . . . Want things I've heard of and never had before—a rubber-t'ard buggy, a cut-glass sugar bowl. Want things I cain't tell you about—not only things to look at and hold in yer hands. Things to happen to you. Things so nice, if they ever did happen to you, yer heart ud quit beatin'. You'd fall down dead!" (24). Ali sells her a bottle of "Elixir of Egypt," saying that the potion will help her to "see everything clear" (25). Laurey takes a sniff of the elixir, which puts her to sleep and induces the "Dream Ballet." Ali's magic tonic thus generates this dance sequence and the plot twist that drives the entire second act.

Ali is similarly the author of Jud's fantasies:

PEDDLER: What I'd like to show you is my new stock of postcards.
JUD: Don't want none. Sick of them things. I'm going to get me a real
    woman. . . . I'm t'ard of all these pitchers of women!
PEDDLER: All right. You're tired of them. So throw 'em away and buy some
    new ones. (46)

Instead of more pictures of women, Jud wants a "little wonder," a kaleidoscope of pornographic pictures that hides a blade: "It's a thing you hold up to your eyes to see pitchers, only that ain't all they is to it . . . not quite. Y'see it's got a little jigger onto it, and you tetch it and out springs a sharp blade" (46). Ali is taken aback at Jud's request: "I—er—don't handle things like that. Too dangerous." The device represents Jud's anger, which seeks to explode the bounds of the musical theater utopia that Ali props up. The "little wonder" also offers a metaphor for the relation between Ali and Jud. By embedding Jud's weapon within Ali's world of "pitchers" and illusion, the play reveals anxiety about the reliability of theatricality and visual evidence. Jud's dark presence and anger expose the welcoming openness of the "white" world as a deception. Jud is the knife within the picture, endangering the illusion. Although Jud and the darkness he represents seem to be successfully eradicated in the triumphant ending, his barely acknowledged death raises questions about the suppression on which *Oklahoma!*'s theatrical illusion is built.

16. Invitation to first-anniversary party for *Oklahoma!* The fourth number in the list features "Mister Ali Hakimstein." Photo from the Theatre Guild Archives, Beinecke Rare Book and Manuscript Library, Yale University.

Jud's one solo, "Lonely Room," provides clues about the suppression represented by his death and complicates his function within the play. A short, tragic operatic soliloquy in an otherwise upbeat score, "Lonely Room" reinforces Jud's marginality:

> The floor creaks,
> The door squeaks,
> There's a fieldmouse a-nibblin' on a broom,
> And I set by myself
> Like a cobweb on a shelf,
> By myself in a lonely room.

As Jud begins to fantasize about "all the things [he] wish[es] fer," he momentarily enters the theatrical world of romance and community. But he quickly returns to his initial solitude, rejecting theatricality as a cruel illusion:

> And the sun flicks my eyes—
> It was all a pack o' lies!
> I'm awake in a lonely room.

While he embodies many of the characteristics and functions of the black man in racist thinking, Jud's inability to survive in the theatrical world makes it difficult to read him as a stereotype. He is associated *not* with "black" entertainment forms in the play, but with elite European performance genres. Jud appears in the ballet, but not in the tap-dance number ("Kansas City"), which is based on a form identified with minstrelsy. Likewise, "Lonely Room" is an operatic aria and not, for example, a blues song. Jud is both uncivilized and too civilized. These contradictory negative characteristics are similar to those ascribed by antisemites to Jews, who were perceived as both poverty-stricken Communists *and* powerful bankers threatening to control the world. Jud is not specifically a black man in a white body but an uncomfortable projection onto a "black" character of the nonwhite and un-American traits Jews feared being persecuted for.

Like the knife and the pictures in the "little wonder," Jud and Ali are inextricably linked. No matter how convincingly Ali looks, plays, and even writes his part as an assimilable "white" ethnic, his success in this role depends on his distancing himself from Jud, the embodiment of the dark qualities Ali fears others will find in him. Jud reminds him of the possibility of exposure and exclusion that always threatens the performance. While Ali represents Jews' hopes of moving into white America, Jud personifies the qualities that Jews feared would make them black. If Jud absorbs the negativity of being black, Ali can move into a more powerful position as part of the white community, despite his immigrant background.[31] Jud's threatening otherness throws the harmlessness of Ali's ethnicity into relief and deflects the xenophobic energy

17. Finale of *Oklahoma!* in the 1943 production. Ali Hakim is close to the center, on the left. Jud Fry is not included. Museum of the City of New York; gift of Harold Friedlander.

★ ★

of the community away from Ali. Jewish desire to assimilate and escape discrimination is thus expressed in this musical at the expense of blacks.[32]

Oklahoma! was instantly accepted as true Americana at a time when Jews in America felt increasingly marginalized. The musical does not reject the racialist language that labeled the privileged members of American society white. In Lynn Riggs's original play, the Indian Territory setting included Natives, African Americans, and European Americans. Rodgers and Hammerstein's *Oklahoma!* contains no blacks and no Indians. Instead, racial otherness, as a trope, is personified in the character of Jud, a sacrificial scapegoat, who refuses to perform in socially acceptable genres and whose death cleanses the community of darkness. The whitewashed landscape then becomes the ideal setting for what one reviewer called "a racial memory in the American mind,"

★
The Apprenticeship of Annie Oakley
★
★
Or, "Doin' What Comes Natur'lly"
★
★
★ ★

I N THEIR 1946 musical *Annie Get Your Gun,* Irving Berlin and Dorothy and Herbert Fields firmly reject the version of "true Americana" on which *Oklahoma!* relies. In a pivotal scene of the play, the newly minted star Annie Oakley discovers an enormous poster with her picture on it. She "walks up to the picture slowly" and exclaims in wonder: "It's me! Was I up there all the time?" (39).[1] She touches the face of the image and then touches her own face, as if to say, "Which is the real Annie?"[2] After gazing at her picture on the billboard for a moment, Annie sings a verse of "There's No Business Like Show Business" in which she recognizes—and even pays tribute to—the confusing relationship between the "real" Annie and the "theatrical" star:

> How I wish the folks at home could only see
> What's come to Annie; how proud they'd be,
> Gettin' paid for doin' what comes natur'lly
> Let's get on with the show. (40)

Annie marvels at the fact that she could be paid, indeed be made a star, for "doin' what comes natur'lly" to her: shooting a gun. Having long considered herself a natural girl and her sharpshooting skill a product of birth, not practice, she is stunned by the way celebrity in the theater has blurred the boundaries for her between the natural (or the real) and the artificial or theatrical. As if in direct response to *Oklahoma!* this play rejects claims of naturalness, instead firmly and unequivocally insisting that America is *theater,* and that only those who understand and embrace America's inherent theatricality are destined for success. Moreover, success in the play is financial, and American theatricality is intimately linked to capitalism. The world of the stage is de-

18. "Was I up there all the time?" Annie—played by Ethel Merman—stands beside her image in the 1946 Broadway production of *Annie Get Your Gun*. Photo by Vandamm. Museum of the City of New York; gift of Harold Friedlander.

★ ★

scribed in the play as "show *business.*" And it is an *advertisement* of Annie that spurs her moment of self-reflection. Her success begins the moment she appears in public as a marketable commodity.

Annie Get Your Gun emerged as a direct result of the work of Rodgers and Hammerstein. With the success of *Oklahoma!* and, soon afterward, that of *Carousel* (1945), Rodgers and Hammerstein were quickly established as the arbiters of the postwar musical theater. Script and lyric writer Dorothy Fields therefore first went to them to propose the idea of a show based on the life of Annie Oakley, starring Ethel Merman.[3] Rodgers and Hammerstein saw *Annie Get Your Gun* as a way of capitalizing on the popularity of their own recent work. But although they were interested in the project's great commercial potential, they chose to produce it, not write it. Rodgers, in his memoirs, recalled that although the play bore a kinship to *Oklahoma!* in its general time period and location, from its inception *Annie Get Your Gun* was stylistically quite different from Rodgers and Hammerstein's recent successes: "The idea of our writing the score was never brought up because neither Oscar nor I thought we were the right ones for it. We had been going in a certain direction with *Oklahoma!* and *Carousel* and this did not seem to be along the same path."[4] They engaged Hammerstein's close friend Jerome Kern to write the music, but Kern died before the project began. In their search for another composer of similar stature, they approached Irving Berlin.

Berlin is considered one of the greatest of all American songwriters. He had an unusually long career, writing the scores for eighteen Broadway shows and nineteen Hollywood musicals and composing such well-known songs as "God Bless America," "Easter Parade," "White Christmas," "Cheek to Cheek," "Blue Skies," and "There's No Business Like Show Business." His biography reads like a paradigmatic American-immigrant success story. He was born Israel Baline in Russia in 1888 and immigrated to the Lower East Side with his family in 1893. His father, a cantor, died when the boy was eight, and Berlin worked as a street singer and singing waiter in saloons to make money for the family. In 1911 he had his first hit with "Alexander's Ragtime Band" and began a songwriting career that brought him enormous fame and wealth at an early age. He married a Catholic heiress, Ellin Mackay, and spent many years trying to ingratiate himself with her antisemitic father and to achieve standing in the uppercrust society of New York City. The Berlins lived on Beekman Place on the Upper East Side, a neighborhood that was home to few Jews during the 1930s and '40s. Berlin was a staunch patriot; he spent years touring his musical *This Is the Army* with the USO during World War II and donated all proceeds from both show and movie to the war effort.[5]

While Berlin was on tour with *This Is the Army* much changed on Broadway, not least because of the enormous impact of *Oklahoma!* According to several biographers, Berlin was reluctant to take on the project. He was not familiar with writing for "book musicals" and did not want to be compared unfavorably to Rodgers. He was uninterested in writing what he called "hillbilly songs"—he had made his name as a writer of hit songs for revues and had little motivation at his age to change his style.[6] In fact, Berlin had achieved his life goal—acceptance within the highest echelons of American society—by writing songs and shows that were distinctly rooted in the older Broadway traditions of vaudeville revue and musical comedy. *Annie Get Your Gun* can be seen as his and Dorothy Fields's response to the new integrated musical theater that had won over theater critics.[7] But Fields and Berlin defiantly resisted the impulse to integrate song and story too closely.[8] Instead, they strengthened *both* elements, allowing story and songs to work with and against one another, without ever conflating the two. While most of Berlin's songs have an obvious connection to the plot of the play, they also work as "hits" which could easily be lifted out of the show and performed on their own. The show actually contained nine songs which achieved commercial success independently: "Anything You Can Do," "Doin' What Comes Natur'lly," "The Girl That I Marry," "I Got the Sun in the Morning," "I Got Lost in his Arms," "I'm an Indian Too," "There's No Business Like Show Business," "They Say It's Wonderful," and "You Can't Get a Man with a Gun." This was a record for both Berlin and Broadway.[9] And unlike Rodgers, who radically changed his composing style for *Oklahoma!* from the classic Tin Pan Alley jazz of "Bewitched, Bothered and Bewildered," to the square, all-American beat of "Surrey with the Fringe on Top," Berlin maintained his signature Tin Pan Alley style despite *Annie's* rural midwestern setting.[10]

In building the play around the precast star, Ethel Merman, Berlin and the Fieldses also distinctly rejected Rodgers' notion of a musical in which "no single element overshadows another." Merman was famous for doing just what Rodgers claimed no element of the musical should do: push itself into the spotlight yelling "Look at me!"[11] She was to perform in nine of the fourteen musical numbers, her presence purposefully dominating the theatrical experience.[12] And while the play is set in the Wild West, this is not *Oklahoma!'s* nostalgic "historical" West but the self-consciously constructed West of Buffalo Bill's Wild West show—a staged West which bears more similarity to musical comedies of the 1930s like *Girl Crazy* than to the sentimentalized, rural West evoked by *Oklahoma!'s* cornfields, barns, and farmhouses. The first scene of *Annie Get Your Gun* is set in rural Ohio, but the action of the play takes place almost exclusively in theatrical locations: dressing rooms, stage sets, trains and boats carrying the touring company from one stop to the next, landing all of the characters finally, and inevitably, in New York City. *Annie Get Your Gun* uses western Americana not to evoke the glories of the vanished frontier, but rather to show and celebrate the pleasures and power of the Broadway stage.[13]

By insisting on an American West posited as a stage set rather than a geo-
graph_____ implicitly critique the *Oklahoma!*
craze_____ _____dvocates an older brand of theat-
ricali_____ *Annie Get Your Gun* is a defense
of th_____ n to the dangerously seductive
appe_____ sage of Annie is a message about
assim_____ ng in the older Broadway musical f_____ Americans on their way up be-
caus_____ process of self-invention. It cer-
tainl_____ eir play serves as a warning that
the i_____ leanings, could end up being a
stum_____ mobility. But if an individual can
harness the power of self-invention, she can become a star. *Annie Get Your Gun*
is a musical about recognizing the conventions of a community and learning to
perform within them. The message is conservative, but also potentially empowering to those who might otherwise be shut out by a naturalism that excluded them on biological (usually racial) terms.

Annie Get Your Gun can be read, then, as a *Bildungsmusical,* a musical of
education, in which, through the theater, Annie realizes her potential and becomes a full member of her community. She learns how to read, how to perform, how to create herself as a marketable and successful American character. The *Bildungsroman* is generally understood to be a novel of formation or
of education.[14] Marianne Hirsch describes the *Bildungsroman* as a novel that
focuses on the growth and development of one central character within the
context of a particular society. Like Annie, the central character generally
emerges from a place of "purity and integrity"—often a rural setting—to confront the challenges of civilization, usually in the city. Society in these novels is viewed as a "school of life," a place to gain experience. The protagonist
grows by encountering the social order, making choices, making mistakes,
and ultimately accommodating to the existing society. The *Bildungsroman* is a
story of apprenticeship that ends when the main character has taken his or
her place in society.[15]

The paradigm of the *Bildungsroman* is Goethe's *Apprenticeship of Wilhelm
Meister,* a novel that uses the theater as a central feature of the protagonist's
education. But *Annie Get Your Gun* is closer in spirit to an American version of
the form, Mark Twain's *Adventures of Huckleberry Finn,* which also has theatrical scenes at its center. Annie and Huck have a great deal in common, not the
least being their ambivalence about "sivilization." *Annie Get Your Gun* also
draws on the rags-to-riches stories of the *un*ambivalent Horatio Alger; but
while the Alger stories are primarily concerned with the practical education of
the capitalist, *Annie Get Your Gun* trains its heroine in an all-encompassing theatrical worldview.

These two types of education are not mutually exclusive. A subcategory of the *Bildungsroman* is the *Kunstlerroman,* a novel about the growth and development of an artist. *Annie Get Your Gun* can be understood as the popular American version of the *Kunstlerroman* in which the training of the artist is a training in entertainment—in becoming a marketable commodity. The artistic goals in this story are inseparable from capitalist ones.

There's No Business Like Show Business

Annie Get Your Gun is loosely based on the story of the real-life Annie Oakley and her husband, Frank Butler. In the play, Buffalo Bill's Wild West Show arrives in Annie's neighborhood looking for a local sharpshooter to match with Frank, the show's star. Annie appears, introducing herself with the anthem "Doin' What Comes Natur'lly." When the local innkeeper witnesses Annie's skill with a rifle, he persuades her to take up the sharpshooting challenge. Annie then meets Frank and is smitten. Frank explains to her that he is looking for someone very different from Annie, a soft, dependent creature he describes in "The Girl That I Marry." Annie, despondent, laments her lack of femininity ("You Can't Get a Man With a Gun"). She then summarily beats Frank in the shooting match. Buffalo Bill and the show's manager, Charlie Davenport, convinced they have a budding star on their hands, urge Annie to join the show ("There's No Business Like Show Business"). Annie signs on as Frank's assistant, and the two soon fall in love ("They Say It's Wonderful" and "My Defenses Are Down"). But just before Frank is about to propose, Annie steals the show with a new trick she has learned. She becomes the toast of the town and so impresses a member of the audience, Chief Sitting Bull, that he adopts her into his tribe ("I'm an Indian, Too"). Frank, whose ego is bruised by Annie's success, quits the show and joins the opposition (Pawnee Bill's show). In Act 2, Annie and Frank come together for a publicity stunt—a sharpshooting contest ("Anything You Can Do"), and Sitting Bull fixes the contest (ultimately with Annie's consent) so that Annie loses the prize but wins Frank. They decide to combine their shows and, by extension, get married, and the chorus sings an appropriately celebratory medley of "There's No Business Like Show Business" and "They Say It's Wonderful."[16]

Dressed in buckskins and speaking with an exaggerated backwoods dialect, Annie first appears in the play as a raw young woman, a clichéd romantic primitive emerging direct from the state of nature. She has been raised, significantly, in Darke County, and indeed she lives "in the dark." Numerous connotations of darkness apply. She is illiterate and uneducated; she is associated with primitive "dark" races; and she has never been exposed to the bright lights of the theater. She actually implies that her siblings are not fully human:

"Kid sisters and little brother ain't used to people yit" (9) and further emphasizes their prehuman state when she tells them to "shake [their] tails." At first,
this "natural" Annie is not even aware of the possibility of theater. Her ideas
are circumscribed by her experience of the natural world, as we see in her first
scene.[17] Dolly, Frank Butler's assistant, is seated on a bench. The following
business ensues:

> [*As Dolly sits on the bench, the green hedge behind her obscures her figure to any-*
> *one behind the hedge. The bird on her hat, however, stands above it, and might*
> *seem as though it were moving on the hedge. Suddenly we hear the sound of a*
> *rifle. Bird flies from her hat. Dolly crosses Left looking to see where shot came*
> *from. Annie Oakley enters. She carries an old rifle; two birds are dangling over her*
> *shoulder. She strides toward the bird and picks it up. Dolly crossing to Annie.*
> *Trying to grab it.*]

DOLLY: I'll thank you to give me that bird!
ANNIE: [*Holding the bird above her head*] What for? It's mine. I shot it!
DOLLY: You shot it right off my hat!
ANNIE: [*Surprised*] I DID! How'd she git up thar? (8)

At the beginning of the play, Annie is unaware of the possibility of theater or
artifice and so assumes that all reality is "natural." She cannot distinguish between a "natural" living bird intended for eating and an artificial bird used for
decoration, because she has never seen—or even imagined—an artificial bird.
And even when Dolly explains to her "it's not an eating bird, it's a wearing
bird," Annie cannot understand the concept of wearing a bird on one's hat, especially in a world in which birds represent food: "Round these parts you'll
have to keep sewin' it on cause folks'll keep shootin' it off." Annie begins to
learn that there is more than one way to sustain the self—more than one use
for a bird. In addition to the straightforward connection between birds and
eating, there is the less direct use of the bird as a consumer object. Annie begins the play shooting birds in order to eat them; she ends by shooting clay pi-
geons for entertainment and money. The scene also sets up a typical "machine
in the garden" moment. Like the pastoral scenes in Hawthorne and Thoreau
that Leo Marx describes, this scene opens with a picture of apparently undisturbed nature: a bird sitting on a bush. Almost immediately, however, the illusion is shattered by the intrusion first of technology—Annie's gun—and second by artifice in the guise of Dolly and her hat. The two intrusions are closely
connected. It is helpful to recall that the word "technology" comes from the
Greek term *technē* (art, craft), and that it originally meant the study of art, especially the practical arts. Annie's shooting is a practical art that can be used
for sustenance, for entertainment, and for violence. Both technology and arti-

fice shatter the pastoral illusion by violently undermining the dream of "the natural."

When Annie offers to exchange one of her dead birds for Dolly's ruined ornament, Dolly reacts with horror, calling Annie a "nasty ragamuffin." The blend of anger and shame Annie feels at this snub sets in motion a process of change and education that will culminate in Annie's far exceeding Dolly in the very world of which she is initially ignorant: that of the theater. In fact, Annie's encounter with the fake bird leads her to suspect that there may be other ways of understanding the world. Leo Marx describes encounters of this type as exposing the "pastoral ideal to the pressure of change—to an encroaching world of power and complexity." The "little event" Marx describes in Hawthorne's notebooks—the intrusion of a locomotive into the natural landscape—"arouses a sense of dislocation, conflict and anxiety."[18] As a "natural" girl who is expert at shooting a gun (a skill which blesses her with theatrical marketability), Annie embodies this tension between the pastoral ideal and the rush of technological and industrial advancement. Her initial response to the encounter with artifice is a defensive justification of "Nature." She flippantly compares what she perceives as the dead "eatin'" bird to the alive but highly artificial Dolly: "She ain't filthy. She looks better than you do and she's got a bullet through her head" (8). In comparing a literal female bird to a metaphorical "bird" (a woman), Annie begins to recognize that just as birds serve different uses, so too do women. The dead bird is more alive than the reified Doll(y), who suffers from a form of death-in-life. In Dolly, the creature of artifice whose name describes the very type of woman Frank will want ("a doll he can carry"), Annie sees an alternate possibility for herself. But she also sees how different she is from Dolly—sees that she would have to commit a form of suicide, killing her true "nature," in order to be attractive to Frank—and she reacts to this implicit judgment with resentment.

Annie launches into her first song, "Doin' What Comes Natur'lly," which elaborates the distinction she has discerned between nature and artifice and extols the virtues of nature. From beginning to end of the play, Annie associates the natural with the uneducated and consequently aligns artifice, performance, and theater with education, specifically with reading:

> Folks are dumb where I come from;
> They ain't had any learnin'.
> Still they're happy as can be
> Doin' what comes natur'lly.
> Folks like us could never fuss
> With schools and books and learnin'.
> Still, we've gone from A to Z
> Doin' what comes natur'lly.

In this first verse of the song, Annie reveals that she has already been affected by her encounter with Dolly and the startling revelation of the fake bird. While on the one hand she asserts that her family is happily ignorant, on the other, she indicates that even she understands life in terms of reading: they have gone not from the natural conditions of birth to death, but from the literary ones of "A to Z."

Annie's blurring of the line between her natural world and what Huck Finn would call the "sivilized" world of literate performers increases in the next verse of the song, where she celebrates the simplicity of sex in the state of nature by making reference to the markers of romance. Annie refers to both sex and romance as "natural." Neither, she implies, requires learning or books:

> You don't have to know how to read or write
> When you're out with a feller in the pale moonlight,
> You don't have to look in a book to find
> What he thinks of the moon and what is on his mind.
> That comes natur'lly.

But, of course, "pale moonlight" is a literary construction. As Oscar Wilde observed: "Nature . . . is an imitation of Art." In "The Decay of Lying," Wilde writes, "What is nature? Nature is no great mother who has borne us. She is our creation. It is in our brain that she quickens to life. Things are because we see them, and what we see, and how we see it, depends on the Arts that have influenced us. To look at a thing is very different from seeing a thing. One does not see anything until one sees its beauty. Then, and then only, does it come into existence."[19] In the same sense, Annie only "sees" the moon because she has been influenced by literary descriptions of its romantic potential.[20]

Although Annie does not yet fully realize it, what she is expressing in this song is not the *difference* between Nature and Art, or a defense of nature in the face of education, but rather the lack of any difference at all. What Annie comes to suspect early in the first act is that nature *is* theater; that the nature she believes in is only natural because she *believes* it to be. At the end of her first song, Annie reveals the distance she has already come in her education. She shows that her supposedly "natural" shooting of real birds for food can, from a different perspective, also be seen as a performance. When asked if she can do fancy shooting, she replies:

ANNIE: Fancy! Shucks, I kin shoot the fuzz off'n a peach! I kin shoot the wart off'n gran'pappy's nose. Most of the time I don't even aim. See that rooster's head up there? [*She points to hotel sign*]
WILSON: Yeh!
ANNIE: [*Shoots gun over her shoulder—rooster head falls off*] Now ye don't! (12)

This time Annie makes no mistake about the rooster—she knows it is made of metal and that her act is a performance. And when asked if she wants to compete with a man in a shooting match, she boasts of her own talent for showmanship: "Whar is he? I can hit anythin' he can hit, and I'll do it standing on my head singin' 'Oh Susannah'" (13). As she learns about and experiences the world, she comes to understand that only by treating her life and her work as theater, with scripts, actors, plots, audiences, and spectacles, will she have any chance of achieving the happiness and success she desires (both of which have also been shaped by literary conventions). An important part of this education will be a development of her performance style. Her boasting in this scene recalls the oral culture of nineteenth-century-style "tall tales"; her more sophisticated performances of Act 2 will depend instead on literate twentieth-century tropes.

For the audience, this point is made even before Annie appears on the stage. The supposedly primitive Annie was played by—and written for—Ethel Merman. Dorothy Fields had been assigned to come up with another project for Merman and had created *Annie Get Your Gun* expressly for her.[21] The actress and the character were inseparable from the beginning. John Chapman wrote in the *New York Daily News:* "Ethel Merman is quite a one, and I predict a great future for her. As Annie Oakley in *Annie Get Your Gun* she wins all sharpshooting matches—and as Ethel Merman she wins out over a big show."[22] Thus, the audience for *Annie Get Your Gun* watched the character Annie Oakley and the real-life show business star inhabiting the same body. The advertising for *Annie Get Your Gun* featured Merman's name above the title, in letters slightly larger than the title and significantly larger than those of Irving Berlin's name. A full-body photograph of Merman, dressed as Annie, stands a bit taller than the text of the poster; this image calls to mind the billboard on which Annie sees herself advertised for the first time. Annie is a living, breathing example of the way in which she is (and was) never just the natural Annie. She is always already a star, because she was, at her very inception, also Ethel Merman.

After a brilliant performance in the shooting match with Frank Butler, in which Annie beats him not just in skill but also in showmanship, she begins to realize the potential of performance to shape, indeed to *be,* her world. Her display has gained her both the attention of Frank Butler and a five-dollar prize. But she still does not see how all-encompassing the world of performance is until she overhears Buffalo Bill, the manager Charlie Davenport, and Frank—who are all stunned by her talents—conversing about whether they should take her into the show. They ask her: "Do you know anything about show business?" Annie responds, "Show business? What's show business?" The line serves not only as a cue for Berlin's famous anthem to the stage, but also as the beginning of Annie's official education in the world of the theater.

Charlie, Bill, and Frank describe to Annie a whole world of new people, places, sounds, smells, sights, and experiences:

> The cowboys, the tumblers, the wrestlers, the clowns,
> The roustabouts that move the show at dawn.
> The music, the spotlight, the people, the towns,
> Your baggage with the labels pasted on.
> The sawdust and the horses and the smell,
> The towel you've taken from the last hotel.

Once you have been exposed to it, they tell Annie, you will inevitably want to be a part of it. This world is exceptional. The show business world cancels out all other worlds: "There's no bus'ness like show bus'ness / Like no bus'ness I know."[23] The stage, as described by Buffalo Bill and the others, is not just a world of exciting experience; it is also a business. The theater represents the way newcomers to America will achieve socioeconomic mobility: through the wonders of the capitalist system. It is infinitely attractive and full of possibility for those willing to grab the chance:

> Ev'rything about it is appealing,
> Ev'rything the traffic will allow;
> Nowhere could you get that happy feeling
> When you are stealing that extra bow.

"Traffic" is defined by Webster's as "the business of bartering or buying and selling" and also as "the volume of customers visiting a business establishment."[24] The world of the stage is circumscribed only by the laws of desire (what is "appealing") and by the constraints of capitalist economics. One can do anything onstage that people ("the traffic") will pay to see. "Stealing" is acceptable so long as it furthers the business of the stage. One is beholden only to the laws of popular taste. The freedom implied by this description of show business is intoxicating.

This world does have a clear set of values. First, one must learn to *act*: "There's no people like show people; / They smile when they are low." But acting is not a constraint on freedom. "The roustabouts . . . move the show at dawn." Every morning, the show moves on to a new town; every day, the performer reinvents him- or herself and moves on. Second, this world is a meritocracy. Show business is a world in which skill matters and hard work is rewarded. Those who perform best are admitted and celebrated, regardless of their "natural" or inherited background. If you act well enough, you will rise:

> Yesterday they told you you would not go far,
> That night you open and there you are,

Next day on your dressing room they've hung a star—
Let's go on with the show!

As the song progresses, Annie is filled with wonder and desire. In their effort to persuade her, the men advertise the glories of show business and celebrity as the site and narrative of the American Dream. Although she has never imagined herself starring in such a narrative, once she glimpses the rosy picture the men draw, she cannot rest until she has achieved what she has just learned to want. She does not yet understand the demands of the theater, but she knows immediately that she wants to be a part of it. She tentatively agrees to their terms: "There's no bus'ness like show bus'ness / If you tell me it's so." Passively accepting the part she is to play, Annie receives from the men the "script" she will follow in her new life, a script that dictates not only what she will experience, but how she will feel—or at least how she will *act* like she feels:

FRANK: Trav'ling through the country is so thrilling
BUFFALO BILL: Standing out in front on op'ning nights
CHARLIE: Smiling as you watch the benches filling,
    And there's your billing—out there in lights.

Despite her "natural" roots, Annie is undisturbed by the privileging of "performed" feelings over "natural" ones. She quickly catches on: "There's no people like show people / They smile when they are low." Annie instantly understands the whole idea of identity as a pose. As an outsider, she easily grasps the notion of double consciousness on which theatricality relies. The men encourage her, explaining the commitment she is making. Interestingly, they make no comment in this song about the fact that she is a woman, and that women's roles in both the theater and the capitalist marketplace differ in important ways from men's. They simply set the risks of the stage as a business proposition against the opportunity the theater offers for fame, wealth, and social acceptance. Yet despite the fact that the lyrics do not specifically address the fact that Annie is a woman, the relentless repetition by the men of subtly coercive phrases demonstrates that resistance to their proposition is futile ("you open," "you watch," "you wouldn't," "you go on," "you know," and so on).

CHARLIE: Even with a turkey that you know will fold.
BUFFALO BILL: You may be stranded out in the cold.
FRANK: Still you wouldn't change it for a sack of gold.

Now Annie is fully integrated, and the group finishes in unison: "Let's go on with the show! / Let's go . . . on . . . with the show!" (24). Here the capitalist message becomes more complicated. The payoff of the stage, it seems, is even better than gold. But if the show is about to fold, why not leave? If you're stranded in the cold, why not trade show business for a sack of gold? What's so great about the theater? Money can be spent, but the skill of selling the self is eternal. What show business offers is a worldview more valuable than a bag of gold. The freedom to recreate the self is the only currency that really matters. Show business—this song implies—rests not on ready cash, but on the shared belief in a set of ideals. A similar message is rendered far less optimistically a couple of years later in Arthur Miller's *Death of a Salesman*. Standing by Willy Loman's grave, his neighbor, another Charley, laments in the final scene: "Nobody dast blame this man. You don't understand: Willy was a salesman. And for a salesman, there is no rock bottom to the life. . . . He's a man way out there in the blue, riding on a smile and a shoeshine. And when they start not smiling back—that's an earthquake."[25] When Willy Loman can no longer sell himself, and hence his products, he disappears, both literally and figuratively, from the stage.

When the men describe to Annie an exceptional world brimming with opportunity—a world where advancement is based solely on merit, where how you act is more important than who you are, where faith in ideals is more important than wealth—they are, of course, describing Irving Berlin's vision of America. Indeed, the power of this song is that it is a *patriotic* song. Acting in the theater becomes, here, a metaphor for becoming an American. Annie will be accepted into this show business community—America—if she makes the commitment to act her part. This song can also be read as a direct response to Rodgers and Hammerstein's vision of America in *Oklahoma!*—a show which is, as we have seen, deeply ambivalent about the role of self-conscious theatricality. Berlin, the older and more experienced showman, the acknowledged embodiment of the success of the American dream, seems to be reacting to Rodgers and Hammerstein's flirtation with realism by insisting that there is *nothing* outside the conventions of show business—that realism, psychology, and integration of song and story lead to less accurate or less transparent renditions of theatrical American characters and landscapes. When Annie's mentors sing "There's no business like show business / Like no business I know," they may actually be saying that nothing compares to show business because there *is* nothing else. *Everything* is show business; everything is theater; theater *is* America. There is no *reality* apart from show business.[26]

Early in the second act, Annie performs a number that indicates the enormous change wrought in her by her training in show business. The company of the Wild West show arrives in New York harbor after a prestigious European tour that has left them flat broke. Buffalo Bill, Charlie, and Sitting Bull hear that Pawnee Bill's show has been playing Madison Square Garden and assume he is rich. They propose a merger between the two shows, a plan that Annie favors as it will ensure that she and Frank will also get a chance to "merge."

They attend a fancy society party thrown by Pawnee Bill, only to discover that Pawnee Bill is also broke and was hoping that Buffalo Bill would be able to finance the merger. The plans are halted, until Annie offers to bankroll the plan with the numerous gold and diamond medals she received from the crowned heads of Europe. Everyone is thrilled. Charlie is concerned that Annie would "give up her only bankroll." Annie responds in song:

> Got no diamond, got no pearl,
> Still I think I'm a lucky girl—
> I got the sun in the morning
> And the moon at night.
> Got no mansion, got no yacht,
> Still I'm happy with what I've got—
> I got the sun in the morning
> And the moon at night.

This opening song for Act 2 mirrors Annie's opener for Act 1, "Doin' What Comes Natur'lly." Again, she sings about nature and her relationship to it. But "I Got the Sun in the Morning" differs from the first song in a number of important ways that demonstrate the distance Annie has traveled since her first sharpshooting contest. This second paean to nature is, in both form and content, a self-conscious defense of the theatrical. While the first song was a comic dialect song, the second is popular swing, performed to the accompaniment of a big band. This song is a star turn, and to create the right atmosphere, Annie is dressed not in buckskins, but in an evening gown with long gloves and high heels. And although she is singing the praises of nature, she is doing so not on a hill in Darke County, but in a hotel ballroom in New York City. Whereas in "Doin' What Comes Natur'lly" Annie sang alone, here she is backed up by a high-society chorus in gowns and tuxedos that, with little irony, supports her performance and her sentiments about nature. And the song *is* ironic, because the entire time she is singing it her chest glitters with the very diamonds and gold she claims she doesn't have. She has agreed to invest her wealth, but she is investing it in *herself* and in the show she wants to do with Frank. The boundaries between Annie's self and Annie's show blur here: the show *is* the self and vice versa. Annie has become her own backer, investing in herself as a business proposition, as a Broadway show. There is little reason to think she will not recoup her investment and make far more.

Annie sings this song about relying on nature on a stage constructed by her success in the theater. The theater has made this paean to nature possible—indeed, the theater has created this view of nature. The lyrics of the song, with their assurance that nature is all Annie needs, reveal that she has ceased to be a primitive object of romanticism. Annie herself has become a romantic.

In an American literary tradition stretching back to Emerson and beyond, Annie has constructed a metaphorical system around the beauty of nature. "I

19. Annie's chest full of jewels. Ethel Merman in *Annie Get Your Gun* (1946). Photo by Vandamm. Museum of the City of New York.

★ ★

Got the Sun in the Morning" *is* in fact an Emersonian expression. Here is Emerson in "Nature": "Give me health and a day and I will make the pomp of emperors ridiculous. The dawn is my Assyria; the sunset and moonrise my Paphos, and unimaginable realms of faerie; broad noon shall be my England of the senses and the understanding; the night shall be my Germany of mystic philosophy and dreams."[27] Witnessing the movement of the moon and sun, Emerson can lay claim to the empire of Nature, an empire far more impressive than the historical empires that gave birth to the great ideas and writers of the ages. Both Annie and Emerson claim elements of nature as private property; both express a distinctly capitalist ethos in relation to such unpossessable items as the dawn, the sun, and the moon. And just as Emerson's view of nature is available only to the educated mind, so Annie's sun and moon are symbols of the nature she has been trained to see. Annie has finally learned to read and write in metaphors. The lyrics of "I Got the Sun in the Morning" refer to a "nature" that lies outside of "show business." But as we now see, the world of the theater is all-encompassing, so the "nature" described in the song must be a product of that world. Annie creates her "sun" and "moon" to serve her own theatrical purposes. In literal terms, she "doesn't have" what she says she does (the sun and moon) and "does have" what she says she doesn't (money). But although she doesn't literally have the sun, she can sing about it, and in doing so bring it into existence. Furthermore, in singing about the sun, she also metaphorically becomes it: she is the light on the stage around which the chorus revolves. She is the star.

In the finale of the song, as performed in the film version, Annie cements the Emersonian connection with a clever dance move. Perched at the top of a staircase, she flips the train of her red gown between her legs, and proceeds to walk down it. In creating her own red carpet for herself (and of herself), she provides a walking illustration of Emerson's value of self-reliance. She also shows how utterly constructed the natural self is: only with the evening gown—the artificial costume that, along with the song, makes her a star—can she dramatically and effectively express her independence.

I'm an Indian Too

The final tableau of the play is a living curtain advertising the combined shows of Pawnee and Buffalo Bill. Annie and Frank pose in the center holding their guns; just below them, in a small oval, is Sitting Bull.[28] The displaced Indian, who has inexplicably taken an interest in the theater, serves as the foundation on which Annie and Frank's union rests. He has been Annie's tutor in the ways of the theater, he has served as their matchmaker, and he has given them his blessing. Whereas in the earlier plays *Whoopee* and *Girl Crazy* the Jewish comedian played an Indian as well as a number of other ethnic types, here we have a return to the convention of the nineteenth-century Indian plays discussed by Werner Sollors: the Indian himself appears in the play to legitimize American romantic love. Sitting Bull adopts Annie and helps her to become a woman, a performer, and an American.

Becoming an American is, in this play—as in *Oklahoma!*—a process of distancing oneself from all signs of "darkness." When Annie and Frank are dis-

20. "Living curtain" at the end of *Annie Get Your Gun* (1946). Photo by Vandamm. Museum of the City of New York; gift of Harold Friedlander.

★ ★

cussing romance, just before Annie begins to sing "They Say It's Wonderful," she tells Frank that her main ambition is to "be a pink and white woman like the kind ye said ye liked." Frank replies, "You're gettin' pinker and whiter every day!" (30). Part and parcel of Annie's theatrical education is the assumption that she will learn to be white. Annie Oakley's transformation offers a nostalgic rendering of the path many an immigrant Jew traveled, as she transforms herself from "dark" country bumpkin to "white" star sharpshooter. She is a "greeneh"—a new immigrant—who must be taught how to dress, how to perform, how to read and write English. Charlie Davenport convinces Frank to take Annie into the show by describing how he will transform her: "'Course she looks lousy now. But we'll dress her up" (22).

While Charlie and Buffalo Bill invest in Annie's education because of the obvious commercial potential of her talent, Sitting Bull's interest in Annie is less clearly motivated. More than anyone, Sitting Bull is Annie's most important tutor and agent of change. At the end of the first act, Annie asks Sitting Bull to read Frank's letter to her:

ANNIE: Say Papa Bull, can you read writing?
SITTING BULL: Papa Bull read four books.
ANNIE: Can you make this out?
SITTING BULL: [*reading*] Dear Annie . . . (49)

The scene recalls numerous immigrant dramas in which illiterate immigrants procured the services of those more established in America for reading and writing letters. The irony, in this case, is that the apparently exotic Indian chief is more familiar with the English language—indeed he is more American—than Annie. Yet Sitting Bull is figured here not as a "natural" American, but as another version of the immigrant who has learned to be an American.[29] His reading ability is, after all, still limited. He has read only four books. Sitting Bull, therefore, is the best teacher for Annie because he has made the transformation himself from natural/immigrant to theatrical/American. Despite his Indian persona, we can read Sitting Bull as serving the same function as the Jewish comics in earlier plays who become the voice of, indeed the embodiment of, theatrical performance of the self.

In a sideplot to the main action, Sitting Bull gradually reveals himself to be a Jewish-style master of theatricality. Inspired by Annie's extraordinary talent, he decides to invest in Buffalo Bill's show, and by extension in Annie's project of self-creation.[30] Investing in Annie, Sitting Bull is buying into American selfhood. And as he becomes increasingly involved with Annie's career, he undergoes a remarkable transformation. He begins to resemble more and more the earlier, self-consciously theatrical Jewish stage comics. Sitting Bull becomes not only a stereotypical businessman; he also plays a romantic enabler similar to Henry Williams, Gieber Goldfarb, and Ali Hakim. Yet in contrast to the earlier characters, this romantic enabler actually *is* an Indian. Or is he? Sitting Bull's interest in moneymaking, for example, leads to jokes that satirize—and combine—Indian and Jewish stereotypes:

CHARLIE: Pawnee Bill playing the Garden?
MAN: Sure, three weeks now.
SITTING BULL: How . . .
MAN: How!
SITTING BULL: No, no, how's business? (53)

The move from "How" as a stereotypical Indian greeting to "How's business?"—the stereotypical Jewish one—indicates that Sitting Bull has been transformed by being a theater producer. It seems that he cannot be a producer without becoming at least a little bit Jewish.

As Henry does for Sally *(Whoopee),* Gieber does for Molly *(Girl Crazy),* and Ali does for Laurey *(Oklahoma!),* Sitting Bull becomes Annie's protector. When she performs a fancy trick of shooting while standing on a motorcycle, Chief

21. Ethel Merman as Annie just after being adopted into Sitting Bull's tribe, in *Annie Get Your Gun* (1946). Photo by Vandamm. Museum of the City of New York; gift of Harold Friedlander.

Sitting Bull decides to reward her skill by initiating her into his community—the Indian tribe:

> BUFFALO BILL: He wants you to be his friend.
> SITTING BULL: Not my friend. I make her my DAUGHTER!
> ANNIE: What did the man say?
> BUFFALO BILL: It's a great honor! He wants to adopt you into the Sioux
>   Tribe as his daughter! (46)

In this scene and the song that follows, Sitting Bull teaches Annie an important lesson of the theater. Race is a performance, not a "natural" and immutable characteristic. Sitting Bull can make Annie into an "Indian"—or at least a vaudeville-style stereotype of an Indian—regardless of her racial background. Annie is adopted into the Indian tribe and "becomes" a Sioux simply by donning the appropriate costume, repeating a few lines, smoking a pipe, and, of course, singing a song:

> Just like Rising Moon,
> Falling Pants, Running Nose,
> Like those Indians,
> I'm an Indian too,
> A Sioux, ooh-ooh! (49)

Annie makes it clear from her song that she realizes Sitting Bull is making her not a *real*—that is, racial—Indian, but rather a theatrical *acted* version of an Indian ("*like* an Indian"). Her silly play on Indian names places her routine squarely in the arena of burlesque. Sitting Bull uses this adoption scene to show her the way one enters a new community. Just as Annie is indoctrinated into the world of "Show Business" by Frank, Charlie, and Buffalo Bill, here Annie is similarly integrated, emphasizing that she will be an Indian because she can act like one:

> And I'll wear moccasins,
> Wampum beads, feather hats,
> Which will go to prove,
> I'm an Indian too.

Sitting Bull also decides that he must intervene in order to help Annie get Frank. When, in the second act, the merger of Pawnee Bill's show with Buffalo Bill's is called off for lack of funds, it is Sitting Bull who suggests to Annie that she offer her medals to the cause ("I know paleface with chest full of gold and jewels"). He also convinces Charlie to devise the theatrical "fix" that ensures the marriage at the end: an alteration of Annie's guns so that when she competes against Frank, she will fail to hit her mark:

SITTING BULL: She show him up again . . . he leave her again.

CHARLIE: How do you figure that?

SITTING BULL: Annie win match today lose Frank: Annie lose match—win Frank. We fix guns!

CHARLIE: Why, S.B., you old S.B. Give me those pliers. (71)

The conflated Indian/Jew character here represents a significant change from the marginal Jewish comics of the earlier musicals. The Indian/Jew is no longer an outsider; he is not only an important investor in the Wild West Show—he is the one character who is capable of teaching Annie how to succeed in the new world she has entered. Sitting Bull has come a long way from Indian to investor! His position as both Annie's mentor and her backer underlines the specifically commercial nature of the show business world in which she longs to succeed. Sitting Bull's shift from outsider to insider can be understood in terms of the historical context of the play. The "Americans All" wartime propaganda that promoted American tolerance and diversity had a profound effect on the attitudes that soldiers of immigrant backgrounds brought home during demobilization. The military served as a great equalizer for Americans of Jewish, Polish, Italian, and Irish descent who returned home to find that they had become white. Strategies for combating prejudice and antisemitism changed in response to this new sense of racial identity.[31] Returning Jewish soldiers felt that they had finally "arrived" in America and were less willing to tolerate exclusions, quotas, and other forms of social discrimination. Thousands of Jewish men took advantage of the G.I. Bill for Education, and Jews quickly became one of the most educated ethnic groups in the country. Jews as a group also experienced remarkable upward mobility after the war.[32] In popular representations of the war, Jewish actors like John Garfield and writers like Norman Mailer increasingly assumed the roles of "typical Americans."[33]

Irving Berlin and Dorothy and Herbert Fields clearly felt that in following the American Way—in assimilating to American norms, in participating as patriotically and vigorously as possible in the war effort, in pursuing material and spiritual independence—they, and Jews like them, had discovered the key to success and acceptance in America. The war marked the "arrival" of Berlin, in particular, as an assimilated American. In late 1945 he received the Congressional Medal of Honor for his service during the war as writer of and performer in his all-army show *This Is the Army*. According to Laurence Bergreen, the occasion was "the sweetest moment in Berlin's entire career": "In receiving the Medal of Merit, he finally, at the advanced age of fifty-seven, completed his drive for assimilation. Attaining that goal was worth the financial sacrifice he had made during the war, for it was a matter of honor. . . . Honor was the one distinction Berlin took more seriously than wealth, and the one he had harbored the most doubts about attaining in his adopted country. Thanks to the war, his goals and the nation's had become one. Honor was his at last."[34] It was only a few weeks after this gratifying homecoming that Berlin received the call from Rodgers and Hammerstein asking him if he wanted to work on *Annie Get Your Gun.* Berlin clearly felt both grateful to and safe in America as he composed the songs for the show.

Sitting Bull becomes Annie's mentor because it is he who understands the wisdom of the Jewish experience in America (and in the theater). He opens Annie's eyes, teaching her how to fit into a new community by recognizing its norms and conventions and learning how to play within its boundaries. In this way, *Annie Get Your Gun* is truly an immigrant story, but the American who teaches the new immigrant how to behave in her adopted country is an Indian who acts like a Jew. Just as many ethnic groups were in the army together, they are now in the show together. Sitting Bull is a particularly complex example of this transformation of ethnic identity.[35] The historical Sitting Bull defeated Custer. When William F. Cody (Buffalo Bill) brought him into his Wild West show as a curiosity in the 1890s, Cody ran the risk of being arrested for harboring a dangerous criminal.[36] In *Annie Get Your Gun,* Sitting Bull is no longer an enemy or dangerous, because he is no longer a racial other. He has shed his primitive biologically defined "naturalness" and become Americanized—that is, theatrical. He is a member of the cast and sings with the ensemble; he is a producer of the very show Annie wants to join. Sitting Bull, Indian/Jew/ethnic, is the perfect character to bless the union of Annie and Frank. As the representative of the Americanized ethnic immigrant, he can offer Annie the wisdom of theatricality: follow conventions—know your part, learn your lines, sing the notes you are given. If you can do that better than anyone else, you will become a star.

The Girl That I Marry

The theatrical education Annie receives from Sitting Bull is not always a straightforward rendering of the paradigmatic immigrant tale, because her story is fundamentally shaped by the fact that she is a woman. Her illiteracy at the beginning of the play encompasses ignorance not only of theatrical convention, but also of socially approved gender roles. In order to achieve success in the theater, Annie must learn to read nature as art; in order to achieve success in love, she must learn to write herself as a woman.

In Annie's first meeting with Frank Butler, she reveals her illiteracy. Frank sees Annie shining up her gun and, in a protective attitude, cautions her against playing with dangerous weapons. Annie, amused by his assumption that she doesn't know how to handle a gun and unaware that Frank is the sharpshooter against whom she will be competing, blurts out that she needs the gun to "win a shootin' contest off'n a big swollen-headed stiff out of the Wild West show." Frank, put off by Annie's blithe use of heavily loaded phallic imagery (both the polishing of the gun and the reference to a "big swollen-headed stiff"), tries to dissuade her. Annie, already smitten by Frank's beautiful eyes, attempts to impress him:

> FRANK: You mean Frank Butler? . . . But he's a champion.
> ANNIE: What's that?
> FRANK: Why, he's the best.
> ANNIE: He was!
> FRANK: Well anyway—Butler wouldn't shoot against a girl.
> ANNIE: He ain't got no choice. He challenged anybody. 'Sides, I don't shoot like a girl. . . . I shoot like a man! (14)

In trying to impress Frank, Annie emphasizes the very elements of her character—her strength, her confidence, her "masculine" skill—that are least likely to appeal to Frank. Annie's gender identity is a source of confusion and anxiety throughout the play, both for her and for Frank. The minute she sees Frank, she desires him; but Frank cannot return this desire while Annie wields a gun. The phallic implications of Annie's gun are strikingly apparent; as long as she "shoots like a man" (and swaggers like one), she will never be able to play the role of the romantic heroine.

Frank enlightens Annie by describing the problem bluntly: "I like you fine, but you're not enough woman for me. I like the dainty kind—the kind that faints when she sees a mouse" (14). In "The Girl That I Marry," Frank outlines for Annie the character she needs to play in order to win his heart:

> The girl that I marry will have to be
> As soft and as pink as a nursery.
> The girl I call my own
> Will wear satins and laces
> And smell of cologne.

Annie is clearly not the picture of fluffy femininity that Frank needs to support his own fragile masculinity. Annie is not Dolly. Dejected, Annie watches Frank go, with the dawning realization of the terrible problem she faces. She wants him, but to have him she will have to give up the very talent that brought her close to him in the first place. Indeed, she will have to give up her role as star of this musical; the type of ingenue Frank desires could never have a musical named after her. Annie laments:

> I'm quick on the trigger,
> With targets not much bigger
> Than a pin point

I'm number one.
But my score with a feller
Is lower than a cellar—
Oh, you can't get a man with a gun.

In the song, Annie articulates the classic dilemma of the 1940s career woman: men don't like women who can fend for themselves. Men especially don't like women who show them up.

This dilemma had particular resonance in 1946, when *Annie Get Your Gun* opened on Broadway. The contingencies of war had caused dramatic upheavals in gender roles and relations in America. In World War II, for the first time in the nation's history, women had served in uniform: as members of the Women's Army Corp (WAC). On the home front, women had flocked to jobs vacated by men called into the army. Massive public relations campaigns had encouraged women to join the war effort by taking jobs in factories. Many of the women who had taken these high-paying blue-collar jobs felt proud and empowered to march under the banner of "Rosie the Riveter." But in 1946 veterans were returning home in droves, expecting their jobs back. The process of demobilization led to a rapid shift in attitudes toward women's employment. What had been considered a patriotic duty only a few months earlier suddenly became an affront to the masculinity of the returning veterans. Within six months after the end of the war, 2.25 million women workers had quit their jobs. Another million women were laid off. Many women still needed to work, but were forced out of the high-paying factory jobs demanded by returning veterans and into lower-paying jobs considered more appropriate for women, like secretarial services and sales help.[37] Some wanted to quit; many were persuaded to do so by a vigorous "back to the home" public relations campaign encouraging women to give up their jobs as their last contribution to the war effort.

The war thus represented a brief window of opportunity for women eager to define themselves outside conventional gender boundaries. But as the war was drawing to a close, the "back to the home" movement encouraged women to adopt a version of femininity even more circumscribed than that of prewar society. It was time to put down their guns and embrace domesticity, women were being told. During the early years of the war effort, the Office of War Information (the propaganda arm of the War Department) encouraged major magazines to include advertising that would generate positive attitudes toward childcare centers and encourage women to find ways to cut down on housework so that they would be available for work outside the home. By the middle of 1944, these campaigns had ceased and were being replaced by ads dramatizing the unhappiness of children with working mothers. An advertisement for Adel Precision Products in the *Saturday Evening Post* (May 6, 1944) features a little girl asking "Mother, when will you stay home again?" The text of the ad provides the answer: "Some jubilant day mother *will* stay home again, doing the job she likes best—making a home for you and daddy, when he gets back." The text then emphasizes women's postwar role as consumers of household goods: "She's learning the vital importance of precision in equipment made by Adel. In her post-war home she'll want appliances with the same high degree of precision." As manufacturers shifted to the production of consumer goods, Maureen Honey reports, advertisers increasingly ran negative depictions of working mothers. In a State Farm Insurance ad from March 1945, a hysterical girl is being taken to a foster home because her mother has to work. By 1945, the *Saturday Evening Post* had completely dropped the industry recruitment themes that had dominated advertising for the previous two years. Instead, Honey writes, "women in ads were all, with the exception of servicewomen, in traditional fields or had no occupational role."[38]

So when Annie stands mystified in front of the advertisement of herself midway through the play, wondering where to find the "real Annie," she may also be expressing confusion about what the poster is trying to tell her regarding her proper role as a woman in a changing world. Annie's character is constructed of the jumble of contradictions and ambivalence that surrounded images of women in the immediate postwar period. Her attachment to and skill with her gun is viewed as *both* useful and unnatural. During the war years, the image of the brave, strong, independent pioneer woman was a common figure in advertising, and women as soldiers a common trope.[39] But such a woman was generally pictured as using her strength (and her gun) to protect her family from danger, not to make a career for herself. Annie's self-confidence and pride in her ability are presented as both useful (in achieving fame) and damning (in love).

Significantly, the idea for the musical sprang from the head of Dorothy Fields as a response to the drama of demobilization. Fields saw Ethel Merman as the ideal Annie—an actress whose own femininity was problematic throughout her career. A powerful presence in show business *and* a new mother (she had recently given birth to a son), Merman was a perfect focal point for the ambivalence of 1940s America toward strong independent women.[40] Annie, then, can be seen as a composite of the many American women who suddenly found themselves constrained by an imposed domesticity after the war. *Annie Get Your Gun* reinforces the ideology of demobilization, but it also offers a theatrical strategy for managing this sudden change in roles. First, Annie must learn what is expected of her; in other words, she must understand the theatrical conventions that dictate her role as romantic heroine. Then she needs to imagine herself within those expectations—within the boundaries of that script. This process involves finding a way to reconcile her desire with the conventions of her community. The theater turns out to be crucial for her in more ways than one: in learning to *act* like a woman, Annie also manages to retain some of the power implicit in role playing, even as she apparently submits to Frank's (and the play's) patriarchal vision of family relations.

In order to figure out how to act, Annie must learn to "read" her part in the play. Annie is, in fact, obsessed with learning to read. The historical Annie Oakley was also self-educated, but had learned to read by the time she was a teenager.[41] So the emphasis on literacy in the play was a choice made by Dorothy and Herbert Fields. She cannot participate in the love story until she knows what a love story is; in the play, to learn to read *is* to be in love and vice versa. Her first love scene with Frank revolves around the problem of reading. Annie has engaged her little brother Jake to "larn" her: "Ye gotta larn me, and ye gotta larn me fast! What's Frank think if'n he knew I couldn't read'n write? You gotta 'ejjicate' me, Jake!" (28). As Frank enters, Annie is clutching a newspaper review that mentions her, but she cannot read it. Trying to cover for her ignorance, she asks Frank if he wants to read it. When he demurs, she coyly insists: "No, you read it. I wanna hear how it sounds when you speak it!" (29). In asking Frank to read it to her, Annie—ironically—reveals that she has actually begun to learn to "read." She is starting to understand the role of the woman within the romantic love plot. Correctly interpreting the structure and dynamics of the moment, she *acts* far more strategically than she did in her first encounter with Frank. Shedding her boastful self-confidence, she plays instead the role of the dependant feminine heroine in order to attract Frank. Annie experiments with giving Frank the power to read for her and about her, and is surprised to find that it works.

When Frank actually does read the clipping, we learn that Annie is not even mentioned by name: "Mr. Butler's assistant, whose name is not on the program, performed only one trick, but she promises to become a fine marksman" (29). Annie is not yet developed enough to have a *written* name of her own. Calling her a "marks*man*" even effaces her gender. Annie herself has acknowledged, in a reprise of "Show Business," that she cannot yet write her name. Facing the audience, she sings:

> This is so exciting but I'm filled with fright
> The show is over and on that night
> Someone wants my autograph but I can't write
> Let's go on with the show.

Annie has not yet acquired a public name; she is known only in relation to Frank, and he would like to keep it that way. The reviewer, and society as a whole, likewise do not know what to call her. Annie, however, is consumed with learning to *autograph*—to write herself. The musical seems to be asking its audience to assist Annie in inventing a new vocabulary that can express

the apparent contradiction of a powerful woman—of a female star who shines more brightly than her male counterpart.

Frank, while pleased with Annie's "development," is concerned that she learn to read the right material and that she not attempt to write new scripts for herself. Above all, he wants to be sure Annie's name never eclipses his own. If Annie can play along with the traditional marriage plot—which usually requires relinquishing her name—Frank will be more than happy to encourage her. But Annie's narratives require constant shaping and monitoring:

> FRANK: What'd you say if some day I might even be willing to make you my partner. [*He looks out as though he could see a theatre sign.*] "BUTLER AND OAKLEY."
> ANNIE: [*Overcome*] Oh, no!
> FRANK: Never wanted a partner before, but now maybe I might.
> ANNIE: [*Dreaming*] "OAKLEY AND BUTLER."
> FRANK: [*Not dreaming*] "BUTLER AND OAKLEY."
> ANNIE: [*Innocently*] What's the difference?
> FRANK: You've got to do it in alphabetical order. Annie . . . Have you ever loved anybody? (30)

Still a novice reader, still largely ignorant of the complex set of conventions that govern the narrative she is trying to enter, Annie dreams outside the "alphabetical order" that Frank uses (and society supports) to enforce his power in the relationship. Annie's problem is that she is trying to play the starring role in two competing narratives simultaneously: the traditional romantic-comedy plot and the American rags-to-riches success story. The first requires her to act within the bounds of conventional femininity; the second requires her to step outside them. This passage indicates a possible compromise: Annie does not have to give up her name and career to be with Frank; she just has to agree to *act* within the bounds of theatrical (and societal) conventions that give the man top billing. As long as Annie accepts this pragmatic bargain—that their names must be listed "in alphabetical order"—Frank can immediately move on to a discussion of love.

Frank relishes coaching Annie in the conventions that ensure his dominant position. For him, love can be understood only by the book, within the strict formula of the romantic musical comedy. The only love song that Frank and Annie sing reinforces this notion of love. Annie has not been in love before, but she has "heerd tell about it." It is from these stories that she will take her cues on how to behave, even how to *feel* about love: "I've heerd tales that could set my heart aglow / Wish I knew if the things I hear are so." Although she cannot read, she has been deeply influenced by the stories "they" tell: "They say that falling in love is wonderful, / It's wonderful, so they say." She acknowledges here that the "natural" moon of "Doin' What Comes Natur'lly" is an element in a stage set, a bit of atmosphere necessary for a sentimental love story: "And with a moon up above it's wonderful, / It's wonderful—so they tell me." Annie then reinforces her own illiteracy, insisting that she must have heard romantic stories, since she is incapable of reading them: "I can't recall who said it. / I know I never read it." Annie is also making a transition here from older, orally transmitted literary genres like folktales and fairy tales to more recent, written literature, thus becoming modern and "sivilized" in this way as well.

Frank verifies the stories "they" tell. He begins by establishing his own position as wise teacher: "Ev'rything that you've heard is really so, / I've been there once or twice and I should know." Frank writes Annie's script for her by outlining how she should behave and what she should feel when she plays her role in this romantic plot:

> You leave your house some morning,
> And without any warning,
> You're stopping people shouting that love
> Is grand.

Annie is eager to enter into the story, to play this role; and so, briefly at least, she is willing to let it be the story that Frank tells. Like her initiations into show business and the Indian tribe, "love" becomes one more world into which she is integrated.

Almost as soon as Annie learns to read, however, she wants to write as well. Once Annie has discovered the power of the theater and has begun to learn the tricks of acting a particular part, she thinks she can also become playwright and director. Determined to get Frank to marry her, Annie decides to surprise Frank with a new trick she has been practicing. The manager, Charlie, helps Annie write the script for a romance with Frank that begins onstage:

CHARLIE: Has he ever asked you to marry him?

ANNIE: Not yit, he ain't broke out in a sweat cold enough to ask me that. I gotta git him, Charlie. . . . How kin I git him?

CHARLIE: That's what I'm trying to tell you. . . . You gotta dazzle him. . . . Drive him crazy. When he sees you step out in front of an audience in a beautiful costume with lights and music and you do this trick you been savin' just for him . . .

ANNIE: He'll be so proud of me, he'll bust out in that cold sweat.

CHARLIE: Sure . . . Monday afternoon he'll be expecting you to shoot the egg off the poodle's head . . . but you don't do that. Instead you come out . . . do this trick on the motorbicycle, save the show and marry Frank!

ANNIE: Jes' like in a fairy tale! (32)

Annie has developed from a girl who cannot read to a woman who imagines her own life as a fairy tale. As Charlie well knows, however, the story can work only if all of the actors are following the same script. But Frank is unwilling to cede to Annie the power to write his story or to allow Charlie and Buffalo Bill to interfere in his education of Annie. When he sees the enormous billboard of Annie that Charlie has put up outside the show tent, Frank is furious that Annie may upstage him. "She's my project," he protests, "I'm gonna be the boss."

Annie relentlessly elaborates on her fairy tale throughout the rest of the play and is repeatedly disappointed by the way Frank fails to follow her plot. Annie encourages Frank to watch her carefully during the show so that he doesn't miss her new trick. She is convinced of the power of her performance to bring to life the script she has written:

> ANNIE: I mean when you see me out there with the music playin' an' all
> them lights on me, you'll . . .
> FRANK: What'll I do?
> ANNIE: You'll almost bust. Then like the end of a fairy tale you'll be so
> proud of me you're gonna ast me to "do something" and "be some-
> body" and I'm gonna "do it" and "be it"!
> FRANK: Honey, I could ask you that right now.
> ANNIE: No. Not now. That ain't the way I planned it. (40)

But Annie's trick is not what Frank has planned. Annie has stepped out of the romantic fairy tale narrative and into the American success story without realizing it, and Frank is disappointed and threatened. In his eyes, her education has failed: she has become the wrong type of woman. He is shocked and troubled by her success and hastily departs, leaving a short note explaining that Annie is too smart for him.

Ironically, the "too smart" Annie cannot read Frank's note. Chief Sitting Bull reads the note aloud, but Annie mistrusts his "reading" of the missive: "What's he mean—too smart fer—Are you sho you can read? [*Tears letter in half*] No, I'm gonna keep it—some day I'll be able to read it" (50). Annie cannot understand what she has done wrong. She thinks she can script for herself a new way of being a woman that will work in the two competing plots in her head: she wants to be a star *and* marry a prince. Annie has misread Frank and the conventions that control the play in which she performs. She keeps the note— which chides her for failing to read the part of "woman" appropriately—as a reminder of her failure, and as a resolution that she will learn to play her role in this show more effectively in the future (that is, she will learn to read). As we shall see, Annie will learn to read by learning to deny her ability to read.

Act 2 opens with Annie making a mistake similar to the one she made with the bird in Act 1. Imagining her reunion with Frank, she writes a passage of dialogue and plays both parts in a love scene in her head. "I'll say: 'What do ye want here ye big swollen-headed stiff? Git!' Then he'll say: 'I jes come out to meet ye honey.' Then I'll say: 'I don't want to git met by you. . . . Git away from me! Take yer hands off'n me! I hate ye!' Then he'll say: 'Now, honey . . .' Then I'll say: 'Don't Honey me! You thought I double-crossed ye . . . thought I was tryin' to show ye up!'" (52). Annie plays both parts in the scene so well that she convinces herself all has been forgiven and the two are together again:

> ANNIE: Then, by rights he oughta say: "Annie, . . . I love ye so! Then I guess I won't be able to stop myself from sayin': "I love ye too!" Then there won't be nothin' left fer him to say, but . . . "Annie!" Then I'll jes say . . .
> [*A man enters with a ten-gallon hat, very much Frank's build. In the twilight she is sure it is Frank. She runs to him and throws her arms around him*]
> Frank!
> [*She pulls back and looks at him and realizes her mistake*]
> You ain't Frank!
> MAN: Nobody said I was. (53)

As with the bird on Dolly's hat in Act 1, Annie's assumptions do not match reality. But now she sees the world theatrically and is eager to experiment with her own theatrical skills. She not only plays the part of herself in this little drama; she also plays the role of Frank. But when the man she seems to have conjured up is revealed to be someone else, Annie is startled to find that she does not have total control over the theatrical environment. The man's response to Annie's surprise that he isn't Frank is telling: "Nobody said I was." In fact, Annie did say he was. But she is neither writer nor director of this play. It is not her job to cast the parts. No matter how hard she tries, someone else seems to be writing the script for her. Annie does not yet realize that, empowering as theatricality is in terms of self-invention, the theatrical worldview operates according to strict conventions and narratives over which she seems to have little control. And these conventions determine that to star in the love scenes she imagines, Annie must *act* like the conventional woman Frank desires.

This realization does not occur until the very end of the play. In the last scene, after a brief attempt at reconciliation, Annie and Frank insist on a shooting contest to determine who is the true champion. Sitting Bull, who wants Annie to be happy, and Charlie, who wants the two shows to merge, have "fixed" Annie's guns so that she will lose the contest and Frank will be satisfied. The contest begins, and Annie—who has never missed a shot before—repeatedly shoots wide of the mark. She takes a break to consult with her mentor:

ANNIE: What's the matter with me, Papa Bull?
SITTING BULL: You do fine. Keep missing—you win.

Annie doesn't get it. Sitting Bull is trying to teach her about a subtle connection between gender relations and the theater:

SITTING BULL: Be second best, Annie.
ANNIE: Huh!

Annie still doesn't see what he means. Just *act,* he is trying to tell her. Finally, it sinks in:

SITTING BULL: Remember in big tent . . . you say "you can't get a man with
    a gun"?
ANNIE: Yeh!
SITTING BULL: You get man with this gun. [*Pointing to sights. A great light
    dawns on Annie*]
ANNIE: Why didn't I think of that? Gimme that gun! . . . PULL!
BUFFALO BILL: MISS!
[*Annie grins at Sitting Bull*] (77)

Remember the song ("You Can't Get a Man with a Gun"), Sitting Bull reminds Annie, referring her back to the musical itself for her cues. By losing the match, Annie wins Frank. To miss a shot is to be labeled, triumphantly, "Miss" and to have her femininity restored. By *acting* the role of the weaker sex, Annie finally allows the play to reach its necessary and conventional resolution. In short, acting allows her to be stronger.

And Annie makes it clear to all that she is indeed *acting.* Throwing up her arms at her repeated misses, she exclaims: "I cain't! I cain't! I quit! I give up! [*Suddenly she stops dramatically*] I concede this match to Frank Butler! The greatest sharpshooter in the world. . . . Might as well go back to Darke County. I ain't no champeen no more. I'm jest second best. Ain't I, Papa Bull? [*Winks at Sitting Bull*]" (77). Interestingly, no one is fooled by her act. Dolly quips, "Somebody got to those guns," and Frank sharply replies, "Shut up, Dolly." Annie does not need to convince anyone that she is *actually* second best. All she needs to do is show that she is willing to play the part. All Frank wants is to be sure that Annie is able to be his theatrical partner—that she understands the form.

The moral system of the show business world does not judge Annie negatively for faking the contest. On the contrary, she is rewarded for finally acting her part. Her "lies" about being second best would receive Oscar Wilde's hearty approval. In his essay "The Decay of Lying," Wilde laments the rise of realism and argues for a cultivation of what he calls the art of lying, which in this play we could call the art of show business:

> Lying and poetry are arts—arts, as Plato saw, not unconnected with each other—
> and they require the most careful study, the most disinterested devotion. Indeed,
> they have their technique, just as the more material arts of painting and sculpture
> have their subtle secrets of form and colour, their craft mysteries, their deliberate
> artistic methods. . . . Here, as elsewhere, practice must precede perfection. But in
> modern days while the fashion of writing poetry has become far too common . . .
> the fashion of lying has almost fallen into disrepute.[42]

Annie has been practicing the art of "lying" since she first met Frank. Now she
has finally learned to read the note hidden in her pocket at the end of Act 1. As
Annie overacts her "despair," Frank gallantly and theatrically comes to the rescue, finally allowed to deliver the lines he, and everyone else, has been waiting
for all along:

> FRANK: Don't worry honey, I'll take care of you. From now on we're gonna
>   be partners.
> ANNIE: Butler and Oakley . . . in alphabelitical order! (78)

Annie finally gets it. In self-consciously referring to her previous reading mistakes, she shows that she has finally learned how to interpret, and act within,
theatrical conventions. Yet her reference to the alphabet is a malapropism,
alerting us to the complexities of her acquiescence to literary conventions. After conceding to the conventions, Annie becomes almost immediately their
enforcer. Frank turns Annie's box of medals over to Buffalo Bill:

> FRANK: Bill, we're gonna combine the shows, and this'll start 'em off.
> ANNIE: Oh Frank, I love ye fer that. That's the nicest thing ye ever
>   done . . . but if'n ye hadn't a done it, I'd a shot ye right in the belly
>   button! (78)

Annie is thrilled to find that when she speaks the right lines, in the right tone
of voice, Frank responds in kind.

Immediately following this scene, the curtain closes and the entire ensemble sings a chorus of "There's No Business Like Show Business." The stage directions instruct the singers to begin in "a whispered voice," which gives the
effect of revealing a secret to the audience. In juxtaposing Annie's capitulation
to Frank with a reprise of "Show Business," the cast is winking at the audience
on Annie's behalf just as Annie winked at Sitting Bull. To wink is, of course, to
keep one eye closed while the other is open. A wink is an agreement *not* to see
as well as to see. The chorus implies here that although Annie appears to have
given in, to have agreed to the role of second fiddle, she has, in actuality, just
learned the ropes of show business, the art of lying. By learning, manipulating,
and brilliantly performing the norms of the community and conventions of the
genre, Annie finally gets everything she wants: love, success, fame, wealth.

The return to "There's No Business Like Show Business" reinscribes the

writers' utopian vision of America: a meritocratic world in which success derives from performance skills. Despite the fact that women's roles are being
dramatically revised in supposed accordance with biological terms in the
postwar period, this musical insists on the power of the theater to resist "natural" or biological categories. It offers a way for women to imagine themselves
out of constricting gender definitions by imagining themselves, indeed asserting themselves, as actresses. What the cast is implying is that in "show business," women always have the upper hand. Recall D. A. Miller's "law of the musical theater," in which he argues that men and women are not equals on the
musical stage. Women, Miller argues, have an advantage because they are also
seen as *representing* the stage, as its "essence and its glory." Men in musicals,
on the other hand, exist merely to enhance a woman's talents, often by down-
playing their own.[43] Annie can lose the shooting match, but Frank will always
be second best. Annie's last name may come after Frank's, but it is her first
name that is in the title of the show. In asserting the primacy of the woman
as actress, as star, the play offers the fantasy of an alternative for women
frustrated by the indignities associated with postwar demobilization. While
women may have to concede to men in their professional or public lives, the
play seems to say, their concession to these conventions actually gives them a
far greater power: the starring role on the private stage of the home. They can
be the best by paradoxically *acting* as if they are not.[44]

The ending thus offers a disturbing vision of a triumphant actress coerced
into playing a constricting gender role. The play suggests that women must accept this subordinate role. Although women must accept the inequities of
marriage, the play implies that because they have done so self-consciously—
because they are only *playing the role* of the weaker sex, they are really in control. For women losing jobs during demobilization, for women accommodating
themselves to inequitable marriages, such a pose of weakness was no sort of
strength. No matter how they played their roles, these women were still out of
jobs and treated as inferiors. But in the play, where posing and role playing *are*
the sources of power, Annie's compromises are less clear-cut. Annie can out-
perform anyone; she can master even submission. In her contest with Frank
she boasts: "I can sing anything *softer* than you" (my emphasis). And when she
does so, the audience applauds.

The question we are left with is why, if Annie is so theatrically powerful, she
needs or wants to make this bargain. What does she really get in the end,
when she "gets" Frank? Can a relationship based on this performance of submission possibly work? The tension in the ending between actually being
weaker and simply appearing to be weaker reveals a larger tension in the vision of America presented by Irving Berlin and Dorothy and Herbert Fields. In
raising questions about the compromises women must make to play out the
marriage plot, the ending throws into question the viability for women of the

"You've Got to Be Carefully Taught"

The Politics of Race in *South Pacific*

I N THE second act of *South Pacific* (1949), Lieutenant Joe Cable sings "You've Got to Be Carefully Taught," a song about racial prejudice. Rodgers and Hammerstein were counseled repeatedly in tryouts to remove the song, which was considered by many to be too controversial, too preachy, or simply inappropriate in a musical. They resisted the pressure. As James Michener, author of the book on which the play was based, later recalled: "The authors replied stubbornly that this number represented why they had wanted to do this play, and that even if it meant the failure of the production, it was going to stay in."[1] During a touring production of the show in Atlanta in 1953, the song raised the hackles of some Georgia legislators, who introduced a bill to outlaw any entertainment that had, as they put it, "an underlying philosophy inspired by Moscow."[2] State Representative David C. Jones claimed that a song justifying interracial marriage was implicitly a threat to the American way of life. Hammerstein replied that he was surprised by the idea that "anything kind and humane must necessarily originate in Moscow."[3]

One of Rodgers and Hammerstein's most popular musicals, *South Pacific* has been acclaimed for its sensitive and courageous treatment of the subject of racial prejudice. Preaching tolerance and a universalist humanism, the musical is often celebrated for representing interracial romance and apparently eradicating (on the musical stage, at least) the differences that separate ethnic and racial groups.[4] It seems curious that Rodgers and Hammerstein would insist on including a message about racial tolerance in a commercial Broadway play a number of years before the civil rights movement was headline news.[5] Their earlier works, *Oklahoma!* (1943) and *Carousel* (1945), showed little overt evidence of interest in the issue. While the source material for the play, James

Michener's *Tales of the South Pacific* (1946), briefly touches on the issue of racial difference, it does not give the topic the central place accorded it in the play. There are no African Americans in the play, but, as the Georgia legislators made clear, American race relations are clearly being addressed nonetheless. Why, then, did Rodgers and Hammerstein choose to focus on racial tolerance?

We can begin to explore the question by revisiting the red-baiting accusations of the Georgia legislators. *South Pacific* appeared in 1949, at the height of the post–World War II Red Scare. The House Un-American Activities Committee (HUAC), under the leadership of Martin Dies, was in high gear, rooting out perceived Communist subversives. In 1948 alone, the news was full of the Alger Hiss and Gerhard Eisler espionage cases and the conviction of the Hollywood Ten.[6] In 1949, Nationalist China was "lost" to the Communists, and the Soviet Union revealed that it had the atom bomb. Under the Smith Act, the Communist Party (CP) was effectively made illegal in a highly publicized trial of party leaders in 1949, and anyone who was or had been even remotely associated with the party was in danger of being investigated by the FBI and subpoenaed by HUAC.

Liberals who had been supporters of left-wing causes in the 1930s and 1940s needed to find a way to assert their anti-Communist credentials without compromising their political positions. One solution was to redefine the fight for racial equality as a way to fight Communism. In maintaining a class of black laborers who were disaffected, segregated, and underprivileged, they argued, America was setting itself up for potential Communist infiltration. By awarding equal rights to all, Americans could protect themselves from revolution from below.[7] American Jews—and, in particular, assimilated New York Jewish artists like Rodgers and Hammerstein—had a personal stake in asserting this connection between anti-Communism and civil rights. Jews were commonly associated with the Communist Party and other left-wing groups. Vocal anti-semites, like Congressman Martin Dies and his HUAC successor John Rankin, associated the Communist menace with Jews, insinuating that Jewish influence was corrupting American politics and culture.[8] Even Jews with impeccable anti-Communist records were wary of Cold War hawks and feared the connections they perceived between anti-Communist demagoguery, neofascism, and antisemitism.[9] Indeed, the Georgia legislators' complaints about *South Pacific*—complaints which equated antiracism with pro-Communism and which implied that the New York (often a code word for Jewish) theater was receiving its directions from Moscow—articulated the very rhetoric Jews of the day understandably feared. Centrist Jews, in order to protect their hard-won status as loyal Americans, therefore needed to dissociate Jewishness from Communism and to establish their own anti-Communist credentials, while critiquing the methods and rhetoric of anti-Communist demagogues. They redefined the terms of the debate, claiming that the best protection against Communism was a reinforcement of the American values of equality and democracy. By championing civil liberties, they felt, Jews could demonstrate that they were good Americans while also protecting themselves from antisemitism.[10]

When explored within its particular historical context, then, *South Pacific* becomes more than a simple example of liberal ideology.[11] Between the lines of its apparently straightforward text and woven into its melodies lies a story of Cold War anxieties and Jewish assimilationist desires. Viewed in terms of theatrical history, *South Pacific* also marks a moment when the musical theater was striving to distance itself from its commercial roots and to redefine itself instead as art. As the quintessential example of what midcentury critics called "middlebrow" culture, *South Pacific* sits between the "low" culture of Tin Pan Alley and the "high" culture of legitimate theater and opera. This chapter will focus on the problem of difference—racial, ethnic, political, and musical—as represented in *South Pacific*. Rodgers and Hammerstein created characters that express the contradictions of Cold War liberalism through the theatrical modes in which they perform. The play is set on a distant island, but the concerns are distinctly American. Traditions of high and low musical theater, of opera and jazz, of European waltzes and burlesque soft-shoe become the language in which difference is expressed.

∗   ∗   ∗   ∗   ∗

South Pacific was a phenomenally successful musical, both commercially and critically. Michener's book won the Pulitzer Prize for fiction in 1947, and the musical won the Pulitzer for drama in 1950 (the year after Arthur Miller won for *Death of a Salesman*). It ran on Broadway for five years and is among the top ten longest-running plays in Broadway history. *South Pacific* toured nationally and internationally for about ten years. The original cast album for the show popularized the 33⅓-RPM format for LPs, selling a million copies and holding the number-one position on the charts for sixty-nine weeks. The sheet music also sold more than two million copies. Before 20th Century Fox bought the movie rights in 1956, *South Pacific* had already earned profits of more than five *billion* dollars. The film version received three Academy Award nominations and the soundtrack album was in the U.S. top ten for two years, with fifty-four weeks at the number-one spot.[12] Mary Martin, who starred in the original Broadway production, created a commercial sensation of her own when she decided to wash her hair onstage for the number "I'm Gonna Wash That Man Right Out of My Hair." Her short hairstyle became a fashion trend and shampoo companies began marketing once-a-day use for their products, relying on Martin's example to sell their product.[13] Throughout the late 1940s and 1950s, *South Pacific* was not only a successful play but also a pervasive presence in American popular culture. Its songs played in American living rooms, its styles directed American women's tastes, and its political ideology helped to shape American popular opinion.

The success of *South Pacific* requires some investigation. The play's enshrinement in American theatrical history is based on claims about its integrated form and its controversial content. As Rodgers himself states in his memoir, in creating *South Pacific* he and Hammerstein decided to dispense with well-worn theatrical formulas.[14] They wanted to push the integrated musical even further than they had in *Oklahoma!* and *Carousel* and to establish it as the new standard for the musical theater. By using a "serious" book and casting an opera star, Ezio Pinza, as the male lead, they intended to raise expectations about the artistic possibilities of the musical form. *South Pacific* is also considered radical in its exposure of racial issues on the American stage. As Philip Beidler has pointed out, the legend of Rodgers and Hammerstein's use of the Broadway theater to make a courageous statement against racial bigotry is the very foundation on which the work is considered a classic.[15] Rodgers and Hammerstein use the different backgrounds of the characters as a way of promoting racial tolerance. By offering a character who has never been a racist (Emile), one who discovers he is a racist (Cable), and one who successfully overcomes her racism (Nellie), Rodgers and Hammerstein aim to show the ways in which, through education and love, prejudice can be overcome. On the surface, *South Pacific* paints an extraordinarily bright picture of a human community that knows no barriers of race or culture. In this natural extension of the liberal utopian vision of *Babes in Arms,* we learn through education that we are all the same under the skin, with the same basic beliefs, needs, desires, and impulses. Whether we are American, Tonkinese, Polynesian, or French (the play implies), as long as we all believe in the fundamental American values of romantic love, marriage, freedom, and equality, we all deserve—and can achieve—happiness.

Racial difference serves as an obstacle to be overcome for both of the central couples in the play. In the main love story, Nellie Forbush, a nurse from Little Rock, Arkansas, has fallen in love with a sophisticated and romantic older man, the French plantation owner Emile DeBecque. When she discovers that he has two children from a previous relationship with a Polynesian woman, Nellie breaks off the engagement. Frustrated by Nellie's refusal, Emile decides to take on a dangerous mission. Anxiously awaiting his return, Nellie realizes the error of her ways and decides she will marry him after all. In the final scene, Emile returns safely to find Nellie serving soup to his "Eurasian" (as they are called in the script) children. In a parallel story, Lieutenant Joe Cable, seduced by Tonkinese saleswoman Bloody Mary's descriptions of a nearby paradise island, travels to Bali Hai, where he meets and falls in love with Liat, Bloody Mary's daughter. When pressed to marry, Joe insists that he cannot bring a Tonkinese woman home to his Mainline Philadelphia family. But after witnessing the damage that Nellie's racism is causing to her relationship with Emile, Joe realizes the folly of his own bigotry. Singing "You've Got to Be Carefully Taught," he implies that if prejudice is learned, it can also be unlearned. Although Joe's realization comes too late (he dies in combat before having the chance to reunite with Liat), the play implies that through education, soul-searching, and love, racism can be overcome.

Peeling back a sunny layer or two, one discovers underneath *South Pacific*'s utopian humanism a strikingly familiar set of racial codes. *South Pacific*'s success actually lies not in political radicalism but in its presentation of familiar racial tropes under a mask of comforting liberal rhetoric. The apparently simple moral of the play—that prejudice is a result of ignorance and can be eradicated through education—is undercut by the use of racial stereotypes and the complex interplay of white Americans with ethnic and racial others. Like Jud in *Oklahoma!* the racial others—the "natives"—do not sing in the "proper" musical theater style (if they sing at all), and hence they have no chance of being integrated into the American community on the island. Like Ali Hakim, the ethnic outsider, Emile DeBecque *is* able to perform in a style that impresses the Americans, and so, although his achievement is ambiguous, he does win the hand of the American leading lady and thus some form of membership in the American community. As in *Oklahoma!* (and earlier for Rodgers in *Babes in Arms*), Rodgers and Hammerstein reinforce a distinction in *South Pacific* between racial difference, which is immutable, and ethnic difference, which is constructed.

In order to uncover the racial logic of the play, one needs to look closely at the theatrical conventions and formulas that drive the action. The vaudevillian approach to race and ethnicity—the use of broad stereotypes—which was widely adopted in the musical comedies of the 1920s and 1930s, served a liberating function when used to its full theatrical potential. By demonstrating the fluidity of racial and ethnic identity on the stage, chameleon-like performers in musical comedies exposed the problems inherent in the biological rhetoric of race. Eddie Cantor, as we have seen, adopted numerous masks in his stage and screen roles, performing as an Indian, a black minstrel, a woman, a Greek, or a stage Jew. His broad characterizations and quick changes highlighted the ways in which these identities were constructed and performed: they were a product of costume and accent, not blood. But in *South Pacific,* the theatricality of these stereotypes is repressed. They are forced into a "realist" structure and twisted to serve a particular pedagogical function. When a theatrical racial type such as Liat or Bloody Mary becomes the basis for a "real" character in a "realistic" play, the stereotype takes on deeply problematic and even sinister nuances. The mask of caricature, which is potentially powerful because it can be shaped, altered, and removed, becomes in *South Pacific* a racist device that undercuts the very message the play is supposed to promote. Forced to don a single stereotypical mask and to interact with white characters within a realist dramaturgy, the Asian characters become not self-conscious performers but "real" examples of the limitations of racial otherness.

The Asian characters in the play are one-dimensional and largely without agency. They have no chance of joining the American community on the island. For the most part, they inhabit a distinctly separate sphere from the Americans and Europeans: they live in an exotic paradise called Bali Hai. This island, figured in the song "Bali Hai" as a woman ("Here am I, / Your special island! / Come to me, come to me!"), is the repository of all of the white man's fantasies about the exotic South Pacific.[16] There the natives enact strange rituals, and the women, eager to sleep with any white man who visits, dance topless in the jungle.[17] Bloody Mary, who introduces Joe Cable to Bali Hai, seems to have come directly from World War II film stereotypes of grinning Chinese peasants with betel-stained teeth.[18] We never learn her real name, only the name given to her by the ridiculing sailors. The language used to describe her in the stage directions is startling in its use of cliché: "She is small, yellow, with Oriental eyes. She wears black sateen trousers, and a white blouse over which is an old Marine's tunic. On her head is a peach basket hat. . . . At the end of the singing, she gives out a shrill cackle of laughter with which we shall soon learn to identify her" (282). Later in the same scene, Hammerstein writes of her "crafty smile" and her "quick scowl" (283), and in the next scene Mary is discovered "grinning a big Oriental grin" (287). Mary's attitudes toward human life and liberty are foreign and distasteful to the Americans. Her only goal is to make a quick buck. To this end she sells shrunken human heads; she also sells her daughter to the "saxy Lootellan," Joe Cable.

The relationship between Joe and Bloody Mary's daughter, Liat, is plagued by similar problems of stereotype. His initial attraction to her is perfectly clear: she is a beautiful, docile, exotic, and willing child-woman who thinks he is a god. Joe and Liat fall in love, but Joe refuses to marry her because of her race. This refusal becomes the moral linchpin of the play. How, the script asks, could Joe turn away the woman he loves simply because of the color of her skin? In doing so, the play implies, he reenacts the crime of American racism. Similarly, in recognizing the error of his ways, he becomes for other white Americans an example of the liberating possibilities of education and understanding. But a close look at Joe and Liat's relationship reveals the conflicted racial ideology operating in this musical.

First and most obviously, Liat embodies the classic stereotype of the exotic oriental woman. Rodgers and Hammerstein were aware that they were dabbling in cliché as they worked on the script: "The more we talked about the plot," Rodgers admitted, "the more it dawned on us that onstage it would look like just another variation of *Madama Butterfly*."[19] According to Rodgers, the solution they arrived at was to leave Liat's character undeveloped while adding the story of Emile and Nellie. Yet the addition of a complex and successful love story between two white people only serves to heighten the formulaic and stereotypical structure of the former one. Unlike Nellie and Emile's relationship, which seems distinctly nonsexual, Joe and Liat's seems only sexual. At their first meeting, they exchange no more than three words and then: "She walks slowly toward him. The music builds in a rapturous upsurge. Cable gathers Liat in his arms. She reaches her small arms up to his neck. He lifts her off her feet. The lights fade slowly as his hand slides her blouse up her back" (323). Because *South Pacific* is at heart a musical comedy, this initial sexual encounter must be explained not realistically as lust but romantically as love-at-first-sight. And so Cable sings to Liat the song "Younger Than Springtime," which explains his love for her.

But Liat cannot answer in song because Rodgers and Hammerstein have rendered her voiceless. In doing so, they deliberately rejected their acknowledged sources for the character: Puccini's opera and Michener's story. In *Madama Butterfly,* Cio Cio San is not only the central character in the play (she dominates Acts 2 and 3, in which Pinkerton makes only a brief appearance); she also has the strongest voice in the opera and her arias are the most powerful in the score. In the Michener story "Fo' Dolla'" on which the relationship between Liat and Joe is based (hardly a racially enlightened text, but marginally more so than the play), Liat is actually an educated woman who speaks fluent French. Cable likewise speaks some French, and their relationship develops through both sexual contact and intimate conversation: "For a while, they sat near the cliff and talked. Strange, but all the things Cable could not write to Bryn Mawr flooded out in half-French, half-English sentences. Liat followed his thoughts with ease and soon she was telling him of Tonkin China."[20] Rodgers and Hammerstein have chosen to make Liat far younger and utterly uneducated. They condemn her to silence, a sentence that in the musical theater is akin to death.[21]

In the only other song involving Liat, "Happy Talk," Bloody Mary tries to convince Joe that he should stay on the island and marry Liat. Ironically, she offers him the opportunity for endless "happy talk" with a girl who cannot speak:

> Talk about a moon
> Floatin' in de sky,
> Lookin' like a lily on a lake;
> Talk about a bird
> Learnin' how to fly,
> Makin' all de music he can make—

To reinforce Liat's silence, the stage directions read: *"Liat now performs a gentle, childish dance."* Director Josh Logan turned the dance into a series of "finger gestures" which Liat uses to mime the words Bloody Mary sings.[22] The effect is that of a dumb show.

In the self-consciously formulaic musicals of the 1920s, which dealt overtly in racial and ethnic stereotype, Liat's silence would be logical, if not unproblematic. Exotic sexual objects are not supposed to have complex thoughts. But in *South Pacific*, Liat is given some of the responsibilities of a "real" character: she is a potential marriage partner for the male lead. And Joe's rejection of her becomes the occasion for the central moral statement of the play. But Rodgers and Hammerstein withhold the tools—a voice, a song—that Liat needs to function as a real character in the musical. This paradox leads to a major plot crisis. By giving Joe a stereotype for a lover, they have set up an impossible situation for him. How, within the logic of this play, could Joe marry Liat? He would first have to prove that they are alike under the skin. In doing this, he would have to erase her exoticism. Then, after dismissing her difference, he would have to find another reason to be attracted to her. If Rodgers and Hammerstein had made a racially different girl into a marriageable American girl, if they had given the racial other both a voice and a blue-blooded American man for a husband, they would have been openly and powerfully advocating miscegenation and integration in an American society still deeply committed to racially separate spheres.[23] Instead, Liat is rendered mute by her stereotypical role, and Joe is killed off as soon as he realizes the problematic nature of his own behavior. Death is the neatest and easiest solution.

Rodgers and Hammerstein both supported liberal and antiracist causes, and clearly never consciously intended to write a racist play. Hammerstein in particular was active in a number of groups that fought against prejudice, including the NAACP. In 1945, under the auspices of the Writers' War Board, he wrote a number of tracts that inveighed against the practice of stereotyping. One was entitled "How Writers Perpetuate Stereotypes"; another was a parody of his song "Old Man River," entitled "Ol' Man Author." In this revision, he imagines a quartet—"an Irishman, a Negro, an Italian, and a Jew"—singing the following lyrics:

> I'm a Jew
> And I like money,
> Wealthy Christians think that's funny!
> I'm a comic, scheming scamp—
> Comic as a Nazi Concentration Camp!
> We keep on tryin', we're in there flyin'
> We're in there fightin', we're in there dyin'
> But ol' man author, he keeps on writing us wrong![24]

22. Bloody Mary (Juanita Hall), Liat (Betta St. John), and Joe (William Tabbert) perform "Happy Talk" in the 1949 production of *South Pacific.* Museum of the City of New York; gift of Harold Friedlander.

Despite Hammerstein's passionate rejection of racial stereotypes for Jews, blacks, Irish, and Italians, he notably (and perhaps logically, considering wartime attitudes toward the Japanese) neglects to include Asians in his group. His ability to fight against racial prejudice on the one hand and unwittingly indulge in it on the other defines the difficulties and inherent contradictions of the postwar Jewish liberal position on race.[25]

Overt racism, defined by Joe Cable as the fear of people "whose eyes are oddly made, / And people whose skin is a different shade" (346), presents a central problem in *South Pacific*. But even more complicated is the treatment of ethnic difference. Racially different characters like Liat and Bloody Mary exist in a marginal space, only occasionally crossing over into American territory. Yet Emile, a white European, operates within the power centers of the American community: fighting on the same side as American troops, entertaining American officers, and ultimately marrying an American girl. The presence of this foreigner among the Americans in wartime provokes surprising reactions that suggest the complex anxieties inherent in Cold War culture. In the late 1940s, as tensions with the Soviet Union escalated, the notion that anyone, and particularly any foreigner, could be a Communist subversive was widespread. Difference, especially difference of a vaguely European intellectual sort, was perceived as a threat. Ellen Schrecker, a historian of McCarthyism, describes the responses to a 1954 poll on why certain individuals might be believed to be Communist: "'He was not like us.' 'Would not attend church and talked against God.' 'He brought a lot of foreign-looking people into his home.' 'I just knew. But I wouldn't know how to say I knew.'"[26]

The problem of difference is highlighted in one of the most popular songs in the play: "I'm Gonna Wash That Man Right Out of My Hair." Mary Martin's rendering was celebrated for its infectious energy in all of the reviews of *South Pacific*'s triumphant opening night in New York. Yet critics have failed to note that, despite its liberating quality, this hit tune is actually a powerful argument *against* difference in relationships (in a play supposedly preaching the opposite). Nurse Nellie is unsure of her new relationship with Emile, long before she knows anything of his "Eurasian" children. Shaken by the suspicions of her mother and her friends, Nellie decides to give Emile up:

> I'm gonna wash that man right outa my hair,
> I'm gonna wash that man right outa my hair,
> And send him on his way.
> > [*She struts around splashing soap out of her hair*]
> Get the picture?

Why this extreme reaction to an apparently charming and attentive lover? Nellie explains that Emile is simply different from her:

23. Nellie Forbush (Mary Martin) "washing that man right out of her hair" in *South Pacific* (1949). Museum of the City of New York; gift of John Toohey.

NELLIE: If the man don't understand you,
 If you fly on sep'rate beams,
 Waste no time!
 Make a change,
 Ride that man right off your range,
 Rub him out-a the roll call
 And drum him out-a your dreams!
NURSES: Oh-ho!

Difference, it seems, is so problematic in the world of *South Pacific* that Nellie must expel Emile from all of the mythical American landscapes that he, as a foreigner, might want to inhabit: the range, the roll call, and, most important, the (American) dream. This difference is defined in terms of one's relationship to American popular culture:

DINAH: If you laugh at dif-f'rent comics
ANOTHER NURSE: If you root for dif-f'rent teams,
NELLIE, DINAH, SECOND NURSE: Waste no time,
 Weep no more
 Show him what the door is for!

But the song quickly moves from pointing out difference to judging it. Difference becomes not just a relationship problem, but the marker of a "bad egg":

NELLIE: You can't light a fire when the wood's all wet!
GIRLS: No!
NELLIE: You can't make a but-ter-fly strong,
GIRLS: Uh-uh!
NELLIE: You can't fix an egg when it ain't quite good,
NURSES: And you can't fix a man when he's wrong!

In the play, the conflict between Emile and Nellie is supposedly rooted in Nellie's childhood prejudices: Nellie cannot countenance Emile's previous interracial relationship. But this song occurs before she even knows about Emile's Polynesian lover. Before any real conflict arises, difference itself is identified as a potential problem. Bouncing along with Nellie as she happily tosses her man out with the soap lather, we too are encouraged to wonder if there isn't something wrong with Emile and the type of difference he represents. Emile is, after all, an outsider. He is not only wealthy, middle-aged, and foreign, but also a political refugee. He left France, as he tells Nellie, because he accidentally killed a petty demagogue who had gained power through unscrupulous means. In the Michener story, Emile directly articulates his political position as antifascist, opposed to the Vichy government of Marshal Pétain.

In order to write about difference, Rodgers and Hammerstein first had to set up a familiar American space into which difference would intrude. In their previous two shows, *Oklahoma!* and *Carousel,* the Americanness of the setting was overt. An Oklahoma farm and a small New England town are clearly American landscapes with obvious insiders and outsiders. But in choosing an exotic South Pacific island, they transformed a clearly non-American space into a normative American one. *South Pacific* presents a roster of familiar American musical types: Nellie, the optimistic and sparkling leading lady; Joe Cable, the romantic hero; Luther Billis, the (sanitized) ethnic comic; the beautiful nurses in bathing suits and the masculine sailors who want to sleep with them. These characters are united by their comfort in sharing a stage and their suspicion of outsiders. They consistently ostracize Emile, who emerges as a palpable threat. Such staging illustrates how Rodgers and Hammerstein used the theater itself to establish American hegemony. By importing familiar conventions of the Broadway musical—both those which signaled the older vaudevillian tradition and those recently created by Rodgers and Hammerstein themselves—into an exotic space, they quickly and efficiently asserted the Americanness of the landscape, creating a familiar community of American "types." These Americans perform in one way; Emile, in another.

Nellie Forbush embodies the gutsy optimism of the new Broadway musical form ushered in by *Oklahoma!*—a form that was quite familiar to audiences by 1948 (via *Carousel, Kiss Me, Kate,* and *Annie Get Your Gun*). In the first scene of the play, the part of Nellie, played by Mary Martin in the original production, clearly requires a leading lady of the Broadway stage. *South Pacific* was, in fact, the first show Rodgers and Hammerstein wrote as a star vehicle. Knowing that Mary Martin would play the part of Nellie Forbush, they were careful to construct a character which would allow her talents to shine (they gave her seven songs, four of them solos). Unlike Emile, whose role in the musical is murky, new, mysterious, and in need of explanation far into the first act, Nellie immediately asserts the simplicity of her persona in the opening scene, claiming her star status and exercising her powers as the symbol of Broadway itself. As expected, she almost immediately stands up, introduces herself to Emile and the audience, and belts out a song:

> You know what they call me? Knucklehead Nellie. I suppose I am,
>   but I can't help it. [*She sings*]
> When the sky is a bright canary yellow
> I forget every cloud I've ever seen—
> So they call me a cockeyed optimist,
> Immature and incurably green!

Nellie establishes herself as the embodiment of American youth, optimism, energy, and power, the life force of the island. Unlike the sexy urban sophisti-

cates in Rodgers and Hart musicals like *Pal Joey* (or in the musicals of Irving Berlin, Kurt Weill, and Cole Porter), Nellie is straightforward, anti-intellectual, and, ironically, antitheatrical. She refuses to put on an act; she can say (or sing) only what is in her heart:

> I could say life is just a bowl of jello
> And appear more intelligent and smart,
> But I'm stuck, like a dope,
> With a thing called hope,
> And I can't get it out of my heart!
> Not this heart!

Nellie the American is open, friendly, and has (she thinks) nothing to hide. She offers herself up to the audience without reservation. As she finishes her song, she asks, "Want to know anything else about me?" She demands that the audience identify with her—a familiar, recognizable all-American girl next door. Her assertive normalcy serves to throw Emile's difference further into relief.

If Nellie represents America by celebrating the new Broadway of Rodgers and Hammerstein, Seabee Luther Billis is Rodgers and Hammerstein's nod to the vaudevillian past. Luther bears a striking resemblance to the Jewish (or ethnic) comics who populated earlier musicals such as *Whoopee* (Henry Williams), *Girl Crazy* (Gieber Goldfarb), and *Oklahoma!* (Ali Hakim). While all traces of ethnic particularity are carefully erased from Luther's character, his performance style clearly connects him with his ethnic predecessors. He serves as comic relief in an otherwise serious play. Enterprising leader of the Seabees on the base, he performs in a broad, bawdy musical style and always has a chorus of sailors and nurses to back him up. Perhaps most telling is his appearance in the number "Honey Bun." For the Thanksgiving show, Nellie and Luther appear together in the finale. Nellie, dressed in an oversized sailor suit, sings:

> A hundred and one
> Pounds of fun—
> That's my little Honey-Bun!
> Get a load of honey bun tonight.

Luther then enters "dressed as a South Sea siren," complete with wig, false eyelashes, and a coconut-shell bra. Luther's performance clearly evokes the Jewish-male-in-drag numbers popular in earlier musicals such as *Whoopee* and *Girl Crazy.* And since Milton Berle's television show began in the same year as *South Pacific,* Luther seems to be making a direct reference to Berle's over-the-top drag routines. Like his predecessors, Luther speaks with the accent of a tough New Yorker: whatever his ethnicity, he is clearly from "New Yawk." When Lieutenant Cable carefully mentions that he went to college at "a

24. Nellie Forbush (Mary Martin) and Luther Billis (Myron McCormick) in drag in "Honey Bun." Anonymous photo from the Billy Rose Theatre Collection, New York Public Library for the Performing Arts; Astor, Lenox and Tilden Foundations.

place in New Jersey," Luther, acknowledging both his familiarity with the New York area and his working-class assumptions, responds, "Where? Rutgers?" (296).

Perhaps most important, Luther serves the same function as the earlier Jewish comics in the musical plot. He is a staunch ally of the leading lady. Luther does Nellie's laundry for her, prepares her shower, and generally sees that she is cared for. When Emile wants to give Nellie some flowers before the Thanksgiving show, Luther intervenes—in this case, not to ensure that Nellie and Emile get together but to protect her from a suspicious outsider. The Americans close ranks around Nellie, solidifying their community against outside influences. Knowing that Nellie is trying to forget Emile, Luther warns him not to bother her during the show:

> EMILE: Pardon, can you tell me where I can find Miss Forbush?
> BILLIS: [*Shrewdly sensing trouble and determined to protect Nellie*] She's on stage now. She's the Emcee. She can't talk to nobody right now. Do you want me to take the flowers in to her?
> EMILE: No. I would prefer to give them to her myself.
> BILLIS: Are you Mister de Becque?
> EMILE: Yes.
> BILLIS: Look, Mister de Becque. Do me a favor, will you? Don't try and see her tonight.
> EMILE: Why?
> BILLIS: We got her in a great mood tonight and I don't want anything to upset her again. (335)

Luther delivers Emile's flowers to Nellie but at first does not tell her who sent them. When he finally decides to show her the card, he assumes she will be upset and offers to help out: "[*Shoving a card at Nellie*] Here's the card that came with them. [*She reads the card, then turns away—deeply affected.*] Are you all right, Miss Forbush? [*She nods her head*] I'll be waiting around the area here in case you need me. Just—just sing out" (345). Luther wants to protect Nellie, and he offers to do so in a manner consistent with his character: he asks her to "just sing out." Luther invokes the familiar trope of American musicals in which community is formed by singing together, but in this case he does so in order to exclude, not include.

Joe Cable offers us another type of American, in another familiar theatrical role: the young romantic hero. He, not Emile, is the natural match for Nellie, and his attention to her further solidifies the American community while pushing Emile to the outside. The script is loaded with references to a possible attraction between Nellie and Joe. When they first meet in the Island Commander's office, all of the men in the room rush to show Nellie to her seat. The script makes a point of noting that Joe succeeds: "The three men rush to help her sit. Cable gets there first. Nellie sits." The officers interrogate Nellie about Emile, but to no avail. Nellie leaves and Commander Harbison muses: "I'm afraid we aren't going to get much out of her. She's obviously in love with him." Cable replies (voicing concerns undoubtedly shared by members of the audience as well), "That's hard to believe, sir. They tell me he's a middle-aged man" (305).

In the next scene, Joe intercepts Nellie reading a letter from her mother. He flirts with her:

> [*Cable enters and watches Nellie for a moment. Nellie is now standing still, read-ing a part of her letter that evokes an occasional groan of irritation from her. Ca-ble grins at her.*]
>
> CABLE: Letter from home? [*Nellie looks up, startled by his voice, then grins back at him*]
> NELLIE: Yes. Do you get letters from your mother, telling you that every-thing you do is wrong?
> CABLE: No. My mother thinks everything I do is right. . . . Of course, I don't tell her everything I do. (308)

Their intimacy is quickly established. Nellie accepts his joking; they speak a similar language, and the scene bounces along easily. Nellie tells him her com-plaints:

> NELLIE: My mother's so prejudiced.
> CABLE: Against Frenchmen?
> NELLIE: [*She smiles to acknowledge that she gets the allusion, then pursues her anti-maternal tirade*] Against anyone outside of Little Rock. She makes a big thing out of two people having different backgrounds.
> CABLE: [*Rather hopefully*] Ages?
> NELLIE: Oh, no. Mother says older men are better for girls than younger men.
> CABLE: . . . This has been a discouraging day for me. (308)

The scene sets up an expectation that Cable is interested in Nellie. His admis-sion of discouragement clearly signals to Nellie that he was hoping he might have a chance with her. Nellie then asks Joe what he thinks of her mother's ad-vice:

> NELLIE: Do you agree with Mother about people having things in com-mon? For instance, if the man likes symphony music and the girl likes Dinah Shore—and he reads Marcel Proust and she doesn't read any-thing . . . Well, what do *you* think? Do you think Mother's right?
> CABLE: Well, she might be. (308)

As they part, Cable throws in another jab at Emile: "Listen, you don't know so much about that guy. You better read that letter over two or three times"

(308). She apparently decides to take his advice. The next time we see Nellie, she is determined to "wash that man right out of [her] hair."

But what makes Emile so different? Why are all of the Americans in the cast, including Nellie, suspicious of him? His foreignness is twofold: he is of different national and ethnic background, and he performs in a different idiom. He is French, not American—he speaks with an accent and has no grasp of American culture. He refers to Nellie's hometown as "Small Rock," a place in the "stick." As Nellie finishes singing "I'm Gonna Wash That Man," Emile appears and asks naively, "That song . . . is it a new American song?" Emile is clearly concerned that Nellie might be singing about him, but instead of directly confronting her, he continues his comments on American music: "It is strange with your American songs. In all of them one is either desirous to get rid of one's lover, or one weeps for a man one cannot have" (313). His history is also murky: he left home under a cloud, and he has, by his own admission, "lived as he could" since he came to the island. He is also an intellectual (usually a suspect category in musicals). He speaks of love "philosophically" (at least according to the stage directions), and he reads Marcel Proust and Anatole France instead of listening to Dinah Shore, as Nellie does. He also seems to have emerged not from the world of musical comedy but from that of opera. He sings "high"-culture music, while Nellie and the others sing low. He is middle-aged, which is acceptable for an opera singer; but in a musical world of youth, energy, and freshness, Emile's maturity is out of place.

Who is Emile in the American landscape of the 1940s? A political fugitive, a radical antifascist, an intellectual with a high-culture background—in fact, Emile strongly evokes the European (mostly German) intellectuals who fled to America in the 1930s and 1940s to escape Nazi persecution. Many of these refugees were connected with the worlds of theater, film, music, and literature, and most were Jews.[27] Emile is a type with whom Rodgers and Hammerstein would have been deeply familiar. In Hollywood, Ernst Lubitsch and the composer Arnold Schoenberg were well known, while Kurt Weill was an important presence in the Broadway theater. Weill, who fled Germany in 1935, wrote the play *One Touch of Venus,* which starred Mary Martin. And the same year that Rodgers and Hammerstein were mounting *South Pacific,* Weill was collaborating with Maxwell Anderson on a show about race issues, *Lost in the Stars,* to be directed by Rouben Mamoulian, who also directed the original production of *Oklahoma!*

Rodgers and Hammerstein's portrayal of Emile suggests deep ambivalence about such European refugees. They seem both in awe of and threatened by his presence in their musical; they appear to admire and to identify with his European intellectual pedigree, even as they distance themselves from his politically and racially murky past. As an outsider, he not only is an object of suspicion but also has the distance necessary to offer sage criticism of American

25. Nellie (Mary Martin) gazes admiringly up at Emile (Ezio Pinza) as he teaches her about high culture, fine champagne, and romantic love. Photo by Richard Tucker. Billy Rose Theatre Collection, New York Public Library for the Performing Arts; Astor, Lenox and Tilden Foundations.

culture. Rodgers and Hammerstein make him the voice of noble democratic rhetoric. Similarly, they give him "high" music to sing but then deny him a leading lady who can sing with him. They give him an apparent advantage by making him "cultured" and Nellie a "hick," but in a musical this is no favor: musicals are famously anti-elitist. And they break form by creating a middle-aged love interest, although they also set up the younger and more musically compatible Joe Cable as his competition. In short, Emile becomes the site of competing anxieties about the racial, cultural, and political world of the late 1940s. His foreign, intellectual, and antifascist background immediately raises a red flag (an unavoidable pun). Certainly many of the German Jewish émigrés had Socialist, if not Communist leanings and most were viewed as potential Communists by the more radical red-baiters. Ellen Schrecker points to Gerhard Eisler, one of the most notorious German Jewish émigrés and the subject of the 1951 Cold War film *I Was a Communist for the FBI,* as the "quintessential embodiment of the specter of international Communism": a Jew, a foreigner, an intellectual with "fancy ideas," and "a man of brilliance and charm."[28] Emile certainly shares some of Eisler's traits; but whereas Eisler was vilified, Emile becomes a hero.

A closer look at Rodgers and Hammerstein's own position in relation to the political and cultural forces of the day helps to untangle Emile's complicated role. HUAC's investigation of Hollywood and the subsequent blacklist sent a shiver down the spines of artists working in theater, television, and film, particularly Jewish artists who may have marched in a leftist rally, signed a petition, or performed in a benefit in the 1930s; any of these activities would now be viewed as subversive by the committee. Neither Rodgers nor Hammerstein had records that HUAC would have considered impeccable, yet both saw themselves as staunch patriots and active defenders of the American Creed. While Hammerstein supported the Welcome House program, which facilitated adoptions of mixed-race children fathered by American servicemen in Asia and which clearly aided the implementation of American Cold War ideology in Asia, he was also affiliated with countless other organizations, many supporting either left-leaning or Jewish causes.[29] He was an active member of the Hollywood Anti-Nazi League (a Popular Front Organization) in the 1930s; a fundraiser for the Jewish Federation, as well as the chair of the Legitimate Theater Division of its New York branch; a vice-president of the NAACP; and a fundraiser for the National Conference of Christians and Jews.[30] Likewise, Rodgers chaired a United Jewish Appeal fundraiser, appeared on a pro-Zionist "Night of Stars" program, and raised funds for the Jewish Federation.[31] In 1947 Rodgers joined a prominent group of artists protesting the HUAC probe in Hollywood; the FBI subsequently opened a file on him.[32] As we have seen, he was also a staunch supporter of Roosevelt and the New Deal.[33] Both were ardent and outspoken patriots—how could the creators of *Oklahoma!* be judged otherwise?—yet through their affiliations, they were connected with a liberal social agenda which could raise suspicions among those who claimed to be exposing Communists "in the interest of national security."

Emile, a foreigner living among Americans, also provokes the suspicions of those charged with protecting America's sovereignty. The military officers Brackett and Harbison want to know not what he has done, but what he believes. They want to determine not if he is a criminal but if he adheres to the American Creed. Early in the first act, Commander Harbison and Captain Brackett call Nellie into their office to ask her to act as an informer:

HARBISON: . . . Find out as much as you can about him, his background, his opinions, and why he killed this man in France.
NELLIE: In other words, you want me to spy on him.
BRACKETT: Well, I'm afraid it *is* something like that.
NELLIE: Why? . . . Do you suspect him of anything?

BRACKETT: No, it's just that we don't know very much about him and
he's—er . . . Will you help us, Miss Forbush? (305)

Harbison and Brackett want to know Emile's political philosophy in order to
determine if he can be trusted on a secret mission. This careful investigation
of a foreigner seems logical—there is, after all, a war going on. But in 1949,
when the play was produced, this type of investigation would have also re-
minded audiences of the highly publicized HUAC hearings. Nellie dutifully proceeds to cross-examine her friend at their next meeting:

EMILE: You know very little about me.
NELLIE: That's right! [*Getting down to business*] Would you sit down?
[*Emile sits. Nellie paces like a cross-examiner*] Do you think about poli-
tics much . . . And if so what do you think about politics?
EMILE: Do you mean my political philosophy?
NELLIE: I think that's what I mean. (314)

Rodgers and Hammerstein shape this scene as a sort of anxious parody. They
inject humor into a tense moment by having Nellie deliberately imitate the
stance of a HUAC cross-examiner. And her naiveté—she is not even sure what
answers she is looking for—points to the absurdity of the whole project. At
the same time, clearly eager to create an indisputably anti-Communist play,
they also take the investigation of Emile to a certain extent seriously. Brackett
and Harbison are not villains—they are friendly characters who are sincerely
concerned with Nellie's interests and the interests of the American people.
The play implies that their suspicions are not unfounded. Emile's difference is
a problem that must be resolved. Foreigners, especially those with strident
antifascist backgrounds (Emile left France because he killed a fascist demagogue), might, after all, be Communists.

Rodgers and Hammerstein's parody of an investigation subtly reveals the
real problem many Jewish liberals had with HUAC: the goal of protecting
America from Communism was acceptable; the methods were not. It was difficult for liberals like Rodgers and Hammerstein to stick to a firm anti-Communist position in the face of the flagrant violation of civil liberties practiced by
the House Un-American Activities committee. Many assimilated Jews worried that the "rooting out" of Communist subversives was tinged with antisemitism. They feared that they would be suspected simply because they
were Jewish. Most also viewed the leaders of the anti-Communist purges with
suspicion, convinced that under their patriotic rhetoric lurked populist demagoguery, always bad for Jews. In the face of competing pressures, Jewish
groups often disagreed about how best to combat this potential antisemitic
threat. Some urged group opposition to HUAC and its activities; others insisted it was not a Jewish issue at all. In a 1948 letter to actress Florence

Eldridge (the wife of Frederic March), Rodgers responded to her accusations of disloyalty to the tribe. Eldridge was apparently angry with Rodgers for not adequately supporting the Hollywood Ten and had implied that as a Jew he should defend them and fight HUAC. Rodgers insisted that his Jewishness had no bearing at all on his politics: "I said I was sick of *this kind* of anti-semitism, and I am. You are attempting to put people like us in an intellectual ghetto when you tell us we must think and act *your* way because we are Jews. I insist on acting and thinking like an American primarily, and a Jew if I want to. . . . Actually, the tone of your attitude was set some time ago when you told Dorothy that she would be a fascist if she weren't a Jew. That stinks, dear."[34]

Rodgers' argument that he is an American first and a Jew when he chooses to be is a familiar one. The fact that he felt a need to make it so forcefully, even to a personal acquaintance, indicates that he, like many others, feared that his Jewishness would be conflated with Communist sympathies. Rodgers repudiates the link between Jewishness and Communism and labels it a form of antisemitism. At the same time, in his memoir, Rodgers indicates his contempt for Senator Joseph McCarthy and condemns his tactics. He claims that while he initially supported Dwight Eisenhower (a personal friend) for president, he switched his allegiance to Adlai Stevenson when Eisenhower "failed to take a stand against the contemptible behavior of Senator Joseph McCarthy."[35] This conflict between supporting moderate anti-Communism and decrying the type of rabid anti-Communist witch-hunts provoked by Dies, Rankin, and McCarthy was typical of the response of many assimilated Jews of the time.[36]

In *South Pacific,* Rodgers and Hammerstein dramatize the strategy the Jewish establishment adopted to resolve this conflict. Jewish organizations such as the Anti-Defamation League, the American Jewish Congress, and the American Jewish Committee adopted a careful anti-Communism that stressed a commitment to liberal social causes. They insisted that racial tolerance, equal rights, and the protection of civil liberties represented the highest values of American democracy and would serve as the best defense against Communist influences. Jewish organizations therefore found a way to express their patriotism and anti-Communism while simultaneously protecting the interests of minorities like themselves.[37] In *South Pacific,* likewise, racial tolerance is presented as the true expression of Americanness and the best way to teach democracy and avoid Communist infiltration both at home and abroad.[38] According to this lesson, Emile, the suspected subversive, turns out to be the best American of all, because he not only believes in American democratic ideals but also practices them more genuinely than Americans do. Emile responds to Nellie's inquiries by asserting his belief in the fundamental American ideals of freedom and equality:

EMILE: Well, to begin with, I believe in the free life—in freedom for everyone.

NELLIE: [*Eagerly*] Like in the Declaration of Independence?
EMILE: C'est ça. All men are created equal, isn't it?
NELLIE: Emile! You really believe that?
EMILE: Yes.
NELLIE: [*With great relief*] Well, thank goodness! (314)

In the second act of the play, Emile becomes the sounding board for American racial angst. Nellie, distraught over Emile's former alliance with a Polynesian woman, breaks off the engagement:

NELLIE: It means that I can't marry you. Do you understand? I can't marry
you.
EMILE: Nellie—Because of my children?
NELLIE: Not because of your children. They're sweet.
EMILE: It is their Polynesian mother then—their mother and I.
NELLIE: . . . Yes. I can't help it. It isn't as if I could give you a good reason.
There is no reason. This is emotional. This is something that is born
in me. (346)

Joe Cable, who has just refused to marry Liat on the same grounds, looks on. Nellie turns to him for support, but to no avail:

EMILE: [*Shouting the words in bitter protest*] It is not. I do not believe this
is born in you.
NELLIE: Then why do I feel the way I do? All I know is that I can't help it. I
can't help it! Explain how we feel, Joe—
[*Joe gives her no help. She runs to the door of the dressing shack.*] (346)

Emile then turns to Joe for explanation. He cannot understand this thing called American racism. He most emphatically does not believe it is biological. He prods Joe to respond, and Joe has an epiphany:

EMILE: What makes her talk like that? Why do you have this feeling, you
and she? I do not believe it is born in you. I do not believe it.
CABLE: It's not born in you! It happens after you're born . . .
[*Cable sings the following words as if figuring this whole question out for
the first time*]
You've got to be taught to hate and fear,
You've got to be taught from year to year,
It's got to be drummed in your dear little ear—
You've got to be carefully taught! (346)

Joe, the American, is explaining Nellie's racism to Emile, the European, during World War II—as if Emile had never encountered racism in Europe. In the face of Nazi concentration camps and death marches, this scene seems absurd, even offensive. But when understood in terms of American Jewish *postwar* concerns, the scene makes sense. Emile, an outsider both in France and in this American community, can grasp the problems of racism more clearly than those who live within the system. In questioning Joe about his beliefs, he helps Joe to work through his irrational racist behavior and to recognize that if racism must be learned, it can also be unlearned. Like the Jews working for civil rights, Emile serves as a conscience for the American community. Because, like American Jews, he has been treated as an object of suspicion and has suffered because of racism, he understands the dangers of demagoguery and is committed to fighting for equal rights for all.

Yet Emile's horror at American racism is, like Rodgers and Hammerstein's, laden with contradictions. He himself lives a lifestyle that is dependent upon racial inequality. He owns a plantation—a word which in itself evokes an economy based on racial oppression—that uses underpaid native labor. Early in the play, Captain Brackett forbids Bloody Mary to employ natives to make souvenir grass skirts, because she pays them so much that they no longer want to work for the low wages the French planters are willing to offer. Bloody Mary succinctly replies, "French planters stingy bastards!" (297). Emile employs only natives as servants. He hires a native couple to perform an exotic dance at his party, but the script implies that all of the invited guests are white (327). When Emile reveals to Nellie that he lived with a Polynesian woman, he supports his choice: "I want you to know I have no apologies." But then he continues by adding an apology anyway: "I came here as a young man. I lived as I could" (331). Just as a good liberal like Hammerstein can write songs protesting stereotypes yet not see the ways in which his own work perpetuates the very problem he laments, so Emile props up the system he claims to abhor.

Unlike the Jewish immigrant of the early twentieth century, who was easy to parody because he was ignorant and penniless, immigrants (or émigrés, as they were more often called) like Emile had many qualities admired by upwardly mobile second- and third-generation American Jews. They were educated, sophisticated, and often wealthy. Emile, the European, is Nellie's tutor in the art of social graces. With him she drinks her first brandy, tastes her first wild chicken. Nellie puts three lumps of sugar in her espresso; only after she leaves does Emile chuckle at her childishness. On the other hand, Nellie offers Emile a refuge from his world-weariness. Emile sings: "This is what I need, / This is what I've longed for, / Someone young and smiling / climbing up my hill!" (277). The relationship evokes an obvious cliché: pretty girl wants rich sugar daddy to keep her in style; older man wants young girl to make him feel youthful.[39] But the sexual quid pro quo implied in such a relationship is strangely missing here. Nellie is apparently uninterested in money, and Emile proposes marriage without so much as giving her a kiss or even placing an arm around her shoulders. As he sings the last line of "Some Enchanted Evening" ("Never let her go!"), he does not even touch her. Where a kiss might be expected, the stage directions read: "There follow several seconds of silence. Neither moves" (279). Their apparent passion for each other is hard to glean from either the dialogue or the stage directions. Emile offers a restrained, almost depressing marriage proposal: "I am older than you. If we have children, when I die they will be growing up. You could afford to take them back to America—if you like. Think about it." As Nellie prepares to go, she "holds out her hand to Emile." Departing, she "turns suddenly and walks off very quickly" (280). Their love seems to be based on little besides a mutual affection for lovely landscapes and a vague sense of "enthusiasm." When Nellie tries to articulate why the two of them should be together, she seems to be woefully stretching:

> NELLIE: Emile, you know, my mother says we have nothing in common.
> But she's wrong. We have something very important in common.
> EMILE: Yes, we're both in love.
> NELLIE: Yes, but more than that. We're—we're the same kind of people
> fundamentally—you and me. We appreciate things! We get enthusiastic
> about things. It's really quite exciting when two people are like that.
> We're not blasé. (329)

This is scarcely an argument for marriage. The connection between Emile and Nellie is hard to render in romantic terms because it is neither sexual nor financial—it is dramaturgical. Regarding the direction that the Rodgers and Hammerstein musical might take, Nellie and Emile represent two approaches: the populist and the elitist. The aging European opera form needs new life, and the American musical needs legitimacy.[40]

Unlike the other songs in the play, Emile's numbers require an operatically trained voice. Rodgers and Hammerstein were clearly enamored of Ezio Pinza's operatic pedigree, and the songs they wrote for Emile allowed him to display considerable virtuosity ("Some Enchanted Evening," "This Nearly Was Mine"). By turning Emile into an opera singer, Rodgers and Hammerstein aimed to move *South Pacific* (and their own careers) out of the musical comedy sphere and into the world of high art.[41] Yet at the same time, they were deeply defensive about the status of popular music in American culture. And for good reason: as we saw in Chapter 3, beginning in the 1930s the commercial musical theater was scrambling for a place in the American cultural landscape. Hollywood was rapidly eclipsing Broadway as the premier producer for commercially successful musical comedy. Nonprofit organizations like the Group Theatre and the Federal Theatre, in contrast, prided themselves on creating socially conscious and artistically sophisticated works of theater that were not subject to the demands of the marketplace. At the same time, a growing body of (largely Jewish) critics and intellectuals began to dissect and critique the concept of mass culture and to associate the commercial

Broadway musical with what Clement Greenberg labeled "kitsch."[42] Clearly aware that the Broadway musical, while still potentially profitable, was no longer mass entertainment, Rodgers and Hammerstein actively worked to distance it from the commercialism that tainted other forms of mass culture and to establish it as an indigenous American art form which was popular because of its democratic appeal. For example, *Oklahoma!*—which they thought of as a "folk" musical—was originally produced by the Theatre Guild, a nonprofit organization that had also presented *Porgy and Bess*. Refugees like Emile brought with them an appreciation of high culture and often a certain disdain for the musical tradition in which Rodgers and Hammerstein were trained. In the 1940s, popular composers like Rodgers and Hammerstein were subjected to frequent attacks from European and American intellectuals, who defined musicals as middlebrow culture.[43]

As an outsider, Emile is not only alone politically; he is also alone musically. The biggest problem with Nellie and Emile's relationship is their incompatible performance styles. The fact that they almost never sing together means that their love is never quite believable. Because Martin was apprehensive about singing with the operatically trained Pinza, Rodgers assured her that she would not have to compete vocally. Rodgers writes of Martin's reaction to their offer: "She'd played opposite musical-comedy juveniles and leading men but, my gosh, this was Don Giovanni himself! How could we possibly expect her to sing on the same stage with Ezio Pinza? Because there was some logic in what she said, I assured her that we'd write the score without a single duet for her."[44] And so, despite the fact that they share the stage, Martin stars in one musical—the *South Pacific* of "Cockeyed Optimist," "Honey Bun," "I'm Gonna Wash That Man Right Out of My Hair"—and Pinza in another: the *South Pacific* of "Some Enchanted Evening" and "This Nearly Was Mine."

Further emphasizing the distance between Emile and Nellie is the fact that Nellie performs easily with other characters in the play. An important feature of the musical theater is that it establishes a metaphorical community onstage by bringing together characters in song and dance. Those who sing and dance together belong together. Nellie and Joe, for example, *do* sing together in the film and in the original score of the show. The song "My Girl Back Home" was performed in the out-of-town previews, cut from the original New York production, and reinstated for the film and for a digitally remastered original-cast album.[45] In this surprisingly bouncy number, Nellie and Joe lament their failed relationships and ponder how far away their American homes seem from "coconut palms and banyan trees / and coral sands and Tonkinese." The ease with which their voices and energies mesh in this short but appealing number raises further questions about Nellie's choice of Emile. Nellie also performs easily and playfully with the chorus of nurses, in both "Wash That Man" and "Wonderful Guy" and with Luther Billis in "Honey Bun." The musical structure of the play thus sets up a community of Americans—Nellie, Joe, Luther, the sailors and nurses—who sing together. Those who sing alone, like Emile, are implicitly excluded from that stage community.

The dynamics of Emile and Nellie's musical interaction are instructive. For the most part, Emile sings romantic arias and Nellie sings upbeat show tunes. But Emile has a powerful and complicated effect on Nellie's singing style. After Nellie rejects Emile with the most American music in the show—the almost jazzy "I'm Gonna Wash That Man Right Out of My Hair"—Emile appears and, criticizing American music, re-seduces Nellie with an ardent assertion of his belief in individual freedom, capped by a description of his escape from France. He then asks her to marry him. Nellie assents by singing a lead-in to a reprise of Emile's song "Some Enchanted Evening." Emile picks up the verse and takes over the song, with Nellie offering a couple of lines as counterpoint:

NELLIE: I've known you a few short weeks and yet
   Somehow you've made my heart forget
   All other men I have ever met
   But you . . . but you . . .
EMILE: Some enchanted evening
   You may see a stranger,
   You may see a stranger
   Across a crowded room,
   And somehow you know,
   You know even then
   That somewhere you'll see her
   Again and again . . .
NELLIE: Who can explain it?
   Who can tell you why?

They never actually sing simultaneously, but a musical dynamic has been established. From the moment Emile asks Nellie to marry him, Emile's musical style will dominate. And, after this moment, whenever they share the stage, Nellie will defer to Emile musically. Nellie offers the final lyrics of the song: "Once you have found him / Never let him go." But Emile sings the recapitulation, allowing him the final triumphant notes: "Once you have found her / Never let her go." After Emile exits, Nellie demonstrates the marvelous new musical synthesis she has discovered in falling in love with him. Adopting the European-influenced waltz meter, but belting the song in true Broadway form, she breaks into the triumphant, rousing "A Wonderful Guy."

"A Wonderful Guy" celebrates the powerful theatrical possibilities latent in a union of the older European and younger American lovers (and musical styles). In their next scene together, Emile and Nellie play with this newfound creativity, reviewing all of the songs they have sung in the show so far and even tentatively testing the boundaries of singing together. But it is clear that in this marriage, whether they sing in an American or European style, it is Emile who will have the last word.[46] They waltz to "A Wonderful Guy," and Nellie begins a reprise of her final triumphant line: "If you'll excuse an expression I use / I'm in love, I'm in love, I'm in love . . ." Emile then breaks in and finishes the line for her: "I'm in love, I'm in love, / And the girl that I love, / She thinks I'm a wonderful guy." Nellie then sings two lines from "Twin Soliloquies." Emile responds with four lines of his own. The orchestra, apparently eager to hear more from Nellie, begins to play "A Cockeyed Optimist" under their dialogue. Nellie picks up the cue and Emile joins in:

NELLIE: I hear the human race
   Is falling on its face . . .
EMILE: And hasn't very far to go!
NELLIE: But every whippoorwill
   Is selling me a bill
   And telling me it just ain't so. (329)

Conceding just one moment of harmony, the two of them then sing together, "'Sweet Adeline' fashion," in one of the few self-consciously theatrical moments in the play. The theatricality and the brief instance of simultaneous singing make their union momentarily believable. But the moment is short-lived. Emile steps over the line. He makes fun of Nellie, imitating her singing "I'm Going to Wash That Man." Nellie loves it, but Emile's implicit criticism of Nellie's type of music reminds the audience that he is different, that he does not understand what he calls "your American songs"; and his rendering of the song in a heavy accent punctuates his difference further. His imitation of her song sets up the revelation of even greater difference: as he finishes the song, Ngana and Jerome, the Polynesian children, enter. Emile explains that they are his. Nellie is flustered, then horrified. She runs off into the night as Emile slips back into his own musical mode, finishing the scene with the final verse of "Some Enchanted Evening." When we next see Nellie in "Honey Bun," she too has reverted to her own musical style, a thirty-two bar Tin Pan Alley tune. The representation of difference here is complicated: Emile's critique of Nellie's popular music is undemocratic and elitist; in this case his difference sets him apart from the community. But his acceptance of his mixed-race children demonstrates his affinity for the ideals of American democracy, a difference that can be perceived as moral leadership. Thus, although he is an outsider who cannot understand American music (like the German Jewish intellectuals whom he evokes), he is also an exemplary American (like the liberal Jewish anti-Communists fighting for civil rights).

After "Honey Bun," Nellie does not sing again for seven scenes. In silence she thinks, deliberates, and then decides to marry Emile after all. She voices her decision in his terms and then barely sings again. Standing alone, looking out over the sea, she prays for Emile to return safely and sings a verse from "Some Enchanted Evening." Even though Emile is absent, she still does not sing his final line:

> Some enchanted evening
> When you find your true love,
> When you feel him call you
> Across a crowded room—
> Then fly to his side,
> And make him your own,
> Or all through your life you may dream all . . .
> [*Music continues. She speaks*]
> Don't die, Emile.
> [*. . . the last line of the refrain is played . . .*] (359)

Nellie lets the orchestra take his line, indicating that she understands her new subservient position in the relationship.

In the last scene of the play, Emile's two children teach Nellie a French children's song while they await their father's return. She at first refuses to sing, claiming that her accent is no good. (Nellie can belt out "Wonderful Guy" and "Honey Bun," dress in drag, and sing like a man, but a French children's song is apparently too difficult for her.) When they insist, Nellie finally agrees to sing with them if they will help her. The three sing:

NELLIE, NGANA, JEROME: Dites moi
  Pourquoi
  [*Nellie is stuck. The children sing the next line without her*]
  La vie est belle.
NELLIE: [*Repeating, quickly, to catch up to them*] La vie est belle . . .
  Dites moi
  Pourquoi . . .
  [*She turns to the children*]
  Pourquoi what?

While they are singing, Emile appears in the background. He hears Nellie ask and responds, singing, "La vie est gaie!" Emile and the children finish the song, the children drink their soup, and Emile clasps Nellie's hand. The curtain descends.

The group of four is transformed into a nuclear family, differences are overcome, and problems are resolved. Or are they? The scene contains an odd stage direction that throws the neat resolution into question. After Emile sings "La vie est gaie!" the script reads: "Nellie gazes at him, hypnotized—her voice gone." Emile and the children sing alone, and Nellie is not heard from again. So powerful is Emile that in the final moment of the play, he renders Nellie, the star, speechless. How are we to understand this choice? It was not necessary

26. The nuclear family in the finale of *South Pacific* (1949). Ezio Pinza, Barbara Luna, Michael Deleon, and Mary Martin. Museum of the City of New York; gift of John Toohey.

★ ★

to silence Nellie. A finale with all four singing together would certainly have been justified, as it is in other Rodgers and Hammerstein works. Rodgers and Hammerstein exploit Emile's European high-culture style, to co-opt its legitimacy; but in making Emile's musical presence in the play so powerful, they end up overwhelming Nellie's popular American style.

There is no rousing finale at the end of the play. No chorus celebrates the union of Nellie and Emile, in contrast to that of Curly and Laurey in *Oklahoma!* The simple snapshot of a family at dinner implies that with the proper kind of love, racial and ethnic difference can be overcome. But the show itself does not support its own professed ideology. The European has not learned the American songs and the American has stopped singing altogether. Meanwhile, the Eurasian children simply repeat the same French song they sang at the opening of the show. What has been learned? What transformation has taken place here? The image is one of global harmony. But the music indicates that the image is superficial: the family that does not sing together cannot stay together.

Coda

"I Whistle a Happy Tune"

A T THE very end of Rodgers and Hammerstein's musical *The King and I* (1951) the King of Siam lies on his deathbed, surrounded by his wives and children who have come to pay their last respects. The King asks his eldest son, the Crown Prince, what he will do when he is on the throne. "I would make proclamations," the young Prince answers. He then says he does not believe that people should prostrate themselves before the King. The King turns to the British governess, Anna, and asks if this proclamation is "her fault." "Oh, I hope so, Your Majesty, I do hope so," she replies. The Prince then elaborates: "No bowing like toad. No crouching. No crawling. This does not mean, however, that you do not show respect for King. You will stand with shoulders square back, and chin high . . . like this." As the Prince speaks, Anna and the audience realize that the King has died. The Prince, oblivious, continues: "You will bow to me—the gentlemen, in this way, only bending the waist." He demonstrates a bow. "The ladies will make dip, as in Europe." The Prince asks his mother to demonstrate. Then the stage directions read: "Lady Thiang crosses to the center and drops a low curtsey before the women. As the music swells, all the women and girls carefully imitate her, sinking to the floor as the curtain falls, a final obeisance to the dead King, a gesture of allegiance to the new one. Curtain."[1]

When this scene is played effectively, there's not a dry eye in the theater. But what, exactly, is it that so moves the audience? The death of the King is itself a poignant moment, but the way in which it is framed heightens the emotional impact considerably. The King dies of a broken heart—he has been crushed by the realization that he will never be able to enter the Promised Land of Western civilization. He dies in order to make way for his son, who strides confidently into a new age of enlightenment. The Prince's speech convinces Anna, the King, and the audience that her mission—to teach the royal children Western values—has been successful. The American audience, watching this American play in an American theater, is triumphant as the play ends, witnessing a Siam on the road to Western-style individualism and American-style democracy.

But what in this last scene indicates that the Prince has absorbed the values of American democracy? What exactly has he learned? He has learned the proper way to bow: from the waist. And the proper time to do so: at the end of the play. Indeed, as soon as the bow is properly performed, the curtain falls. In short, the Prince has learned from Anna one of the most important conventions of the stage. The ability to bow is considered such a powerful symbol that it stands in for all of the democratic values Anna is supposed to impart. Throughout the play, in fact, Anna teaches about democracy by using the conventions of the theater. Only when the Siamese can learn to perform in the manner of the musical theater, this play implies, can they successfully transcend their otherness and become just like us. The children succeed in learning the proper performance skills, and in this way acquire the necessary Western values to be accepted in the developed world. The King, on the other hand, is too circumscribed by his racial otherness, which prevents him from successfully learning new behaviors. Because he cannot perform properly, he—like Moses, with whom he is obsessed—must die without ever seeing the Promised Land.

The King and I is based on the novel *Anna and the King of Siam* (1944), by American writer Margaret Landon. The novel is a fictionalized account of the experiences of Anna Leonowens, a British widow who was hired by the King of Siam in the 1860s to teach his children Western culture. In the play, Anna and her young son, Louis, arrive in Bangkok ("I Whistle a Happy Tune") and set up house in the royal palace, contrary to Anna's wishes: she expected a home of her own. Anna adapts to her foreign surroundings and quickly learns the strange ways ("Getting to Know You") of the harem, befriending Tuptim—a Burmese slave girl who dreams of freedom and romantic love—along the way. Anna and the King have a fiery relationship, and Anna refuses to behave as the King's other subjects do. She is particularly averse to bowing low to the ground when the King enters the room. But when the King is informed that the British are threatening his sovereignty, he turns to Anna to help him plan a ball for the visiting diplomats. In the process, she gains his deep admiration and respect. As they dance together after the ball, they appear to be falling in love ("Shall We Dance"). But the mood is broken by the discovery that Tuptim, who tried to escape, has been found. Anna, horrified at the King's cruel threat to whip Tuptim, refuses to see or speak with him. At the end, as the King lies dying, he calls for Anna. They reconcile their differences, and the play concludes with the young Prince, Anna's best student, demonstrating his new grasp of Western ways.

Despite its exotic foreign setting, Rodgers and Hammerstein's *King and I* is actually a rewriting of the basic themes and issues of American immigrant melodramas like *The Jazz Singer*. The play features a racially defined Old World father who cannot assimilate the new ways and so dies in order that his son may march unfettered into the so-called New World. As in *The Jazz Singer*, the son's New World ideas are expressed in theatrical terms, and while the son remains respectful of his heritage, he, like Jack Robin, does not inherit the stigma associated with his father's racial otherness. Anna revisits the minstrelsy of *The Jazz Singer* with the children by having them perform a pan-Asian version of *Uncle Tom's Cabin*. The children easily combine their racially specific dance steps and musical styles with American values such as freedom, liberty, and equality. Indeed, in taking on the masks of the black characters in *Uncle Tom's Cabin*, the children reenact the Jews' theatrical rite of passage—their assimilation into America. The King, on the other hand, like his predecessor Cantor Rabinowitz, sees the performance as a blasphemous threat, and because of his inability to accept New World conventions is excluded from the Promised Land.

In 1951, when *The King and I* opened on Broadway, the United States was in the throes of the Red Scare at home and the Korean War abroad. According to the reigning Cold War ideology, Asian countries like South Korea were in danger of falling prey to Communist domination and needed U.S. assistance to defend themselves against the aggression of the Soviet Union. As Americans rushed to help Koreans and, later, Southeast Asians, they were forced to adjust their racial outlook to accommodate this new development. Americans needed a way to assimilate Asians into their anti-Communist alliance. In a dramatic turnaround from the war years, U.S. policymakers decided that as long as Southeast Asians and Koreans were willing to adopt the Western principles of democracy and learn the basic features of Western civilization, they could join the American family. In 1952, the year after *The King and I* appeared, Congress passed the McCarran-Walter Act, repealing the thirty-year ban on Asian immigration and removing the racial qualifications for citizenship that had formerly excluded Asians.[2] Notably, however, the act underlined the antisemitic subtext of the Red Scare, maintaining the immigration restrictions on Jews and other eastern Europeans implemented by the National Origins quotas of 1924. With the arrest of Julius and Ethel Rosenberg in 1950 for spying on behalf of the Soviet Union, Jewish anxiety about the conflation of anti-Communism and antisemitism reached an all-time high.

As we saw in the previous chapter, American Jews, Rodgers and Hammerstein included, had a stake in distancing themselves from these perceived alien (Communist) interlopers. Here they did so by actively moving the Jewish immigration story out of the present and into the past. Distancing themselves from contemporary stories of Jewish refugees from Europe, Rodgers and Hammerstein instead chose to rewrite the Jewish immigrant myth as a model for other immigrant groups. In doing so, they asserted not only that Jews born in the United States were fully assimilated Americans, but that their assimilation experience could set the standard for the making of new Americans. By shifting the elements of the Jewish immigration story onto Asian subjects, *The King and I* rejects the image of the Jew as alien threat and argues that the Jewish model of immigration and assimilation is actually the best template for creating Americans and hence defeating Communism. The Asian children replace Jews as the model minority of the future.[3] Rodgers and Hammerstein seem to have become obsessed with this formula. Their 1958 musical *Flower Drum Song* pushes the substitution of Asian for Jewish immigrant even further, offering a story of generational conflict among immigrant residents of contemporary San Francisco's Chinatown—complete with young people who perform in a "modern" American nightclub, much to the chagrin of the more traditional parents. Chinatown in this play differs from the early twentieth-century Lower East Side only in accent and costume. The attitudes, personalities, storylines, and conflicts mirror those of the earlier immigrant stories exactly. Even *The Sound of Music* (1959) draws on similar themes, with Maria and the Von Trapp children figured as model immigrants who—of course—sing and dance. With the help of the Jewish theater producer Max, they teach the older generation—namely, the straitlaced father—the benefits of performing in the modern theater. Unlike the King of Siam, however, this father *does* learn how to perform along with his children—perhaps because he is already white—and so can join them in their flight over the Alps and into America. The fact that Rodgers and Hammerstein wrote a play about escape from the Nazis in which the heroes are not Jews, but Austrian Catholics, is further proof of their apparent need to distance Jews from contemporary immigrant stories.

Despite the fact that *The King and I* is set in Siam and its central character, Anna Leonowens, is British, this musical can easily be read as an American creation. It was written, composed, directed, choreographed, designed, and acted (mostly) by Americans on the American stage for an American audience.[4] And the character Anna, despite her British origins, draws on American narratives and symbols to make her points—particularly in her liberal evocation of Abraham Lincoln when she argues against slavery. In fact, Anna can be read as the voice of the American public: changing the title from *Anna and the King of Siam* (as it was in the novel) to *The King and I* allows Anna to become not just a character in the story, but the "I" of the play, the voice of the authors and the onstage representative for the audience. Also distinctly American is the musical's performance style, in particular that of the *Uncle Tom's Cabin* minstrel show—an invention of the Rodgers and

Hammerstein adaptation—used to "impress" the British visitors. In short, Rodgers and Hammerstein dramatically rewrote the original story to reflect their particular political and cultural concerns.

Unlike *South Pacific,* which featured a community of Americans who only occasionally interacted with the Polynesian natives, *The King and I* thrusts the audience directly into the heart of a foreign world. Like *The Jazz Singer* and other immigrant melodramas, which offered audiences a peek into the "exotic" lives of inhabitants of the Jewish slums, *The King and I* functions as a voyeuristic and pedagogic journey into another culture. Likewise, Anna distinctly resembles the Americanization teachers who worked with immigrants on the Lower East Side of New York at the turn of the century.[5] She serves as the audience's guide into the ghetto and as a beacon of modernity for a backward culture. Anna (like the audience, the play implies) considers the Siamese performance style and value system to be outmoded and barbaric. So foreign and unacceptable did Rodgers and Hammerstein find traditional Siamese customs that they began Anna-style missionary work long before the play reached the stage. Rodgers recalls in his memoir: "Not only would I have been incapable of creating anything authentically Siamese, but even if I could, I wouldn't have done it. Western audiences are not attuned to the sounds of tinkling bells, high nasal strings and percussive gongs, and would not find this kind of music attractive. If a composer is to reach his audience emotionally—and surely that's what theatre music is all about—he must reach the people through sounds they can relate to."[6]

Despite the fact that in *South Pacific* the authors insist that knowledge can dispel prejudice, Rodgers himself clearly did not believe that *actually* getting to know the Siamese would help to overcome bigotry in any way (or at least it would not make for a commercial success). In an article for the New York *Herald Tribune* in 1951, discussing his choice to avoid doing research for *The King and I,* Rodgers remarks:

It seems more than likely that if one were to attempt to reproduce with accuracy the court of the King of Siam in the year 1860, he might have to show the king as an individual quite unattractive (physically, at least) to the Western eye. The palace itself might show a certain weird charm, but there would probably be a strange odor about the place coming from the kitchen where strange and not entirely palatable foods were being prepared. Continue this technique and let it include the philosophies, the physical discomforts and the appearance of the Siamese women and it seems probable that you would end up repelling completely the Western eye, ear, nose and sense of touch. . . . In 1942 I had never been in the state of Oklahoma and I suppose it may be truthfully said that *Oklahoma!* doesn't contain a single bar of authentic Southwestern music. It doesn't seem to have hurt the overall effect.[7]

The presentation of the Siamese court, according to Rodgers, must be altered to fit American theatrical expectations. Rodgers and Hammerstein began the process by writing a script and score that would be, as Rodgers implies, attractive to the Western eye. Anna completes the job by teaching the Siamese how to perform like an American musical theater cast. Her moral anthem "Getting to Know You," is ostensibly, like "You've Got to be Carefully Taught," a song about the importance of education in reducing prejudice. Yet the insistence in the play that Anna, the white European, is "I," the subject, and the Siamese are "you," the objects, continually reinscribes the fact of Asian otherness in the language of the play. The Western eye ("I") determines the way the Asian "you" will be performed and known.

As an Americanization teacher, Anna is a living symbol of the powers of theatricality to define identity. Christina Klein offers an extended reading of Anna's character as a mother figure whose mission is to bring the children of Southeast Asia into the Western family. Klein argues that by protesting the harem and demanding a home of her own, Anna "casts the abstractions of Western liberal political ideology in the terms of middle class domesticity: romantic love, exclusive sexuality within marriage, and the nuclear family."[8] Klein's argument is compelling but limited. Anna casts the abstractions of liberalism just as powerfully in theatrical terms as in domestic ones. Focusing on manners, customs, language, and dress, Anna teaches her students how to perform like Americans.

In the first scene of the play, Anna teaches her son, who is frightened by the strange Siamese men, her guiding philosophy. The best way to meet life's challenges is to strike a pose and sing (or, in this case, whistle):

> Whenever I feel afraid
> I hold my head erect
> And whistle a happy tune,
> So no one will suspect
>   I'm afraid
> While shivering in my shoes
> I strike a careless pose
> And whistle a happy tune,
> And no one ever knows
>   I'm afraid. (373)

So powerful is theatrical performance, Anna implies, that when executed well it can allow both actor and audience to overcome the fear of difference and foreignness:

> The result of this deception
> Is very strange to tell,
> For when I fool the people I fear
> I fool myself as well!

Anna, like Nellie Forbush, is a cockeyed optimist, so a key to the success of the performance is that it be not only well performed, but also uplifting:

> I whistle a happy tune,
> And every single time
> The happiness in the tune
> Convinces me that I'm
> Not afraid!

Here, theatrical performance has the power to affect real and important change. It not only masks fear but actually dispels it, transforming the frightened person into a brave one. Furthermore, if the "fear" Americans felt in 1951 was the fear of Communism, this song insists that a tune, and by extension a musical play, can serve as an antidote to that fear.

At the end of the play, we witness the successful transmission of this philosophy to the Siamese children. Begging Anna not to leave, the children cry that they will be afraid without her. The King, speaking in the halting English of a dignified Bloody Mary *(South Pacific)*, admonishes them: "Hush children. When you are afraid, make believe you brave." And then to Anna: "You tell them how you do. Let it be the last thing you teach." Anna haltingly begins a verse of "Whistle a Happy Tune." The children begin to follow her direction, holding their heads up and striking insouciant poses. The stage directions read: "Anna whistles. The King motions to the children. They all try to whistle but cannot. Finally, something like a whistle comes from the twins. This is too much for Anna. She kneels and throws her arms around them, weeping freely" (447). Her lesson has been understood. For Anna, the children's ability to pose and whistle implies their acquisition of American optimism, bravery, and self-reliance.

Throughout the play, Anna functions as a theater director. When the King needs to find a way to impress a group of European diplomats, Anna suggests they throw a grand ball. As their excitement builds, the King and Anna sound like two kids from *Babes in Arms* planning their show in the neighborhood barn. Anna exclaims, "We shall start now, this minute. Work! Work! We have only eighteen hours, but I shall do it somehow!" (411). Anna uses all of her theatrical skills to ensure that the party is a success: she makes the costumes, arranges the sets, secures the music, teaches the women proper gestures, language, and behavior, directs the planned entertainment, and even feeds the King cue lines so that he will appear well informed on Western topics. The British diplomats enjoy the performance thoroughly and leave convinced that the King and the Siamese people are capable of overcoming their racial difference and assimilating to the Western world.

Anna's brand of theatricality is clearly triumphant in the play. But just as Rodgers and Hammerstein make Nellie a highly theatrical character who claims to be antitheatrical (or incapable of pretense), so they also complicate the virtues of performance in this play. Sometimes the play privileges the "real" person underneath the costume and makeup; other times it celebrates the act of performance. Theatricality is linked at times with deception, yet it also becomes the symbolic glue that holds communities together. Through the conventions of theatricality, the Siamese children acquire Western values. At the same time, however, the doctrine of individual rights is expressed in psychological, distinctly nontheatrical terms: one must be permitted to be true to oneself, to choose one's own romantic partners, to express one's feelings freely.

The character of Tuptim embodies this ambivalence. A Burmese slave girl brought to the Siamese court as a present for the King, Tuptim is in love with another man. Because she is an outsider, she is able to see the ways in which theatricality operates in the Siamese culture she despises. Her song, "My Lord and Master," valorizes her "true" Burmese self and derides the act she must put on for the Siamese King:

> Though the man may be
> My lord and master,
> Though he may study me
> As hard as he can,
> The smile beneath my smile
> He'll never see
> He'll never know I love
> Another man.

Tuptim informs the audience that *she* is a consummate performer. The King will never see "the smile beneath [her] smile." But to the audience she reveals her "true" self. Later in the play, Tuptim dons yet another costume and another role: she dresses as a monk in order to escape from the palace with her lover. Performance in the Siamese style for the benefit of the King is deception; but performance in the American style and in an American play, in order to fulfill dreams of freedom and romantic love, is right and true. The play thus illustrates a double consciousness, and specifically privileges certain kinds of performance—those that promote American democratic ideology—over those that are seen as deceitful, pretentious, cowardly, or outmoded.

Hiding her secret authentic self beneath a mask of obedience and custom, Tuptim uses theatricality to promote and finally to achieve freedom.[9] Not surprisingly, she turns to minstrelsy, the theatrical form that perhaps most directly relies on and expresses double consciousness, to accomplish her goals. She adapts *Uncle Tom's Cabin* for the stage, and serves as the narrator for the performance. In the dance sequence, the children appear in reverse blackface: "their faces painted chalk-white." Despite the insertion of a number of clichés from Southeast Asian dance and Chinese opera, the story follows closely the minstrel version of *Uncle Tom's Cabin* that was performed widely in the United States for more than fifty years after the publication of the book. Tuptim uses her disguise in the play to argue vehemently against slavery:

> I too am glad
> For death of King.
> Of any King who pursues
> Slave who is unhappy and tries to join her lover!
> [*The dancers look frightened. Tuptim's emotions are running
>   away with her*]
> And, Your Majesty,
> I wish to say to you . . .
> Your Majesty—
> [*A chord is struck. Tuptim collects herself.*] (429)

The powerful abolitionist argument of Stowe's novel was almost completely eliminated from the theatrical version, and the protest is even further watered down in the sequence performed in the musical. Gone is all of the discussion of the evils of the slave economy. All that remains is the demonic Simon Legree's chase of Eliza across the frozen river; a brief dance by Topsy; and an utterly unmotivated death of Little Eva (who now lives in the eponymous cabin with Topsy and Uncle Tom). In fact, those slaves who are not under Legree's control—Topsy and Uncle Tom—are (like the natives in *South Pacific)* "very happy people." Nonetheless, the dance sequence serves the same function as the blackface performance in *The Jazz Singer:* it gives immigrant outsiders the opportunity to express their own racial history using American theatrical conventions. In the 1950s, the racialism of *The Jazz Singer* was outdated for Jews because Jews were no longer considered a race. But for Asians, newly defined as a racial group with the "invention" of the Mongoloid race, the *Jazz Singer* template still held.

This ability to link racial heritage with American theatrical conventions makes the Siamese children, like Jack Robin and other children of Jewish immigrants, assimilable. They can learn the ways of Western culture (as figured through stage conventions). They easily connect their Old World habits and beliefs to the American value system, while the older generation, which clings tenaciously to traditional ways, is locked in a racially defined otherness. Ironically, though all of the Siamese are ostensibly of the same "race," racial limitations circumscribe only those who are too old and fixed in their ways to change. "Race" in this play has been conflated with "generation." Race circumscribes those raised in the Old World; it aids those who are young enough to assimilate to the New. The parents make attempts to learn the performance skills Anna teaches—which, as we now see, also symbolize American democratic values—but their racial otherness is an insurmountable barrier to integration. They cannot achieve a place in the new community that their children will inhabit.

While the children learn English, sing songs, and dance new dances with ease, the King's wives have a much harder time acquiring these skills. Anna coaches them about how to wear their hoopskirts and how to greet the English ambassador. Yet when the moment arrives for their performance, they fail miserably. The Englishman looks at them through a monocle that they fear is the evil eye. The women raise their skirts to cover their faces as they rush out the door. The "I/eye" of the title inspects the Asian women and reinforces their marginality, literally sending them offstage. Unfortunately, Anna has forgotten to give them undergarments. And so, as they rush off, the women reveal the nakedness of their bare (putatively dark) skin. These women are incapable of effectively playing a role; their true selves, racially figured in the color of their naked skin, are always exposed. In contrast, when Anna removes her shawl and reveals her gown, the wives gasp in admiration. The King, staring at Anna's bare shoulders, asks, "This is what you are going to wear?" (415). Anna's body is a costume. Her skin is exposed, but because she knows how to wear her costume properly—as a white woman—her bare white shoulders become a tool for her to use in her performance.

The most complicated figure in the play is the King himself. Like Emile (*South Pacific*), the King is a wealthy and powerful older man, an intellectual from a foreign culture who is often found reading in his enormous library. He is powerful, charismatic, and deeply sympathetic. His desire to learn is admirable and his attempts to perform in a modern idiom are surprisingly elegant. Yet he is incapable of achieving his goal of assimilating "what is good in Western culture" because he is too closely identified with his racial past. His obsession with Moses and the Bible connects him immediately with the Old World Jewish patriarchs of the immigrant stories. While he resembles Jack Robin's cantor father in some ways, he seems in others to be a precursor of Tevye in *Fiddler on the Roof*. The King is, after all, an affectionate father trying desperately to understand the modern impulses of the younger generation. In the King's soliloquy "Is a Puzzlement," the final prayer to Buddha ("If my Lord in heaven Buddha show the way") sounds remarkably like davening (Jewish chanting); and if one listens closely to Yul Brynner's rendition of the song on the soundtrack, one hears cadences strikingly similar to those of Tevye's plea "If I Were a Rich Man," which echoes Jewish niggun (traditional melody). The King's exoticism, however, is markedly different from that of the Jewish patriarch, in that he is highly masculinized: he is sexually voracious and physically violent. Yet in the paradoxical catch-22 of American racial logic, he is also feminized, though not like the Jewish male. His body is exposed and adorned. He addresses Anna as "Sir" and defers to her on questions of science, logic,

English language, and Western culture. He appears only within the domestic sphere of the palace and the harem. And, like Uncle Tom, he dies a sentimental death at the end of the play. But no matter how handicapped he may have been in the script by being figured as a noble savage and a patriarch of a dying tradition, the King as actually performed by Yul Brynner on Broadway and in the film complicated and humanized the stereotype. In performance, Brynner's King became, like Merman's Annie, a theatrical powerhouse hemmed in by societal roles. Just as Annie/Merman must play the role of the weaker sex in order to become a star, so the stage power of Brynner and the King is contained within the limited role of "barbarian."

The brilliant penultimate scene of the play promises (or threatens to bring, depending on your point of view) the consummation of interracial romance. The party is over and the King and Anna can finally relax. They converse about romantic love, and Anna begins to demonstrate how young girls dance at a ball:

> Shall we dance?
> On a bright cloud of music shall we fly?
> Shall we dance?
> Shall we then say "good night" and mean "good-bye"? (435)

When she realizes the King is watching her as if she is a dancing girl, she stops. She explains: "In England we don't—that is, a girl would not dance while a man is looking at her." Incredulous, the king asks, "But she will dance with strange man, holding hands, etcetera, etcetera?" Again, Anna explains the difference between the type of performance she teaches and the type that is customary in the harem. The intimacy of performance for the pleasure of one man is not, in Western terms, appropriate. Indeed, it represents the very decadence that Anna aims to dispel. But when the man and woman perform together in a traditional courtship ritual, for the pleasure of each other and the audience, they create something far more acceptable: they create a public performance—a theatrical spectacle—rather than a private or intimate one. The public performance allows all members of the community to share in the joy of performing the same steps together.

The King asks Anna to teach him the steps. As his confidence increases, he tentatively begins to perform with Anna:

> Or, perchance,
> When the last little star has leave the sky,
> Shall we still be together
> With our arms around each other
> And shall you be my new romance?
> On the clear understanding

> That this kind of thing can happen,
> Shall we dance?
> Shall we dance?
> Shall we dance?

As the number increases in intensity, the King gets bolder, and insists that they not simply hold hands, but rather dance like "real" Europeans:

> KING: One two three *and,* one two three *and.* [*They circle. Suddenly he stops*] But this is not right!
> ANNA: Yes, it is. You were doing . . .
> KING: No! No! No! Is not right. Not the way I see Europeans dancing tonight.
> ANNA: Yes, it was. It was just like that.
> KING: No! . . . Were not holding two hands like this.
> ANNA: [*Suddenly realizing what he means*] Oh, . . . No . . . as a matter of fact . . .
> KING: Was like this. No?
> [*Looking very directly into her eyes he advances on her slowly and puts his hand on her waist*]
> ANNA: [*scarcely able to speak*] Yes. (437)

The sexual tension reaches a peak as the King and Anna whirl about the floor, exulting in the joy of performing together. The stage directions read: "They dance a full refrain and dance it very well indeed, rhythmically and with spirit, both obviously enjoying it. They stop for a moment, stand off and laugh at each other. Then he wants more. He goes back to her slowly." The audience shares in the ecstasy of the moment as all are swept into one celebratory community—a utopia in which racial differences are subsumed, in which a British governess and a Siamese King can fall in love, provided that the king can shed his old self and adopt the theatrical conventions Anna promotes.

The dance is suddenly interrupted by the entrance of the Prime Minister with the terrified Tuptim, who has been found trying to escape. The musical number ends abruptly. The King prepares to whip Tuptim as Anna begs him to show mercy. Furious, he grabs the whip and holds it high. Anna cries, "You *are* a barbarian!" As the King's racial identity is reasserted in this act of violence, all of the joy of the musical moment is dispelled. Anna labels the King an outcast and ejects him from her musical community. Stung by Anna's condemnation, the King realizes his attempts to join the Western world are futile. Despite his joyful participation in "Shall We Dance," the power of self-invention promised by the musical number seems to lie just beyond his reach. He cannot reshape who he is; he is defined by his essence. Unlike Berlin and the Fieldses' Annie Oakley, Rodgers and Hammerstein's barbarians are ultimately uneduca-

27. The sexual tension mounts as the King (Yul Brynner) and Anna (Celeste Holm) perform the number "Shall We Dance" in *The King and I* (1952). Photo by Vandamm. Museum of the City of New York.

ble. And so, like all of the characters in Rodgers and Hammerstein musicals who are defined by racial otherness (and like the Old World Jewish fathers who never learned to assimilate to American culture), the King must die in order for the new musical community—of new Americans—to emerge.

★ ★ ★ ★ ★

With the transference of the immigrant mantle to Asians in *The King and I,* Rodgers and Hammerstein marked the beginning of the end of an era in the American musical theater. Jewish writers and composers consistently produced musicals throughout the 1950s and 1960s that defined the boundaries of the American community in both racial and theatrical terms. But they no longer engaged directly with Jewish anxieties about belonging. Ironically, at the same time that they were distancing themselves from contemporary Jewish concerns, they began to experiment with musicals involving historical Jewish characters such as Fanny Brice and Tevye. The historical distance of the settings of *Funny Girl* (1964) and *Fiddler on the Roof* (1964) allowed Jewish musical writers to sentimentalize the Jewish immigrant without endangering their own highly assimilated identities. A majority of musicals of the 1950s and 1960s actually relied less on contemporary urban settings and became increasingly nostalgic. While writers such as Leonard Bernstein and Betty Comden and Adolph Green continued to write in an edgy modern style, many of the popular musicals of the next two decades—*My Fair Lady* (1956), *The Music Man* (1957), *Camelot* (1960), *Oliver!* (1960), *Hello, Dolly!* (1964), *Man of La Mancha* (1965)—depict a nostalgic version of the mythic past.

The separation of song and story that created the assimilation effect also diminished, as sung-through musicals and psychological realism gained popularity in the later 1960s and came to dominate the Broadway stage by the early 1970s. Stephen Sondheim produced intimate and intensely psychological musical dramas that resembled popular opera and maintained only an ironic (and occasionally nostalgic) connection to the midcentury musical theater.[10] With *Jesus Christ Superstar* (1971), the British team of Andrew Lloyd Webber and Tim Rice introduced the wildly popular rock-opera to the Broadway stage—and marked the end of American Jewish dominance of the musical form.

Attention was shifting away from Jewish otherness on the national stage as well. Jews certainly still felt anxiety about their place in American society during the 1950s, but with the defeat of the Nazis, the founding of the State of Israel, and the censure of Joseph McCarthy in 1954, real threats to Jewish safety largely faded. Antisemitism declined sharply during the 1950s. Universities began to repeal quotas, and corporations began to hire more Jews. By 1949, seven states had passed bills banning discrimination in the workplace and previously restricted neighborhoods began opening up to Jews. Whereas 20 percent of respondents to a 1948 poll said they did not want Jews as neighbors, only 2 percent objected in a similar poll in 1959.[11] Outspoken antisemite John Rankin lost his congressional seat in 1952, and the notion of Jewish racial difference he so vigorously promoted lost currency. Jews were defined instead as a religious group—as one-third of the American triad Protestant, Catholic, Jew—and the rhetoric of religious tolerance became increasingly *de rigueur* in the American public sphere. By the late 1960s, Jewish writers, filmmakers, and activists began to feel comfortable enough with their place in America to critique their own community in the public sphere.

During three chaotic decades of depression, war, and societal upheaval, Jewish musical writers imagined an optimistic, meritocratic, selectively inclusive America shaped by self-invention through song and dance. The communities they invented and the anthems they popularized helped to construct a vision of America that Americans could use to understand themselves and their country as the nation emerged as a global power. The celebratory dances, rousing choruses, wild hilarity, and sobering moments of exclusion that mark the midcentury American musical theater are now an indelible part of the national consciousness. Those musicals also offered a generation of American Jews a road map through a cultural landscape that was occasionally hostile yet often welcoming. The Jewishness of the musical theater creators was central to the popular culture they produced, even if it was not central in their lives. Their intense desire for acceptance and delight in the possibilities that America offered for self-invention gave the Broadway musical its communal energy and optimistic drive.

This hunger for inclusion is the midcentury musical's lasting legacy in American popular culture. In 1975, when Michael Bennett (second-generation American, half-Italian, half-Jewish) launched *A Chorus Line,* he intended to demystify and ultimately destroy a signature unifying image of the musical theater. In a reworking of the backstage musical, the play offers a voyeuristic peek into an audition for the chorus of a traditional musical comedy. The fictional director's goal is to construct a group that appears perfectly unified, that shares a performance style and implicitly a cultural background. One after another, however, the dancers reveal the very secrets about themselves that were obscured in the midcentury musicals. They are an almost absurdly diverse group: one is Italian, others are Jewish, Irish, Hispanic, Chinese, black, gay. They hail from all regions of the country. In short, they are meant to represent the *real* America, not the fairy-tale America of the musicals.

Unlike the musicals discussed earlier, *A Chorus Line* did not appear in a time of triumphant postwar victory. In 1975 the Watergate hearings were drawing to a close, race riots were tearing apart many American cities, and New York was on the edge of bankruptcy. Multiculturalism was in, and patriotism was

28. The multi-ethnic cast of *A Chorus Line* (1975). Photo copyright © by Martha Swope.

MERLE DEBUSKEY & ASSOCIATES

300 West 55th Street ◻ New York, N.Y. 10019 ◻ Circle 7-6634 ◻ Publicity

FROM: Bill Schelble
         Press Agent for "A Chorus Line"

WHEN: Saturday evening, March 16   10 P.M.

WHERE: Shubert Theatre, 225 West 44th Street. Stage Door in Shubert Alley.

WHY: "A CHORUS LINE" celebrates its 4,000th performance. As a souvenir

         of the evening , each member of the audience will be given a

         gold-sparkled hat. At the end of the performance, the audience

         will rise and doff their hats to the cast. We have been given

         permission to shoot the audience from on stage. A party will

         follow with champagne and cake (in the form of 4000). Among

         those invited are Michael Bennett, Joseph Papp, Marvin Hamlisch

         etc.

         Please call Bill Schelble at 247-6634 to confirm.

29. At the four-thousandth performance of *A Chorus Line* (1985), the connection between audience and cast is made explicit. Press release, 1984–1985. Museum of the City of New York.

30. Poster for *A Chorus Line*. Contrary to Michael Bennett's intentions, "One" became the advertising strategy. Papp/NYSF Collection, Box 6, Folder 10; Billy Rose Theatre Collection, New York Public Library for the Performing Arts; Astor, Lenox and Tilden Foundations.

★ ★

distinctly out. *A Chorus Line* reflects this sense of disillusion and fragmentation, as each cast member offers his or her own relationship to the theater in songs such as "I Can Do That," "Nothing," and "Dance Ten, Looks Three." In the final number, "One," the entire cast performs the dance from the fictional musical for which they have been auditioning. Forming a traditional kick line, dressed in identical gold tuxedos and top hats, the distinct personality of each dancer, so carefully crafted in the play, is elided in the final sequence. The director, Michael Bennett, wanted this moment to horrify audiences:

> You're going to get to know all these dancers as individuals and care about each one. Then, at the very end of the play, they're all going to come out in tuxedos and top hats, and you're not going to be able to tell one from another. They're going to

blend. They're going to do everything you've ever seen anyone in a chorus line do. It's going to be the most horrifying moment you will ever experience in a theatre. . . . If I do this right, you will never see another chorus line in a theater.[12]

Bennett apparently did not "do it right," because audiences reacted to "One" just the way they reacted to the finale of *Oklahoma!* They loved it, they cheered it, and they left the theater humming the song.[13] Though Bennett intended the chorus line as an exercise in anonymity, his audiences reacted to it as a celebration of self-invention, unity, and community. The star, the "one singular sensation" of the number, is clearly America herself—the America that demanded assimilation as the price of acceptance.[14] Audiences refused to accept the empty homogeneity that Bennett tried to represent through absence (the "star" never appears on stage). Instead, their overwhelming embrace of the final number implies that they let their memories of other musicals fill in the blank. *A Chorus Line* ascribes fixed racial, sexual, and class identities to each member of the company. But in the end—in the one "old-fashioned" musical comedy number—the company members reinvent themselves as glamorous, glittering show people. Rather than decry the homogeneity, audiences celebrate the transformation. For years, the advertisement for the show featured the title of the song "One!" in bold type and a photo of the cast members in their gold costumes.

Even this swan song to the American musical demonstrates the theatrical power of the Jewish-created musical comedy. Bennett's impulse to subvert the form simply could not overcome the desire for self-invention inherent in the musical comedy form. Bennett overlooked the *hunger* of the dancers he represented. Ultimately, no matter what their backgrounds, the only thing these dancers want is to be a part of the show. Dancers and audience alike want, indeed need, to believe in the social mythology which the musical represents. Like George and Ira Gershwin, Irving Berlin, Dorothy and Herbert Fields, Richard Rodgers, Lorenz Hart, and Oscar Hammerstein, the dancers and audience of *A Chorus Line* still trust—against all odds—in the promise of American meritocracy. They believe in their hearts that if they can only perform those steps perfectly ("kick, step, step, kick"), they will be welcomed into the chorus of America.

★ ★
★   ★
★   **Notes ★ Credits ★ Index**   ★
★   ★
★ ★

Notes

Overture

1. Anonymous review, *Philadelphia Record,* 1930, in *Girl Crazy* scrapbooks, Billy Rose Theatre Collection, New York Public Library for the Performing Arts. The Stage Manager's Guide to *Girl Crazy* describes Howard's impersonations as "all ad-lib"; see liner notes to recording of *Girl Crazy* (Elektra Nonesuch, 1990).

2. Seymour Martin Lipset defines the "American Creed" as America's "political religion," characterized by a belief in liberty, egalitarianism, individualism, populism, and laissez-faire. The values of meritocracy, opportunity, and social mobility are also built into the fabric of the Creed. See Lipset, *American Exceptionalism* (New York: Norton, 1996), introduction.

3. Stephen Greenblatt, *Renaissance Self-Fashioning: From More to Shakespeare* (Chicago: University of Chicago Press, 1980), p. 3.

4. I have chosen to focus on writers and composers, but Broadway musical producers, backers, promoters, and agents were also overwhelmingly Jewish. The Shubert Brothers, for example, are only the best-known example of a long list of Jewish producers. While this is not a traditional business history akin to Neal Gabler's work on Hollywood producers (*An Empire of Their Own: How the Jews Invented Hollywood* [New York: Doubleday, 1988]), there is no way to separate the "business" of show business from the creation of the plays, all of which were intended as commercial products. Indeed, the relationship between theater promotion and business promotion is a central theme of my chapters on *Babes in Arms* and *Annie Get Your Gun.*

5. Gerald Mast writes in *Can't Help Singin': The American Musical on Stage and Screen* (Woodstock, N.Y.: Overlook Press, 1987): "Porter was the one *goy* in American popular and theater music. . . . Porter jokingly said that to be successful in American theater music meant writing 'Jewish music'" (185). For more on these figures, see Laurence Bergreen, *As Thousands Cheer: A Life of Irving Berlin* (New York: Viking, 1990); Philip Furia, *Ira Gershwin* (New York: Oxford University Press, 1996); Hugh Fordin, *Getting to Know Him: A Biography of Oscar Hammerstein* (New York: Da Capo

Press, 1995); Herbert G. Goldman, *Banjo Eyes: Eddie Cantor and the Birth of Modern Stardom* (New York: Oxford University Press, 1997); Frederick Nolan, *Lorenz Hart* (New York: Oxford University Press, 1994); Deborah Grace Winer, *On the Sunny Side of the Street: The Life and Lyrics of Dorothy Fields* (New York: Schirmer, 1997); and Meryle Secrest, *Somewhere for Me: A Biography of Richard Rodgers* (New York: Knopf, 2001). For brief details on the Jewishness of other Broadway personalities, see Howard M. Sachar, *A History of the Jews in America* (New York: Vintage, 1992), pp. 366–373 and 763–768.

6. The function of racialist thinking in American Jewish history has received serious attention in the past few years. Crucial texts on the topic include Michael Rogin, *Blackface, White Noise* (Berkeley, Calif.: University of California Press, 1996); Matthew Frye Jacobson, *Whiteness of a Different Color* (Cambridge, Mass.: Harvard University Press, 1998); Karen Brodkin, *How Jews Became White Folks* (New Brunswick, N.J.: Rutgers University Press, 1994); and Jeffrey Melnick, *A Right to Sing the Blues* (Cambridge, Mass.: Harvard University Press, 1999).

7. *The New Grove Dictionary of Music,* vol. 12 (London: Macmillan, 1980), conflates musical comedy with musical theater: "Musical comedy . . . consists of a loose plot combining comic and romantic interest and a musical score of catchy songs, ensembles and dances. . . . The term 'musical play' indicates a work with a more substantial plot and musical score, as in Leonard Bernstein's *West Side Story.* The term 'musical' has become current since World War II to cover the two forms, but 'musical comedy' is still conveniently used for the whole genre from the 1890s to the present day. There is no precise or internationally consistent distinction between musical comedy and operetta, but the latter term usually indicates an older-style work with a romantic Ruritanian story and a score using nineteenth-century European musical styles" (815). The musical theater, therefore, is understood to encompass a wide variety of theatrical forms—revue, operetta, musical comedy, opera, and rock opera, to name just a few. Musical theater has received only limited scholarly attention, and the genres that make up this diverse field are still waiting to be carefully delineated. Among those who have begun to articulate generic distinctions are Stephen Banfield, *Sondheim's Broadway Musicals* (Ann Arbor: University of Michigan Press, 1993); Gerald Bordman, *American Musical Theatre: A Chronicle* (New York: Oxford University Press, 1992); Kurt Ganzl, *The Musical: A Concise History* (Boston: Northeastern University Press, 1997); Andrew Lamb, *150 Years of Popular Musical Theatre* (New Haven: Yale University Press, 2000); and Joseph P. Swain, *The Broadway Musical: A Critical and Musical Survey* (New York: Oxford University Press, 1990).

8. Northrop Frye observes that comedies are traditionally inclusive. Outsiders, he argues, who might initially form obstacles to the emergence of a new society, are generally converted and accepted by the end. Frye, "The Mythos of Spring: Comedy," in *Comedy: Meaning and Form* (New York: Harper and Row, 1981), p. 84.

9. These musical romantic comedies clearly conform quite closely to paradigms of New Comedy (as adapted in Shakespeare and commedia dell'arte) and so can be understood as a part of the larger tradition of Western dramatic comedy. See Frye, "Mythos of Spring," p. 84.

10. Sacvan Bercovitch, *The Rites of Assent* (New York: Routledge, 1993), p. 355. Both

Frye and Bercovitch are interested in the mythic dimensions of literary representation. But whereas Frye describes traditional comic worlds that depend on the reconciliation, eradication, or conversion of difference for their resolution, Bercovitch argues that the New World myth of America can tolerate contradiction.

11. Eric Lott, *Love and Theft: Blackface Minstrelsy and the American Working Class* (New York: Oxford University Press, 1993), p. 4.

12. Bercovitch, *Rites of Assent,* p. 359 (emphasis added).

13. Here I am following Sander Gilman: "The Jew is one perceived and treated as a Jew." Gilman in turn is paraphrasing Jean-Paul Sartre's definition of the Jew as one who is seen as a Jew. For Gilman's discussion of the origin of and reactions to this definition, especially Fackenheim's objections, see his book *Jewish Self-Hatred* (Baltimore: Johns Hopkins University Press, 1986), pp. 11–12.

14. Scholars have also remarked on the role of Jews in the development of the radio, television, book and newspaper publishing, fashion, and popular-music industries. See Stephen Whitfield, *In Search of American Jewish Culture* (Hanover, N.H.: Brandeis University Press, 1999); Irving Howe, *The World of Our Fathers* (New York: Schocken, 1976), pp. 555–573; Kenneth Kanter, *The Jews on Tin Pan Alley* (New York: Ktav, 1982); Melnick, *A Right to Sing the Blues;* Gabler, *An Empire of Their Own;* and Rogin, *Blackface, White Noise.*

15. Henry Feingold, *A Time for Searching: Entering the Mainstream, 1920–1945* (Baltimore: Johns Hopkins University Press, 1992), p. 80.

16. "The International Jew," in *The Dearborn Independent* (Dearborn, Mich.: Dearborn Publishing, 1920). My thanks to Jeffrey Shandler for first drawing my attention to the problems raised by the debate over the term "disproportionate."

17. Howe, *World of Our Fathers,* pp. 557–558. Feingold offers a number of reasons for the profusion of Jewish creative energy in interwar America but only a few remarks about the theater. More attention has been given to the involvement of Jews in the film industry. Arthur Hertzberg, in *The Jews in America* (New York: Simon and Schuster, 1989), writes: "Jews had to take the risks of beginning new pursuits. The movies were exempt from the endemic anti-Semitism which kept Jews out of [other] white collar jobs" (210). Gabler also argues that the level playing field and lack of antisemitism in the entertainment industry allowed Jews to carve out a niche for themselves, making the familiar argument that immigrant Jewish studio heads were outsiders trying to become a part of mainstream America. The idealized America they offered in their films was so influential, he asserts, that it came to define American self-image and values in the mid-twentieth century. Lary May, in *Screening Out the Past: The Birth of Mass Culture and the Motion Picture Industry* (Chicago: University of Chicago Press, 1980), similarly explains Jewish success in film by arguing that Jews' historical status as outsiders conditioned them to "seize new commercial opportunities that were not already monopolized by people of the host culture who might discriminate against them" (170).

18. See, for example, Scene 2 of Lorraine Hansberry's play *A Raisin in the Sun,* in which the family cleans house to a blues program blasting from the radio.

19. The music of musical comedy obviously merits consideration on its own terms as music. While I draw attention to salient musical features, an in-depth musicological

study—of orchestration, harmonization, lyric, instrumentation, and so on—is beyond the scope of this project. For those interested in the work done so far in this regard, see Swain, *The Broadway Musical;* Geoffrey Block, *Enchanted Evenings: The Broadway Musical from Show Boat to Sondheim* (New York: Oxford University Press, 1997); Graham Wood, "The Development of Song Forms in the Broadway and Hollywood Musicals of Richard Rodgers, 1919–1943" (Ph.D. diss., University of Michigan, 2000); and Deena Rosenberg, *Fascinating Rhythm: The Collaboration of George and Ira Gershwin* (New York: Dutton, 1991). David Michael Kilroy, "Kurt Weill on Broadway: The Postwar Years (1945–1950)" (Ph.D. diss., Harvard University, 1992), deals primarily with Kurt Weill but also touches on *Oklahoma!* Mast, *Can't Help Singin',* offers some discussion of musical form. For studies of American song which include many of the songs addressed in this book, see Alec Wilder, *American Popular Song: The Great Innovators, 1900–1950* (New York: Oxford University Press, 1990; orig. pub. 1972); and Allen Forte, *The American Popular Ballad of the Golden Era, 1924–1950* (Princeton, N.J.: Princeton University Press, 1995). Charles Hamm's writings are also crucial on American song, especially on the work of Irving Berlin. See Hamm, *Putting Popular Music in Its Place* (New York: Cambridge University Press, 1995); idem, *Yesterdays: Popular Song in America* (New York: Norton, 1979); and idem, *Irving Berlin—Songs from the Melting Pot: The Formative Years, 1907–1914* (New York: Oxford University Press, 1997). Other musicologists who have written extensively on the musical aspects of musical theater in various books and articles include Stephen Banfield, Kim Kowalke, and Ralph Locke.

20. Mel Brooks, in accepting a Tony Award for *The Producers,* thanked his collaborator, Thomas Meehan, for helping him figure out "where it talks and where it sings" (Tony Awards ceremony telecast, 3 June 2001, PBS.) This notion that a show talks and sings in different places is a throwback to the midcentury musical, and, based on the success of *The Producers,* clearly still popular.

21. Northrop Frye explains that in New Comedy "tragic actors expect to be applauded as well as comic ones, but nevertheless the word *plaudite* at the end of a Roman comedy, the invitation to the audience to form part of the comic society, would seem rather out of place at the end of a tragedy. The resolution of comedy comes, so to speak, from the audience's side of the stage" ("Mythos of Spring," p. 85).

22. Bertolt Brecht, "The Modern Theatre is the Epic Theatre" (1930), in *Brecht on Theatre,* trans. John Willett (New York: Hill and Wang, 1964), pp. 37–38.

23. On Brecht's years in America, see Patty Lee Parmalee, *Brecht's America* (Columbus: Ohio State University Press, 1981).

24. For a discussion of a contemporary representation of theatrical education, see the analysis of Whitman's *Franklin Evans* in Alan Ackerman, *The Portable Theater* (Baltimore: Johns Hopkins University Press, 1999).

25. Brecht, "The Modern Theatre," p. 37.

26. "Musicals nights" at piano bars and sing-along screenings of *The Sound of Music* are recent public manifestations of this phenomenon. For a wonderfully honest discussion of one writer's own experience imagining himself as a Broadway musical star, see D. A. Miller, *Place for Us: Essay on the Broadway Musical* (Cambridge, Mass.: Harvard University Press, 1998).

1. Acting American

1. Richard Rodgers, *Musical Stages* (New York: Da Capo Press, 1995), p. 4.

2. On the debate over whether "non-Jewish Jews" should be studied as a part of Jewish culture, see Stephen J. Whitfield, "The Paradoxes of American Jewish Culture," David W. Belin Lecture in American Jewish Affairs, University of Michigan, 6 April 1992. Sander Gilman, *Jewish Self-Hatred* (Baltimore: Johns Hopkins University Press, 1986), and John Murray Cuddihy, *The Ordeal of Civility* (Boston: Beacon Press, 1987), make a strong case that those who reject Judaism are important to the larger story of Jewish history and culture. For well-articulated arguments against this position, see Harold Bloom, "The Pragmatics of Contemporary Jewish Culture," in John Rajchman and Cornel West, eds., *Post-Analytic Philosophy* (New York: Columbia University Press, 1985); and Robert Alter, "The Jew Who Didn't Get Away: On the Possibility of an American Jewish Culture," in Jonathan Sarna, ed., *The American Jewish Experience* (New York: Holmes and Meier, 1986). Bloom and Alter favor limiting the definition of Jewish culture to subjects who have a direct and apparent continuity with the Jewish past. As this book makes clear, their criterion may be too limiting to allow for a complex understanding of American Jewish history, since it leaves little room for the many Jews who create culture in the non-Jewish community but are still profoundly affected by being raised as and perceived as Jews.

3. Judaism was outlawed by the Spanish Inquisition in the late fifteenth century, and Spanish Jews were forced to either convert to Catholicism or leave the country. Many publicly converted, but continued to practice Judaism in secret. These Jews were called Marranos. In the mid-seventeenth century, Sabbatians, followers of the mystic Shabbetai Zevi, launched a massive movement declaring Zevi the Messiah. Word swept through Jewish Europe and the Middle East that the Diaspora was about to end and Jews eagerly prepared to move to the Land of Israel. When, under threat of death in Turkey, Zevi chose to convert to Islam rather than martyr himself, his act shook the foundations of the Jewish world. Drawing on Marrano experience, his most devoted followers refused to believe in his apostasy and insisted that Zevi was leading a double life, professing Islam publicly, but privately practicing Judaism. See Gershom Scholem, "Redemption through Sin," in Scholem, *The Messianic Idea in Judaism* (New York: Schocken, 1971), p. 84.

4. Sigmund Freud, *Jokes and Their Relation to the Unconscious,* trans. James Strachey (New York: Norton, 1963), p. 80.

5. Mary Antin, *The Promised Land* (Princeton: Princeton University Press, 1985), p. 18.

6. Ibid., p. 20.

7. Ibid., p. 25.

8. W. E. B. DuBois, *The Souls of Black Folk* (New York: Penguin, 1995), p. 3.

9. For a discussion of the processes of performance in everyday life, particularly among marginalized groups, see Judith Butler, *Gender Trouble: Feminism and the Subversion of Identity* (New York: Routledge, 1990); and Erving Goffman, *The Presentation of Self in Everyday Life* (New York: Doubleday, 1959). For connections between musical theater and gay self-fashioning that draw on the notion of performative identity, see John Clum, *Something for the Boys: Musical Theater and Gay Culture*

(New York: St. Martin's Press, 1999); D. A. Miller, *Place for Us: Essay on the Broadway Musical* (Cambridge, Mass.: Harvard University Press, 1998); and Stacy Wolf, *A Problem Like Maria: Gender and Sexuality in the American Musical* (Ann Arbor: University of Michigan Press, 2002).

10. The dramatic writings of Antonio Enríquez Gómez and Joseph Penso de la Vega are particularly interesting for their secular themes. See Israel Zinberg, *History of Jewish Literature* (Cleveland: Case Western University Press, 1972–1978), vol. 5, pp. 117–136, for details on these plays.

11. See ibid., vol. 8, ch. 5, on Isaac Euchel's *Ein Familien Gemälde* (A Family Portrait) and Aaron Wolfsohn-Halle's *Leichtsinn und Frömmelei* (Frivolity and Bigotry).

12. In the forewords to Noah's *She Would Be a Soldier* (1819) and Phillips' *Camillus; or, The Self-Exiled Patriot* (1833), the writers discuss their nationalist aims. Both works can be found in the Rosenbach Rare Book Collection of the American Jewish Historical Society, Waltham, Mass. Jonathan D. Sarna, *Jacksonian Jew* (New York: Holmes and Meier, 1981), describes the extraordinary commitment of a number of prominent Jewish men to developing an American national drama and reveals Noah's passionate involvement with the early American stage.

13. Menken's background is murky and her Jewish lineage uncertain. Important in this context, however, was that she was considered Jewish by her public and fervently expressed her devotion to Judaism in her adult life. See Alan Ackerman, "Adah Isaacs Menken," in Paula Hyman and Deborah Dash Moore, eds., *Jewish Women in America* (New York: Routledge, 1997), pp. 910–912.

14. Jacob R. Marcus, *The Rise and Destiny of the German Jew* (New York: Ktav, 1973), notes that Otto Brahm brought the naturalism of Ibsen and Hauptmann to the German stage at the turn of the century (149). Reinhardt, who succeeded Brahm as the dominant figure in German and Austrian theater (he cofounded the Salzburg Festival), was committed to Jewish causes as evidenced by his production of the pro-Zionist pageant *The Eternal Road* in New York in 1937. See Stephen Whitfield, "The Politics of Pageantry, 1936–1946," in *American Jewish History* 84 (1996): 221–251. For more information on the life of Oscar Hammerstein I, see Vincent Sheean, *The Amazing Oscar Hammerstein* (London: Weidenfeld and Nicolson, 1956). Georg Morris Cohen Brandes, a Danish-Jewish theater critic, was also significant in the late nineteenth century for his championing of Ibsen.

15. On the Theatrical Syndicate and the Shuberts, see Don B. Wilmeth and Christopher Bigsby, eds., *The Cambridge History of American Theatre* (Cambridge: Cambridge University Press, 1999), vol. 2, pp. 212–218.

16. Between 1860 and 1900, the proportion of the total U.S. population living in urban centers doubled, from 20 to 40 percent. By 1920, this figure had risen to more than half. A total of 28 million people immigrated to the United States between 1861 and 1920. Between 1901 and 1915, 407,000 Irish came to America, as well as nearly 4 million Italians, 300,000 Greeks, 3.2 million people from the Austro-Hungarian empire, and 1.1 million from Russia. David Ward, *Cities and Immigrants* (New York: Oxford University Press, 1971), p. 7; Helen Hornbeck Tanner, *The Settling of North America* (New York: Macmillan, 1995), p. 115.

17. One typical Lower East Side block in 1900 comprised thirty-nine six-story tenement houses with 605 apartments, providing accommodation for 2,781 people. Only forty

of these apartments had hot water, and there seems to have been only one bathtub in the entire block. Of the total number of rooms, 27.7 percent were completely without windows and 40 percent were ventilated only by narrow air shafts. Deborah Dwork, "Immigrant Jews on the Lower East Side of New York," in Sarna, *The American Jewish Experience,* p. 108.

18. Abraham Cahan, *Yekl and the Imported Bridegroom* (New York: Dover, 1970), p. 36. "Yekl" was the basis for Joan Micklin Silver's 1975 film *Hester Street.* See also Henry Roth, *Call It Sleep* (1934), where the wife is likewise disoriented, but more by her husband's demeanor than by his clothing.

19. Andrew Heinze, *Adapting to Abundance* (New York: Columbia, 1990), p. 167.

20. Alan Trachtenberg, *The Incorporation of America* (New York: Hill and Wang, 1982), p. 119.

21. This description of the city as a confusion of surfaces and reality is taken from Trachtenberg. He shows how questions of truth and spectacle were linked in the Horatio Alger story *Ragged Dick:* Dick "teaches that the city is indeed manageable with the right combination of savvy, alertness, and native virtue. Street-wise to the city's crooked ways, Dick instructs Frank that what is visible is not a reliable guide to what is true" (106). This vision of the modern urban world originated in the late eighteenth and early nineteenth centuries, in cities like Paris and London. For a discussion of the American context, see Karen Halttunen, *Confidence Men and Painted Women* (New Haven: Yale University Press, 1982).

22. As late as 1969, this sense of doubleness was still active among American Jews. When Philip Roth published *Portnoy's Complaint* he was criticized by rabbis and communal leaders not so much for the forthright sexuality of the work, but for exposing the "inner" Jew to the outer, Gentile world (Gilman, *Jewish Self-Hatred,* p. 354). Similarly, in *Annie Hall* (1977), Woody Allen imagines that his Jewishness has been externalized (in the form of sidelocks, a beard, and a large black hat) during a dinner with the family of his non-Jewish girlfriend.

23. In the mid-nineteenth century, large numbers of Jews from German lands immigrated to the United States to escape persecution and to better their economic and social position. By the 1880s and 1890s, when Jewish immigrants began arriving from eastern Europe, many of these German Jews were well established in middle-class lives in America. Between 1881 and 1914, more than two million Jews—one third of the Jewish population of eastern Europe—came to America (Dwork, "Immigrant Jews," p. 102). See Hasia Diner, *A Time for Gathering* (Baltimore: Johns Hopkins University Press, 1992), and Naomi Cohen, *Encounter with Emancipation* (Philadelphia: Jewish Publication Society, 1984), for further details on German-Jewish immigration. For a description of the rise of German Jews to middle- and upper-class status, see Barry Supple, "A Business Elite: German-Jewish Financiers in Nineteenth-Century New York," in Sarna, *The American Jewish Experience,* pp. 73–86. See also Stephen Birmingham, *"Our Crowd": The Great Jewish Families of New York* (New York: Dell, 1968).

24. See Jonas Barish, *The Antitheatrical Prejudice* (Berkeley: University of California Press, 1981).

25. Of Zangwill's nine plays, his best-known work is *The Melting Pot* (1908). In the 1890s, Herzl was well known as the author of the Viennese plays *Tabarin* (1895) and *The*

New Ghetto (1898), among others. See Jacques Kornberg, *Theodor Herzl* (Blooming-ton: Indiana University Press, 1993).

26. Buber wrote a number of important essays connecting his ideas about Judaism to the drama, as well as a mystery play entitled *Elijah.* See Maurice Friedman, ed., *Martin Buber and the Theater* (New York: Funk and Wagnall's, 1969).

27. See Mendel Kohansky, *The Hebrew Theatre* (New York: Ktav, 1969).

28. Nahma Sandrow, *Vagabond Stars* (Syracuse: Syracuse University Press, 1996); J. Hoberman, *Bridge of Light* (New York: Schocken, 1991).

29. A. H. Fromenson, "Life on New York's Lower East Side," in Jacob Rader Marcus, ed., *The Jew in the American World* (Detroit: Wayne State University Press, 1996), p. 378; Moses Rischin, *The Promised City* (Cambridge, Mass.: Harvard University Press, 1977), p. 133; Irving Howe, *World of Our Fathers* (New York: Schocken, 1976), pp. 460–496.

30. Hutchins Hapgood, *The Spirit of the Ghetto,* rev. ed. (New York: Schocken, 1966), p. 122.

31. Sandrow, *Vagabond Stars,* p. 78.

32. The Yiddish theater had its heyday in the first three decades of the twentieth century. By the early 1930s, its audience was dwindling as children of immigrants turned to the English-language theater for entertainment.

33. A number of historical and ideological pageants, staged by and for immigrants, also served a similar function. See Whitfield, "Politics of Pageantry."

34. Just one of many popular Broadway musicals, *Oklahoma!* receives six hundred separate productions in theaters across the United States each year, more than half a century after its initial opening. Max Wilk, *OK! The Story of "Oklahoma!"* (New York: Grove Press, 1993), p. 257.

35. Michael Denning, *The Cultural Front* (New York: Verso, 1997), 21.

36. Henry L. Feingold, *A Time for Searching: Entering the Mainstream, 1920–1945* (Baltimore: Johns Hopkins University Press, 1992), p. 198.

37. I use quotation marks here to indicate my distance from the racial implications of these words and to highlight the constructed nature of racial language. To avoid distraction, I will forgo the quotation marks in the rest of the text. The reader, however, should take my use of words like "white," "black," "Negro" and "Hebrew" as if they were set off wherever they appear.

38. This discussion of the development of the American racial landscape is deeply informed by Matthew Frye Jacobson, *Whiteness of a Different Color* (Cambridge, Mass.: Harvard University Press, 1998), p. 110. While the status of the "Mongoloid" or Asian race was certainly still an issue in the postwar era, this racial group was perceived as being located mostly outside U.S. borders, not within. As we will see in the later plays of Rodgers and Hammerstein, the "Asian problem" was closely related to the global containment of Communism.

39. Lothrop Stoddard, *The Rising Tide of Color against White World-Supremacy* (New York: Scribner's, 1921), p. 165.

40. Quoted in Walter Benn Michaels, *Our America* (Durham: Duke University Press, 1995), p. 32.

41. André Siegfried, *America Comes of Age* (London: Jonathan Cape, 1927), p. 24.

42. Ibid., p. 27. Another nativist writer, Gino Speranza, in his book *Race or Nation: A Conflict of Divided Loyalties* (Indianapolis: Bobbs-Merrill, 1925), described the Jew as someone who "holds tenaciously to his racial and special culture . . . and . . . realizes that he neither can, nor wants to, merge it with other cultures. He can, of course, be politically a citizen of any state to which he gives his political allegiance; but he cannot, certainly not in the mass, be culturally . . . anything but Jewish" (103).

43. Michaels, *Our America,* p. 10.

44. See Eric Goldstein, "'Different Blood Flows in Our Veins': Race and Jewish Self-Definition in Late Nineteenth Century America," *American Jewish History* 85 (1997): 29–55. Goldstein points out that Jews did not immediately seek to distance themselves from racial self-definition. In the post–Civil War period, racial categories allowed Jews to distinguish themselves from other Americans while still participating fully in society.

45. The National Origins Act (as the Johnson-Reed Act was also known) was clearly slanted against immigrants from eastern and southern Europe, and nearly eliminated Asian immigration altogether. The maximum annual number of immigrants was reduced to about 160,000 people. The combined quota for Poland, Russia, Romania, and the Baltic countries was set at 9,443. Whereas 656,000 Jews came to the United States between 1907 and 1914, only 73,000 were admitted between 1924 and 1931. See Feingold, *A Time for Searching,* p. 29. For the text of the 1920 act, see Paul Mendes-Flohr and Jehuda Reinharz, eds., *The Jew in the Modern World* (New York: Oxford University Press, 1980), pp. 405–407.

46. Israel Zangwill, "The Melting Pot," in *Works of Israel Zangwill* (New York: American Jewish Book Company, 1921), vol. 6, p. 33.

47. Horace Kallen, "Democracy versus the Melting-Pot: A Study of American Nationality" (1915), in Werner Sollors, ed., *Theories of Ethnicity* (New York: New York University Press, 1996), p. 91.

48. Antin, *Promised Land,* p. xxi.

49. Charles Hamm, *Irving Berlin: Songs from the Melting Pot* (New York: Oxford University Press, 1997).

50. Douglas Gilbert, *American Vaudeville* (New York: Dover, 1940), p. 288.

51. Joyce Antler, *The Journey Home* (New York: Free Press, 1997), p. 139.

52. See Allen Woll, *Black Musical Theatre* (New York: Da Capo, 1989), for an extended discussion of the situation of black performers.

53. For an analysis of the racialized perception of the Jew in Germany, see Sander Gilman, *The Jew's Body* (New York: Routledge, 1991).

54. Jacobson, *Whiteness of a Different Color,* p. 99.

55. Ibid., pp. 110–111.

56. For an overview of studies of race and the role of whiteness in American culture, see Shelley Fisher Fishkin, "Interrogating 'Whiteness,' Complicating 'Blackness': Remapping American Culture," *American Quarterly* 47, no. 3 (1995): 428–466. See also Ruth Frankenberg, *White Women, Race Matters* (Minneapolis: University of Minneapolis Press, 1993); Noel Ignatiev, *How the Irish Became White* (New York: Routledge, 1995); and David R. Roediger, *Wages of Whiteness* (New York: Verso, 1991).

57. On the Jewish role in the founding of the National Association for the Advancement

of Colored People (NAACP), see Nancy J. Weiss, "Long-Distance Runners of the Civil Rights Movement," in Jack Salzman and Cornel West, eds., *Struggles in the Promised Land* (New York: Oxford University Press, 1997).

58. For an analysis of similar black-Jewish dynamics in the film industry, see Rogin, *Blackface, White Noise* (Berkeley: University of California Press, 1996). Ann Douglas, in *Terrible Honesty* (New York: Farrar, Straus and Giroux, 1995), offers a far more benign picture of black-Jewish artistic "borrowing" in a number of fields, though she rarely focuses specifically on the Jewishness of the artists she covers. Sollors, in *Beyond Ethnicity,* describes the black-Jewish relationship that informs some immigrant writing, and labels such literature "bluish."

59. Jeffrey Melnick, *A Right to Sing the Blues* (Cambridge, Mass.: Harvard University Press, 1999), provides useful background here in his discussion of African Americans, Jews, and popular music. Most other works on black-Jewish relations in America focus on political alliances and deal only tangentially (if at all) with the arts. Murray Friedman in *What Went Wrong?* (New York: Free Press, 1995), and Jonathan Kaufman, in *Broken Alliance* (New York: Scribner, 1988), describe the complexities Jews and blacks faced working together for civil rights. Hasia Diner, *In the Almost Promised Land* (Westport, Conn.: Greenwood Press, 1977), offers a detailed analysis of images of blacks in the Jewish press, but does not deal with the performing arts.

60. On the rise of antisemitism during the Depression and the war years, see Leonard Dinnerstein, *Antisemitism in America* (New York: Oxford University Press, 1994), particularly chs. 6 and 7.

61. After achieving financial success, Oscar Hammerstein lived on the Upper East Side of Manhattan and on a large farm in Doylestown, Pennsylvania. The Rodgers family bought a weekend home on Long Island after the success of *Babes in Arms,* and a country home in Fairfield, Connecticut, after *Pal Joey.* Irving Berlin owned a large house on Beekman Place in Manhattan.

62. This generational language does not refer literally to the length of time a particular theater artist's family had lived in the United States; while most of the writers and performers discussed in this book were the children of immigrants, some were immigrants themselves, and some were the grandchildren of immigrants. Rather, I use the terms historically, as a way of evoking a particular sensibility.

63. Margaret Mead, "We Are All Third Generation" (1942), in Sollors, *Theories of Ethnicity,* p. 227.

64. Marcus Lee Hansen, "The Problem of the Third Generation Immigrant" (1938), in Sollors, *Theories of Ethnicity,* p. 206.

65. Mead, "Third Generation," p. 218.

66. The first song on which brothers Ira and George Gershwin collaborated gained an audience through interpolation. George, while playing piano for *Ladies First* in 1918, convinced star Nora Bayes to interpolate "The Great American Folk Song (Is a Rag)" into the show, where it met with great success. See Deena Rosenberg, *Fascinating Rhythm* (Ann Arbor: University of Michigan Press, 1997), p. 35. Tin Pan Alley was the name given to West 28th Street between Broadway and Sixth Avenue in Manhattan, the area where most music publishers had their offices around the turn of the twentieth century. The publishers hired "pluggers" to play songs for potential customers

of popular sheet music. The nickname Tin Pan Alley was coined by a writer from the New York *Herald* who thought the din of competing pianos on 28th Street sounded like the beating of many tin pans. See Kenneth Kanter, *The Jews on Tin Pan Alley* (New York: Ktav Publishing House, 1982).

67. See Stephen Whitfield, "Stages of Capitalism: The Business of American Jewish Dramatists," *Jewish History* 8 (1994): 307–322. Whitfield focuses largely on Jewish writers of straight dramas, but introduces a compelling idea perhaps best explored in the musical theater: that the theater's emphasis on community represents a deeply Jewish sensibility. Whereas Whitfield uses this point to demonstrate the way in which late twentieth-century Jewish dramatists mark a failure in American culture, I use it to explore the irrepressible optimism of the early twentieth-century musical.

68. For example, *Oklahoma!* was based on a dramatic play, *Green Grow the Lilacs,* which attempted to portray realistically the lives of settlers in the Oklahoma territory.

69. As Gerald Mast points out, "Hammerstein's music drama redefined the singer of a song—a specific character living in a specific place at a specific moment in history. While the voice, the I, of a Gershwin, Hart or Porter lyric is an undefined surrogate for the lyricist himself, the voice, the I, of a Hammerstein lyric is an Oklahoma rancher, or a nurse from Little Rock, or a Victorian British schoolmarm." Mast, *Can't Help Singin': The American Musical on Stage and Screen* (Woodstock, N.Y.: Overlook Press, 1987), p. 203.

70. Gerald Bordman argues that this claim of originality was highly exaggerated—a number of writers had been moving toward this sort of integration throughout the preceding decade (Bordman, *American Musical Comedy* [New York: Oxford University Press, 1992], p. 159). But although *Oklahoma!* may not have been the first so-called integrated musical, it did mark the beginning of an era when this sort of musical was considered, by critics, to be the height of the form.

71. See Mast, *Can't Help Singin';* Bordman, *American Musical Comedy;* and Ethan Mordden, *Rodgers and Hammerstein* (New York: Harry N. Abrams, 1992).

72. The realistic, historically and psychologically based notion of character described here became a fundamental cornerstone of American drama in the 1940s and 1950s, which adopted the naturalist techniques of Konstantin Stanislavsky, Method Acting, and the Group Theater.

73. Although Richard Rodgers himself cited Wagner as an influence, few critics have noted the ideological implications of rejecting Brechtian theory in favor of the Wagnerian model, particularly for Jews. Historians of the musical theater instead generally write unselfconsciously about the "progress" of musicals from low to high culture.

2. Cantors' Sons, Jazz Singers, and Indian Chiefs

1. Jeffrey Melnick, *A Right to Sing the Blues* (Cambridge, Mass.: Harvard University Press, 1999), p. 109.

2. On Tucker, see her autobiography, *Some of These Days* (Garden City, N.Y.: Garden City Publishing, 1946).

3. *The Jazz Singer* is not a musical comedy. It is a dramatic play with songs. But its plot

centers on the relationship between Jews and the musical theater, so it is an appropriate topic for this study.

4. Irving Howe, *World of Our Fathers* (New York: Touchstone / Simon and Schuster, 1976); Irv Saposnik, "Jolson, the Jazz Singer and the Jewish Mother; or, How My Yiddishe Momme Became My Mammy" *Judaism* 172 (Fall 1994): 432–442; Michael Rogin, *Blackface, White Noise* (Berkeley: University of California Press, 1996); Matthew Frye Jacobson, *Whiteness of a Different Color* (Cambridge, Mass.: Harvard University Press, 1998); W. T. Lhamon, *Raising Cain* (Cambridge, Mass.: Harvard University Press, 1998). For a history of antebellum blackface minstrelsy, see Eric Lott, *Love and Theft* (New York: Oxford University Press, 1995).

5. Samson Raphaelson, *The Jazz Singer* (New York: Brentano's, 1925), p. 28. Subsequent references to the script will be noted in the text.

6. Werner Sollors, in *Beyond Ethnicity* (New York: Oxford University Press, 1986), describes a theory of American ethnicity that is particularly useful for this discussion. He articulates a tension in American self-fashioning between the biological lines of descent and the free choice of consent: "Descent relations are those defined by anthropologists as relations of 'substance' (by blood or nature); consent relations describe those of 'law' or 'marriage.' Descent language emphasizes our positions as heirs, our hereditary qualities, liabilities and entitlements; consent language stresses our abilities as mature free agents and 'architects of our fates' to choose our spouses, our destinies, and our political systems" (6). Sollors argues that American ethnic literature is particularly fraught with tension over these two ways of articulating American identity.

7. The use of blackness as a symbol of race does not in any way reduce the offense to African Americans caused by the blackface stereotype. In fact, when the symbol is thus emptied of immediate political content, it becomes a more adaptable and more insidious tool of racial ideology.

8. I must stress once again that this tool of self-invention was available to Jewish performers only because they could pass as white. Musical comedy in America worked for Jews because it allowed their Jewishness to become transparent—to be redefined as a set of affectations rather than immutable biological facts. This was obviously *not* the case for African Americans. See Allen Woll, *Black Musical Theatre* (New York: Da Capo Press, 1989), for a description of the way African American writers and performers used the same theatrical tropes that Jews did, but to different ends.

9. Daniel Boorstin, *The Americans: The Democratic Experience* (New York: Random House, 1974), p. 246.

10. My use of the male pronoun is intentional here. The Jewish immigrant characters and newcomers I will be describing are almost always male.

11. Boorstin, *The Americans,* p. 9.

12. The music for *Whoopee* was written by Walter Donaldson, the lyrics were by Gus Kahn, and the book was by William Anthony McGuire. The play was produced by Florenz Ziegfeld and starred Eddie Cantor. It opened on Broadway in December 1928. *Girl Crazy* had music by George Gershwin, lyrics by Ira Gershwin, and a book by Guy Bolton and John McGowan. It opened on Broadway in October 1930. Neither

play is published, but both are available from the theatrical licenser Tams-Witmark, and all quotes are from those versions.

13. A reviewer for the *Philadelphia Ledger* (30 September 1930) noted of Willie Howard, the star comic actor of *Girl Crazy:* "The show stopper . . . was Mr. Howard. . . . Last night he had the stage to himself."

14. These comics were also aware that the themes and characters of musical comedies specifically appealed to urban audiences, whereas Westerns were largely geared toward small-town and hinterland audiences. As Henry Jenkins has shown, when Hollywood studios began to convert to sound and to produce movie musicals by the hundreds, exhibitors in small towns protested that their audiences weren't interested in the "Broadway stagey stuff" of the talkies. They wanted more Westerns. These plays clearly lampoon the heroes of Westerns—and by extension the audiences who venerated them—for the entertainment of the "in" Broadway crowd. See Henry Jenkins, *What Made Pistachio Nuts? Early Sound Comedy and the Vaudeville Aesthetic* (New York: Columbia University Press, 1992), p. 163.

15. In this chapter I will be referring to both the play and the movie for my examples. Unlike later movie musicals, the film *Whoopee* reproduces the stage show almost exactly. Except for the addition of a few sweeping shots of Western landscapes and the substitution of a few songs, the film and the show are nearly identical. The casts were the same, and the movie performers behave as if they are performing on stage. "*Whoopee* is not so much a movie as a filmed stage show," says Herbert Goldman in his biography of Cantor. "Unlike similar such efforts, there is not even the pretense of an 'adaptation' to the screen, only a judicious pruning of some dialogue and most of the Kahn-Donaldson stage score" (Goldman, *Banjo Eyes: Eddie Cantor and the Birth of Modern Stardom* [New York: Oxford University Press, 1997], p. 137). Because the comedy in the show depends on numerous "bits" improvised by Cantor, the movie is particularly helpful in preserving the many performance moments never mentioned in the play's script. Where a page number is indicated, the description is taken from the printed script. When there is no page number, I am referring to the film.

16. In his 1974 film *Blazing Saddles,* Mel Brooks picks up on this conceit. As the final Wild West fight scene careens out of control, walls collapse, revealing that the entire story has been played on a movie set.

17. The film is instructive in indicating where Cantor expected to get laughs. After jokes he pauses expectantly, which creates a strange pace for the film but makes perfect sense for a stage play.

18. Isidore Kanter was Cantor's original name—"Itchik" to his family and "Izzy" on the street (Goldman, *Banjo Eyes,* p. 8).

19. Since there are no statistics on the ethnicity of theater audiences, we cannot determine the proportion of the Broadway audience that was of Jewish background. But we do know that the tastes of audiences in New York were clearly different from those in other regions of the country. As Henry Jenkins has shown, when *Whoopee* was made into a film it was a smash in New York and in other major industrial cities, particularly those with sizable ethnic populations. These audiences were familiar

with and appreciated the vaudeville-style humor and broad ethnic characterizations of *Whoopee* and *Girl Crazy.* But throughout the South and the Midwest, the film was a failure. A Michigan exhibitor wrote (in clearly xenophobic language) of "Broadway-style" talking pictures in 1930: "Round up the English and other accents and quietly exterminate them by some humane but effective method. Hunt out all the Broadwayites . . . and send them back to Broadway" (quoted in Jenkins, *Pistachio,* p. 163). By 1932, when *Girl Crazy* was filmed, movie producers had learned their lesson and altered the script to appeal to a broad national audience. Gieber's name became Jimmy and all ethnic references were deleted. A 1943 remake starring Mickey Rooney and Judy Garland eliminated the Gieber character altogether.

20. Gieber and Henry's ingenious escape strategies have a history in the world of Jewish performance. Harry Houdini, a Jewish performer of the vaudeville era, was literally an escape artist. Bugs Bunny, a favorite cartoon character of the war years, also possessed the Jewish facility for "escape" (from a pig, no less!)—as well as the Brooklyn accent of his Jewish voice, Mel Blanc.

21. My use of the word "invisible" here consciously echoes Ralph Ellison's *Invisible Man.* Gieber and Henry choose to disguise themselves as members of visible minorities—i.e., those who look different from mainstream white Americans. But in doing so, they achieve the particular status of Ralph Ellison's narrator: "I am invisible, understand, simply because people refuse to see me. Like the bodiless heads you see sometimes in circus sideshows, it is as though I have been surrounded by mirrors of hard, distorting glass. When they approach me they see only my surroundings, themselves, or figments of their imagination—indeed everything and anything except me." *Invisible Man* (New York: Random House, 1981), p. 3.

22. Busby Berkeley, who choreographed the dance sequences for the film version of *Whoopee* (and numerous other musical films), extended this metaphor of repetition exponentially. He created kaleidoscopic patterns of flowers and stars using lavishly dressed women as props.

23. Of course, Jewish comedians were not the only performers who used feminization as a comic technique in early twentieth-century theater and film. It was a stock element in the routines of Harry Langdon, Charlie Chaplin, Jimmy Durante, Fatty Arbuckle, and others. But the particular history of links between Jewish men and the feminine complicates Cantor's and Howard's performances in important ways. See Daniel Boyarin, "Masada or Yavneh? Gender and the Arts of Jewish Resistance," in Jonathan Boyarin and Daniel Boyarin, eds., *Jews and Other Differences* (Minneapolis: University of Minnesota Press, 1997), p. 306.

24. It is interesting to note that one of the supposed links between women and Jews—dissimulation—is also relevant in the theater. Acting has also often been perceived as dissimulation or lying. For elaboration see Jonas Barish, *The Antitheatrical Prejudice* (Berkeley: University of California Press, 1981).

25. In this chapter I use Sander Gilman's definition of the term "feminized": "a form of 'external pseudo-hermaphrodism.' It is not true hermaphrodism, but rather the sharing of external, secondary sexual characteristics, such as the shape of the body or the tone of the voice. The concept began in the middle of the nineteenth century with the introduction of the term 'infemminsce,' to feminize, to describe the sup-

posed results of the castration of the male. By the 1870s, the term was used to describe the 'feminisme' of the male through the effects of other diseases, such as tuberculosis." Gilman, *Freud, Race and Gender* (Princeton: Princeton University Press, 1993), p. 163.

26. See ibid., particularly chs. 1 and 2, for an extended discussion of Weininger.

27. Ibid., p. 32.

28. Sander Gilman, *The Jew's Body* (New York: Routledge, 1991), p. 63.

29. Quoted ibid.

30. Ibid., pp. 155–156.

31. Quoted in Gilman, *Freud, Race and Gender,* p. 162.

32. This scene is reminiscent of the ending of Shakespeare's *Twelfth Night,* in which Viola and Orsino declare their love for each other while Viola is still dressed as a man. Both scenes give rise to sexual and gender ambiguities which are never fully resolved.

33. D. A. Miller, *Place for Us: Essay on the Broadway Musical* (Cambridge, Mass.: Harvard University Press, 1998), p. 117.

34. Ibid., p. 71.

35. Ibid.

36. Ibid., p. 74.

37. I should note that Miller is largely focusing on postwar musicals, where the role of the male comic is significantly diminished (ibid., p. 73).

38. Ethan Mordden does notice this gendered division of labor in the musical: "The women got all the fun stuff, the dressing up, the leading of the troops in travesty, the dancing of a jig, the giggling, the pining, and the scheming. The men got the athletic stuff—but there isn't that much in the way of sports in the average musical. So the men who were not comedians got less to do than the women who were not comedians. So the women were the romantic stars and the men stars were comics." Mordden, *Broadway Babies* (New York: Oxford University Press, 1983), p. 49.

39. Miller, *A Place for Us,* p. 79.

40. Here Gieber parodies the stereotype of the "pushy Jew" by turning it into an Indian name.

41. For an extended description of these "Indian" plays, see Sollors, *Beyond Ethnicity,* ch. 4.

42. Ibid., p. 141. An Indian character might be played like an ethnic immigrant, for example. Sollors describes at length a burlesque version of the Pocahontas tale created by John Brougham, who played Chief Powhatan as a pipe-smoking Irishman.

43. Anonymous review, *Philadelphia Record,* 1930, in *Girl Crazy* scrapbooks, Billy Rose Theatre Collection, New York Public Library for the Performing Arts.

44. Not only does Gieber successfully cheer up Molly in this scene, but he also accomplishes an extraordinary theatrical victory of his own. After the third exit, when Gieber has impersonated Eddie Cantor (!), the stage directions indicate that even after Kate (Ethel Merman) has entered, Gieber might return for another encore. Merman's stage presence was legendary. Gieber/Howard's ability to cover her entrance with yet another encore was a feat few actors could pull off.

45. Rogin makes the interesting point that in Hollywood Jews adopted the two original

genres of American popular culture—blackface minstrelsy and captivity narratives (the Western)—as a means of gaining access to American culture. He implies that Jews essentially used the already operative racism against blacks and Indians to assimilate to American society (Rogin, *Blackface,* ch. 1). The example of the early musical stage is quite different: I argue that Jewish comics of this era adopted these oppressed personae not to prove their similarity to the majority culture but to subvert it.

46. Quoted in Walter Benn Michaels, *Our America* (Durham: Duke University Press, 1995), p. 39. As Michaels points out, this valuing of Indian ancestry was possible only because by the 1920s the Indians no longer posed any real threat to American sovereignty: "It is because the Indian's sun was perceived as setting that he could become . . . a kind of paradigm for increasingly powerful American notions of ethnic identity" (38). Indeed, *Whoopee* ends with an "Indian spectacle" in which Chief Black Eagle sings an ode to the setting sun and to the disappearance of his people.

47. Michaels, *Our America,* pp. 31–32. Interestingly, both musicals subtly evoke Indian triumph (even while overtly representing Indian disappearance) by making reference to "Custer." Nurse Custer is Henry Williams' love interest, and *Girl Crazy* is set in Custerville.

48. Ibid. Michaels does exaggerate his claim a bit. The Johnson Act reduced the number of immigrants from southern and eastern Europe, but did not eliminate them altogether. It thus did not automatically prevent immigrants from becoming citizens; rather, it limited the number who would have the opportunity.

49. Mel Brooks has carried forward this impulse to the present. The humor in Brooks's movies originates in the idea that *everything* and *everyone* is actually Jewish, and that it is his job to reveal it as such. So the oldest man in the world is Jewish (*The Two Thousand Year Old Man;* 1961), the Indians are Jewish (*Blazing Saddles;* 1974), Sherwood Forest's Merrie Band is Jewish (*Robin Hood: Men in Tights;* 1993), the past is Jewish (*History of the World;* 1981), and the future is Jewish (*Spaceballs;* 1987). My thanks to Leonard Majzlin for this observation.

50. Jonathan Sarna writes: "Other ethnic groups in America claimed founder status based on their putative roles as discoverers of the new world. Jews, I believe, are the only group which has claimed status based on ties to the Indians, the Puritans, and Columbus, as well." Sarna, *Jacksonian Jew* (New York: Holmes and Meier, 1981), p. 205, n. 46.

51. Quoted in Jonathan Sarna, "The Mythical Jewish Columbus and the History of America's Jews," in Bryan F. Le Beau and Menachem Mor, eds., *Religion in the Age of Exploration* (Omaha, Nebr.: University of Nebraska Press, 1996), p. 84.

52. Ibid., p. 86.

53. See Ronald Sanders, *Lost Tribes and Promised Lands* (Boston: Little, Brown, 1978), for a full account of the origins of the Israel/Indian connection.

54. Sarna, *Jacksonian Jew,* p. 136.

55. Ibid., p. 206, n. 49.

56. Sollors, *Beyond Ethnicity,* p. 112.

57. Ibid., p. 123.

3. Babes in Arms

1. Aviators were all the rage in 1937, when Howard Hughes broke the cross-country flight record and Amelia Earhart disappeared over the Pacific.

2. The last moments of the play went through a number of incarnations. The endings of the various scripts (held in the Billy Rose Theatre Collection, New York Public Library for the Performing Arts) vary slightly. Archival notes and reviews give no clear indication as to which ending was actually performed on Broadway, so I will discuss the version that seems the most complete and logical. It is possible that all of the versions were used in tryouts. The ending I have chosen—Flambeau uses his aviation prize money to fund the kids' show—is also the ending chosen by the *Encores* series production at New York City's City Center in 1999, a group which prides itself on accurate revivals of musical scores and scripts. All direct quotes are taken from the 1937 script supplied by the Rodgers and Hammerstein Organization.

3. Cultural products of the 1930s with left-wing or New Deal sensibilities became potentially incriminating once the Cold War turned such sympathies into a crime. The script was obviously revised to remove topical references which might be lost on a 1950s audience, as well as racial stereotypes which by the 1950s were considered offensive; nonetheless, the extent of the revisions is surprising in light of the success of the original. The choice to bury the original in an archive may have been a protective measure on the part of the Rodgers and Hammerstein organization. The original version has recently become available again for production from the Rodgers and Hammerstein Theatre Library in New York.

4. In the years between 1936 and Hart's death in 1943, Rodgers and Hart introduced an extraordinary catalogue of songs that have become jazz standards. In addition to the gems composed for *Babes in Arms,* they wrote "There's a Small Hotel," "Have You Met Miss Jones?" "Falling in Love with Love," "This Can't Be Love," "I Didn't Know What Time it Was," "It Never Entered My Mind," and "Bewitched, Bothered and Bewildered," as well as the jazz ballet "Slaughter on Tenth Avenue," to name just a few.

5. Rodgers' family was largely of eastern European descent, but both of his parents were native-born Americans. The other composers and writers mentioned above were either eastern European immigrants themselves or the children of immigrants, and all spent their childhood on the Lower East Side of Manhattan, an eastern European immigrant neighborhood. Already more assimilated and of a higher socioeconomic class, most Jews of German backgrounds like Hart had immigrated to America in an earlier period. See Moses Rischin, "Germans versus Russians," in Jonathan Sarna, ed., *The American Jewish Experience* (New York: Holmes and Meier, 1986), pp. 120–132.

6. While Rodgers and Hart came from similar backgrounds, they were worlds apart in temperament. As Dorothy Hart, Larry's sister-in-law, remarked in *The Complete Lyrics of Lorenz Hart* (New York: Knopf, 1986): "Richard Rodgers seemed more like a stockbroker than a composer" (xiii). Frederick Nolan, in *Lorenz Hart: A Poet on Broadway* (New York: Oxford University Press, 1994), describes Rodgers as "a com-

plete conformist: punctual, organized, sober, precise, diligent and ambitious" (22). He also calls Rodgers "upwardly mobile," wanting to be "part of the smart set, in society, one of the Four Hundred" (36). Larry Hart, by all accounts, was disorganized and undisciplined, smoked too much, drank far too much, spent too much money, and refused to begin work before noon. And perhaps most important, Larry Hart led a double life. Nolan quotes Josh Logan, who referred to the "special after-dark existence" which Hart spent in unnamed bars, in Turkish baths, and with a group of friends Rodgers barely acknowledged and preferred not to know (238). Although Rodgers claimed he never realized during their decades of working together that Hart was a closeted homosexual, this was understood by most of Hart's other friends. Nolan is quite straightforward about Hart's secret life. He reads the entire partnership with Rodgers, in fact, as a frustrated love affair. Hart's homosexuality is not central to this book, but it adds a layer of complexity to the analysis of his work and deserves closer attention.

7. See Henry Feingold, *A Time For Searching* (Baltimore: Johns Hopkins University Press, 1992), p. 251.

8. On the disappearance of Jewish characters from Hollywood screens in the 1930s, see Patricia Erens, *The Jew in American Cinema* (Bloomington: Indiana University Press, 1984), pp. 134–139; Neal Gabler, *An Empire of Their Own: How the Jews Invented Hollywood* (New York: Doubleday, 1988).

9. Henry Feingold, "American Liberalism and Jewish Response," *Contemporary Jewry* 9, no. 1 (1988): 19–45, 35.

10. In 1936 and 1940, Jewish voters overwhelmingly supported Roosevelt—more than 90 percent of them in 1940 (ibid., p. 34).

11. Ibid., p. 33.

12. Richard Rodgers, *Musical Stages* (New York: Da Capo Press, 1995), p. 184.

13. Many of these features are, of course, also characteristic of the liberalism of non-Jews. But this particular grouping of political positions—as a whole—quickly became associated in the public mind specifically with the politics of American Jews.

14. Gerald Bordman, *American Musical Theatre* (New York: Oxford University Press, 1978), p. 503.

15. Brooks McNamara quotes Brooks Atkinson on vaudeville in 1938: "On the whole, there is nothing wrong with vaudeville except that it is dead." See McNamara, in Don B. Wilmeth and Christopher Bigsby, eds., *The Cambridge History of American Theatre,* vol. 2 (New York: Cambridge University Press, 1999), p. 393.

16. Rodgers, *Musical Stages,* p. 164.

17. Blitzstein adapted Brecht and Weill's *Threepenny Opera* for a successful off-Broadway run. *The Cradle Will Rock* turned out to be one of the last left-wing shows produced by the FTP. Conservatives in the government accused the FTP of communist leanings, and in 1938, the FTP was investigated by the House Un-American Activities Committee, which found it to be "subversive and dangerous." Consequently, the government ended the Federal Theatre experiment in 1939. See *The Cambridge History of American Theatre,* vol. 2, p. 228.

18. *Pins and Needles* held the record for the longest-running show until the following

year, when it was superseded by *Hellzapoppin'*. Facts and figures on this page come from Bordman, *American Musical Theatre,* pp. 503–509.

19. Rodgers and Hart were certainly not the first to use topical issues in a musical, but they were the first to achieve popular commercial success in this political idiom. George and Ira Gershwin produced a string of satirical musicals in the early 1930s, including *Strike Up the Band* (1930), *Of Thee I Sing* (1931), and *Let 'Em Eat Cake* (1933). *Of Thee I Sing* was critically acclaimed—it was, in fact, the first musical to win a Pulitzer Prize—but none of the three musicals had the popular (and lasting) impact of *Babes in Arms.*

20. In the case of *On Your Toes, Babes in Arms,* and *I Married an Angel,* they acquired control over the plays by writing their own books. Even when they worked with other writers, they tended to choose playwrights of acknowledged artistic quality: George S. Kaufman and Moss Hart, John O'Hara (whose stories published in *The New Yorker* became the book for *Pal Joey*), and William Shakespeare (*The Boys from Syracuse* was an adaptation of *The Comedy of Errors*).

21. In *On Your Toes,* Rodgers and Hart achieved a "major theatrical breakthrough" with "Slaughter on Tenth Avenue," a highly original jazz ballet (Stanley Green, *Encyclopedia of the Musical Theatre* [New York: Da Capo Press, 1976], p. 323). Scored by Rodgers, the ballet marked George Balanchine's first major choreography for a Broadway show. In *Babes in Arms,* when Peter wins $500, he also launches into an extended ballet sequence based on the song "Imagine," choreographed again by George Balanchine. *I Married an Angel* included two ballet sequences, both choreographed by Balanchine.

22. David M. Kennedy, *Freedom from Fear* (New York: Oxford University Press, 1999), p. 323.

23. One farmland survey indicated that half of the 6,000 farmhouses in a region of Colorado had been abandoned. Lois Gordon and Alan Gordon, eds., *American Chronicle* (New Haven: Yale University Press, 1999), p. 350.

24. *The Public Papers and Addresses of Franklin D. Roosevelt* (New York: MacMillan, 1938–1950), vol. 6, p. 5.

25. Kennedy, *Freedom from Fear,* p. 314.

26. Cohen, *When the Old Left Was Young,* p. 92.

27. Beth Wenger, *New York Jews and the Great Depression* (Syracuse: Syracuse University Press, 1999), p. 65.

28. Lawrence Levine, *The Unpredictable Past* (New York: Oxford University Press, 1993), p. 214.

29. Alan Brinkley, *Culture and Politics in the Great Depression* (Waco, Tex.: Markham Press Fund, 1998), p. 7.

30. Levine, *Unpredictable Past,* p. 218.

31. Wenger, *New York Jews,* p. 139.

32. The *Oxford English Dictionary* defines "one's place in the sun" as "an individual share in those things to which all have a right; hence, a position giving scope for the development of personal or national life." Ironically, this phrase was also associated closely with the German national movement (the quest for *Lebensraum,* "space for

living," which the Nazis believed the master race required). Bernhard von Bülow, Chancellor of Germany, was quoted in the London *Times* (7 December 1897) as saying: "We desire to throw no one into the shade, but we also demand our own place in the sun" (*Oxford English Dictionary,* CD-Rom, 2nd ed., 1992, s.v. "Place in the sun").

33. Cohen's book, published in 1993, was one of the first to document these student uprisings. He notes that historians of the Great Depression have largely ignored the movement, and he attributes much of the neglect to McCarthyism: "By far the greatest harm that McCarthyism did to the historical record was to prod former leaders of the student movement—in fear of political persecution—to destroy some of the movement's main organizational files and correspondence." Cohen, *When the Old Left Was Young,* p. xviii.

34. As Cohen points out, "By creating new and non-discriminatory institutions, the movement enabled Jewish students to obtain national leadership positions that they could not have achieved in traditional undergraduate institutions. . . . Jews were prominent at all levels of the student movement, both locally and nationally" (268). Among the Jewish leaders of the student movements were the founders of the National Student League—Joseph Clark, Max Gordon, and Max Weiss—and the head of the American Student Union, Joseph Lash.

35. Wenger, *New York Jews,* p. 64.

36. Cohen, *When the Old Left Was Young,* pp. 64–65, 153.

37. Ibid., p. 26.

38. See Paul Jacobs, *Is Curly Jewish?* (New York: Atheneum, 1965), for a first-hand account of the frustrations of factionalism in the left-wing movements.

39. Compare this with Rodgers and Hammerstein's *South Pacific* (1949), in which Nellie has four solo numbers, or Irving Berlin's *Annie Get Your Gun* (1946), in which Annie Oakley is given six solos.

40. The press was particularly impressed by the fact that the cast was young and green. A critic in *Theatre Arts Monthly* wrote: "The young actors in *Babes in Arms,* fully a dozen of them, have a fresh and fluent skill, a theatre presence and a developed power of projection that are distinctly disarming, not to say impressive" (*Theatre Arts Monthly* 21 [June 1937]: 424). Brooks Atkinson wrote in the *New York Times* (15 April 1937): "If it is fresh faces you want, any number of shining ones can be discovered among the bantling performers in this good-humored musical show." And John Mason Brown described the show in the *New York Post* (15 April 1937) as "filled with talented striplings and bubbling over with the freshness and the energy of youth."

41. Review of *Babes in Arms,* New York *American,* 15 April 1937.

42. Cohen, *When the Old Left Was Young,* p. 141, emphasis added.

43. Michael Denning, *The Cultural Front* (New York: Verso, 1998), p. 4.

44. Review of *Babes in Arms,* New York *American,* 15 April 1937.

45. For an extended treatment of this issue, see Henry Jenkins, *What Made Pistachio Nuts? Early Sound Comedy and the Vaudeville Aesthetic* (New York: Columbia University Press, 1992).

46. "The Declaration of the Rights of American Youth," American Youth Congress, 4 July 1936. Robert Cohen Personal Collection, published online at New Deal Network, newdeal.feri.org/students/ayc.htm.

47. Quoted in Kennedy, *Freedom from Fear,* p. 210.
48. Quoted in Cohen, *When the Old Left Was Young,* p. 188.
49. Feingold, *A Time for Searching,* p. 254.
50. Allen Woll, *Black Musical Theatre* (New York: Da Capo Press, 1989), p. 212.
51. At the same time, the Federal Theatre Project institutionalized segregation in the guise of a number of "Negro Units," which gave black actors the opportunity to play the wide range of roles they were barred from on the Broadway stage. Rena Fraden, *Blueprints for a Black Federal Theatre* (New York: Cambridge University Press, 1994).
52. The "sanitized" versions of the show are in many ways more racially offensive than the original. The 1939 Hollywood film version, for example, reverses the liberal race politics of the play. In the film, not only is the entire cast white and the issue of integration excised, but at one point Judy Garland and Mickey Rooney perform a bizarre rendition of an "old-fashioned minstrel show" in blackface, despite the fact that this style of entertainment was becoming increasingly unacceptable and unpopular in the late 1930s.
53. The crying is reminiscent of Jakie Rabinowitz's "soulful" lamentations in blackface makeup, for example.
54. Ralph Ellison captures this dynamic powerfully in his grotesque description of the "battle royal" in the first chapter of *Invisible Man* (1947). The protagonist is invited to give a speech at a gathering of white men. When he arrives, he is forced to participate in a masochistic fight-game with other black boys for the pleasure of white onlookers. When the game is finally finished, the protagonist, bloodied and exhausted, is asked to give his speech. When he finishes, "there is thunderous applause." The boy feels a combination of disgust, pain, joy, and gratitude. He is offered a scholarship to the Negro College: "I was so moved that I could hardly express my thanks. A rope of bloody saliva forming a shape like an undiscovered continent drooled upon the leather and I wiped it quickly away" (32).
55. Robert Coleman notes in the *Daily Mirror* that the Nicholas Brothers "stopped the show completely on numerous occasions with their sensational stepping." Review of *Babes in Arms, New York Daily Mirror,* 15 April 1937.
56. All reviews are dated 15 April 1937 and are pulled from the Review scrapbook for *Babes in Arms,* Billy Rose Theatre Collection, New York Public Library for the Performing Arts. The last three quotes are from the New York *Daily News,* the *New York Evening Journal,* and the *New York World-Telegram,* respectively.
57. Quoted in Cohen, *When the Old Left Was Young,* p. 205.
58. Bertolt Brecht, "The Modern Theatre Is the Epic Theatre" (1930), in *Brecht on Theatre,* ed. and trans. John Willett (New York: Hill and Wang, 1964), p. 37.
59. Ibid., p. 125.
60. The theatrical structure and political goals of musical comedies are different from those in Brecht's plays. In a Brechtian musical like *The Cradle Will Rock,* the aesthetic and political goals are radical: such musicals strive to overturn the traditional musical comedy structure and the principles of the democratic capitalist political system. *Babes in Arms,* on the other hand, wants to preserve and improve both.
61. See his skewering of the romantic love plot in *Threepenny Opera,* for example.
62. The reviewers emphasized Mitzi Green's skill at mimicry, which leads one to sur-

mise that she may have performed other imitations that are not noted in the script. Burns Mantle, in the New York *Daily News,* noted Mitzi Green's "gift for imitation."

63. Wenger, *New York Jews,* pp. 35–42.

64. Quoted in Levine, *Unpredictable Past,* p. 224. Levine points out the significance of the book in understanding Depression-era culture and notes that it sold 729,000 copies in 1937 alone.

65. Ibid.

66. Criticizing Roosevelt's ability to switch roles and positions, Hoover called him a "chameleon in plaid." Jack Bell, covering the White House for the Associated Press, explained Roosevelt's attraction for reporters: "He acted, he emoted; he was angry, he was smiling. He was persuasive, he was demanding; he was philosophical, he was elemental." And the newspaper editor William Allen White told Roosevelt near the end of his second term, "For box office attraction you leave Clark Gable gasping for breath." William E. Leuchtenberg, *The FDR Years* (New York: Columbia University Press, 1995), pp. 2, 13.

67. Frederick M. Binder and David M. Reimers, *All the Nations under Heaven* (New York: Columbia University Press, 1995), p. 184.

68. Although a Republican, LaGuardia ran for mayor on a "fusion" ticket which represented a coalition of Republican and liberal parties. He was seen as a great reformer, who expanded social welfare services and built the first low-cost public housing projects in New York City.

69. *I'd Rather Be Right* (1938), by Richard Rodgers, Lorenz Hart, George S. Kaufman, and Moss Hart, featured Roosevelt as its central character. *Fiorello* (1959), by Sheldon Harnick, Jerry Bock, Jerome Weidman, and George Abbott, celebrated the career of LaGuardia.

4. "We Know We Belong to the Land"

1. The Japanese-Americans of the West Coast were relocated in February 1942, as a result of Executive Order 9066. While this deportation was publicized as a security measure, it was also a concession to racist sentiments. For example, a leader of the California Grower-Shipper Vegetable Association declared: "It's a question of whether the white man lives on the Pacific Coast or the brown man." Quoted in David Kennedy, *Freedom from Fear* (New York: Oxford University Press, 1999), p. 751.

2. Not to mention the Jim Crow segregation laws, which were still in effect in 1943. Among the corporations that refused to hire blacks at the beginning of the war mobilization were North American Aviation, Kansas City Standard Steel, and Boeing Aircraft. In late 1941, after agitation led by Philip Randolph, Executive Order 8802 forbade government and the defense industries to discriminate on the basis of race, creed, color, or national origin. While blacks were able to find work after the issuance of the order, many corporations hired them only for menial labor and refused to promote them above white workers. The armed forces were not desegregated until 1948. See Kennedy, *Freedom from Fear,* pp. 768–774.

3. *Motion Picture Herald* (9 January 1943), p. 15.

4. See, for example, the war films *Air Force* (1943), *Destination Tokyo* (1944), and *Pride of the Marines* (1945).

5. By the early 1940s, Larry Hart's mental and physical health was deteriorating quickly. Rodgers found him increasingly difficult to work with, as he perpetually missed appointments and deadlines. Rodgers had begun to extend feelers to Hammerstein in 1942, and when Hart expressed no interest in adapting *Green Grow the Lilacs,* Rodgers invited Hammerstein to work with him. Older than Hart, far more reliable, and unabashedly sentimental, Hammerstein was a vastly different partner. The change in theatrical style was immediate, as revealed by a simple comparison of *Oklahoma!* and Rodgers' last play with Hart, *By Jupiter.* Hammerstein's background was similar to that of Rodgers and Hart (second-generation, middle-class upbringing; childhood on the Upper West Side of Manhattan; summers at Jewish boys' camps; college at Columbia University), but he was not technically Jewish, since his father was Jewish but his mother was not. Hammerstein's Jewish grandfather, Oscar Hammerstein I, was a well-known opera impresario, and Oscar's Uncle Arthur, who worked with the elder Hammerstein, had a significant influence on Oscar II's career choice. For the purposes of this book, what is important is that Hammerstein was perceived as a Jew by others and that he recognized the social limitations Jews confronted in the 1940s—not that he was religiously Jewish. That Hammerstein was aware of the tenuous social and business status of members of his family because of their Jewish backgrounds is evident in his correspondence with his Uncle Arthur. Discussing the failure of his nightclub in Palm Beach, for example, Arthur writes to his nephew that the "owner doesn't want any tenants who are Jews" (Arthur Hammerstein to Oscar Hammerstein II, 23 June 1936, Hammerstein Collection, Library of Congress, Washington). Other correspondence between the two about the script for a biographical film of Oscar Hammerstein I includes an extended discussion of the need to expunge Jewish storylines in order to get the movie made in Hollywood. For more information on Rodgers and Hammerstein's first meetings, see Hugh Fordin, *Getting to Know Him* (New York: Da Capo Press, 1995), ch. 5; and Richard Rodgers, *Musical Stages* (New York: Da Capo Press, 1995), pp. 216–223.

6. This merging was literal: *Oklahoma!* was based on a dramatic play by Lynn Riggs, *Green Grow the Lilacs* (1931; in *Best American Plays,* supplementary volume, 1918–1958, ed. John Gassner [New York: Crown, 1961], pp. 129–168). Riggs, a gay Cherokee Indian, attempted to portray realistically the lives of settlers and Native Americans in the Oklahoma territory. Rodgers and Hammerstein added songs and reworked characters (removing Native Americans, among others), turning it into the musical play that exists today.

7. The meaning of this term, as used by Rodgers, is a loose rendering of Wagner's notion of *Gesamtkunstwerk.* In line with Wagner's concept, Rodgers believed that the best expression of the American folk culture was a musical drama that fully integrated music, words, and dance.

8. Rodgers, *Musical Stages,* p. 227.

9. Hammerstein acknowledged that *Oklahoma!* deviated from the established norm: "We realized that such a course was experimental, amounting almost to the breach of implied contract with a musical comedy audience." Max Wilk, *OK! The Story of "Oklahoma!"* (New York: Grove, 1993), p. 76. Gerald Bordman, *American Musical Comedy* (New York: Oxford University Press, 1992), argues that the claim of originality for *Oklahoma!* is exaggerated—a number of writers had been moving toward this

sort of integration in the preceding decade (159). More important here, however, is the perception that *Oklahoma!* was the first musical play.

10. Frederick Nolan, *The Sound of Their Music* (New York: Walker, 1978), p. i.

11. Ethan Mordden, *Rodgers and Hammerstein* (New York: Harry N. Abrams, 1992), pp. 24–25.

12. Ibid., p. 49.

13. Timothy P. Donovan, "Oh, What a Beautiful Mornin': The Musical, *Oklahoma!* and the Popular Mind in 1943," *Journal of Popular Culture* 8 (Winter 1974): 480.

14. Richard Goldstein, "'I Enjoy Being a Girl': Women in the Plays of Rodgers and Hammerstein," *Popular Music and Society* (Spring 1989): 1.

15. While American film and stage musicals have many different properties, they share this emphasis on communal acceptance. As Leo Braudy notes in *The World in a Frame: What We See in Films* (Chicago: University of Chicago Press, 1976), the musical, in its valorization of community, is opposed to the Western, the other mythical American entertainment form: "In a musical there is no need for Shane to wander off, left out of the world he has united by his actions; instead the energy of the central character or couple can potentially bring the community together in an array around them" (140). As a musical about the West, *Oklahoma!* seems to foreground the tension between the "farmer" and the "cowman," but the play reveals its musical affiliation in the belief that they "should be friends."

16. Richard Rodgers and Oscar Hammerstein II, *Six Plays by Rodgers and Hammerstein* (New York: Random House, 1959), p. 15. Subsequent references to this edition will be given in the text.

17. In 1943 Franklin Roosevelt's administration was promoting the idea that even the elderly could learn the "new steps" that Roosevelt was teaching the nation. See Kennedy, *Freedom from Fear,* pp. 245–247, for a description of Roosevelt's step-by-step campaign to educate Americans about the New Deal. (Thanks to Jonathan D. Sarna for this observation.) The song's celebration of progress and material prosperity also evokes the optimism associated with the renewed vigor of the wartime economy.

18. This insistence that statehood is the natural and desirable course of events represents a marked departure from the attitude of the original play, which depicted the citizens of Indian Territory as fiercely independent and highly ambivalent about the absorption of Oklahoma into the Union.

19. Rodgers articulated this patriotic climate in his memoir: "People could come to see *Oklahoma!* and derive not only pleasure but a measure of optimism. It dealt with pioneers in the Southwest, it showed their spirit and the kinds of problems they had to overcome in carving out a new state, and it gave citizens an appreciation of the hardy stock from which they'd sprung. People said to themselves, in effect, 'If this is what our country looked and sounded like at the turn of the century, perhaps once the war is over we can again return to this kind of buoyant, optimistic life'" (*Musical Stages,* p. 227).

20. The conductor for the original Broadway production, Jay Blackton (born Jacob Schwartzdorf), reminisced about the first time the song "Oklahoma!" was included in the play: "The first night we did it I was conducting, and so I couldn't see the audi-

ence behind me . . . but I certainly could *hear* them. They went wild! The number stopped the show, dead. The applause was so great that first time we did it that right after the performance Dick came to me and we decided to establish an encore chorus of the song." (Quoted in Wilk, *OK!* p. 203.)

21. The representation of Oklahoma as the site of American bounty and opportunity was both ironic and optimistic in 1943. Only a few years earlier, windstorms had transformed its prairies into the Dust Bowl. It was also among the regions hit hardest by the Depression: the masses of displaced farmers heading west to California in search of work were labeled "Okies." *Oklahoma!* presented a wholesale refurbishing of the image of the American Midwest—a revision for which the state of Oklahoma was particularly grateful. In 1946, when the Broadway touring production opened in Oklahoma City, the *Oklahoma City Times* called it the "homecoming" of the play and described how the governor had headed a parade to welcome the cast and crew. Later, Oklahoma adopted the title song as its state song. (Oscar Hammerstein Collection, Library of Congress, Washington, D.C.: newspaper clippings, and text of the State of Oklahoma's act designating the state song.)

22. By 1943, Zionist ideas were familiar in American Jewish culture, even among the most assimilated American Jews. By 1946, only three years after *Oklahoma!* appeared, an American Institute of Public Opinion poll placed Zionist support among Americans at 76 percent. (See Howard M. Sachar, *A History of Jews in America* [New York: Vintage, 1992], p. 595.) When Israel was declared a state in 1948, an official celebration at Madison Square Garden was so crowded that 75,000 people were turned away. See Sachar, "The Zionization of American Jewry" (ibid., ch. 16), for a detailed account of the Zionist movement in America.

23. Barry Supple points out that by 1860 most peddlers in the United States were Jews. See Supple, "A Business Elite: German Jewish Financiers in Nineteenth-Century New York," in Jonathan Sarna, ed., *The American Jewish Experience* (New York: Holmes and Meier, 1986), p. 74.

24. Ethan Mordden, *Rodgers and Hammerstein,* p. 39. Even in the original play on which *Oklahoma!* was based, the role of the peddler was filled by a Jewish actor: the young Lee Strasberg. This elevation of the status of the Jewish comic was unusual for Rodgers and Hammerstein. With Hart, Rodgers had rarely written for overtly ethnic comics like Bert Lahr, Ed Wynn, Willie Howard, or Sophie Tucker, all of whom were well known on Broadway in the 1930s. Hammerstein, in the 1930s, had written mostly operettas which had no place for ethnic comedy. This shift, however subtle, marks not a return to vaudeville-style comedy, but rather an early example of the nostalgic representation of Jewish immigrants on the Broadway stage—a trend which reached its apotheosis in *Fiddler on the Roof* in 1964.

25. Irving Lewis Allen, *Unkind Words: Ethnic Labeling, from Redskin to WASP* (New York: Bergin, 1990), p. 19.

26. In wartime, this lynching metaphor extended to other racial groups as well. When Japanese Americans, under pressure to leave the West Coast in 1942, began to migrate to the Midwest, the governor of Wyoming predicted that if too many showed up in his state "there would be Japs hanging from every pine tree" (Kennedy, *Freedom from Fear,* p. 753). Lynching imagery had made its way into Broadway songs

and popular music as well in the preceding decade, most famously in Ethel Waters' rendition of "Supper Time," by Irving Berlin, in the revue *As Thousands Cheer* (1933), which Berlin had written with Moss Hart; and in Billie Holiday's rendering of "Strange Fruit" at the left-wing cabaret Café Society in 1939.

27. In wartime America, anyone who appeared to be disrupting the war effort was treated like a "snake in the grass." This certainly included blacks agitating for desegregation, who were the target of white violence in Detroit in 1942, as well as in Mobile, Alabama, and Beaumont, Texas, in 1943. Race riots in Detroit and Harlem in 1943 left forty people dead. But members of labor unions, who went on strike during war mobilization efforts, were also pilloried. When the United Mine Workers (who really did spend their lives "in a hole") went on strike in 1943, newspapers labeled the miners traitors and an Air Force pilot was quoted as saying, "I'd just as soon shoot down one of those strikers as shoot down Japs—they're doing just as much to lose the war for us." (Kennedy, *Freedom from Fear,* pp. 770, 643.)

28. The trial ends differently in *Green Grow the Lilacs.* In *Oklahoma!* (Rodgers wrote) "we tied the strands together a bit more neatly than in the play by having Curly being found innocent of murdering Jud Fry, rather than being given his freedom for one night to spend with his bride" (Rodgers, *Musical Stages,* p. 218).

29. Rodgers and Hammerstein invented the name "Ali Hakim." In *Green Grow the Lilacs,* the character is simply called "the peddler."

30. Invitation to first-anniversary party for Broadway production of *Oklahoma!* Theater Guild Collection, Beinecke Rare Book Library, Yale University.

31. Sander Gilman, in *Freud, Race and Gender* (Princeton: Princeton University Press, 1993), shows that Freud used a similar strategy to combat antisemitism in fin-de-siècle Vienna. By projecting onto women the qualities antisemites associated with the Jewish man, Freud deflected attention from the Jew/Aryan dichotomy and toward the male/female dichotomy, situating himself within the more powerful group.

32. This uneasy relation between American Jews and blacks is conditioned by the racist contours of American culture and has been the norm since the early nineteenth century, despite the alignment of blacks and Jews in the 1960s civil rights movement. Rarely have members of minority groups been able to work together to win tolerance from the majority culture. Racial and ethnic divisions in American culture have made it more expedient for minorities to take on the prejudices of the majority than to ally themselves with other minorities. Ruth Frankenberg's findings suggest that one experience of marginality (i.e., being lesbian or Jewish) does not necessarily lead white women to empathize with oppressed communities they are not part of, and that participation in a nonracial liberationist movement is not a sure sign of antiracist convictions. See Ruth Frankenberg, *White Women, Race Matters* (Minneapolis: University of Minneapolis Press, 1993), p. 20.

33. Patterson Greene, *Los Angeles Examiner,* 7 May 1946. On this point see Jace Weaver, *That the People Might Live: Native American Literatures and Native American Community* (New York: Oxford University Press, 1997), p. 99: "That one could write such a play about Oklahoma, whose very name means 'land of the Red people,' without any Indians is remarkable." Weaver offers an interesting analysis of *Green Grow the Lilacs,* arguing that Curly is actually a Cherokee Indian and that the fight between cow-

boys and farmers is a coded reference to struggles between Indians and European Americans.

5. The Apprenticeship of Annie Oakley

1. All page references are to the version of the script published by the Irving Berlin Music Corporation in 1967, following the 1966 Lincoln Center revival of the play. The Fieldses and Berlin did make some changes to the script for the revival, streamlining certain scenes, cutting a minor subplot (young lovers Winnie Tate and Tommy Keeler), and adding one new song, "An Old Fashioned Wedding." But the development of the character of Annie that is central to the argument of this chapter remains almost unchanged in the two versions, and so for the sake of those interested in reading the script, quotations are taken from the accessible 1967 version.

2. This was the reaction of Annie (played by Betty Hutton) in the 1950 film version. The stage directions for the play also indicate a similar move.

3. Dorothy Fields was one of the very few woman songwriters to achieve notable success on Broadway and in Hollywood in the years before and after World War II. She wrote lyrics with composers Jimmy McHugh, Jerome Kern, Harold Arlen, Sigmund Romberg, Arthur Schwartz, and Cy Coleman. Some of her better-known songs include "On the Sunny Side of the Street," "I Can't Give You Anything But Love," "I'm in the Mood for Love," "A Fine Romance," "The Way You Look Tonight," and "If My Friends Could See Me Now." In addition to writing the book for *Annie Get Your Gun,* Fields wrote the lyrics or libretto for *A Tree Grows in Brooklyn* and *Sweet Charity* and for the Astaire-Rogers film *Swing Time. Sweet Charity* reworks the message of *Annie Get Your Gun* described in this chapter. Charity is, like Annie, paid to "do what comes naturally."

   Fields came from a legendary Jewish stage family. Her father, Lew Fields, was one of the most successful men on Broadway, performing as part of the comedy team Weber and Fields in the early days of vaudeville and later managing and producing countless Broadway productions. Her siblings all had careers as writers and performers. Fields was raised on the Upper West Side of Manhattan, in the same haute bourgeois neighborhood as Richard Rodgers, Oscar Hammerstein, and Larry Hart. Like Rodgers, Hammerstein, and Berlin, Fields was part of a highly assimilated Jewish social circle. For more biographical details, see Deborah Grace Winer, *On The Sunny Side of the Street: The Life and Lyrics of Dorothy Fields* (New York: Schirmer, 1997).

4. Richard Rodgers, *Musical Stages* (New York: Da Capo Press, 1995), p. 246.

5. The best biography of Berlin is Laurence Bergreen, *As Thousands Cheer* (New York: Da Capo, 1996). Mary Ellin Barrett's memoir of her father, *Irving Berlin* (New York: Simon and Schuster, 1994), is also useful.

6. Bergreen, *As Thousands Cheer,* pp. 450–451; Barrett, *Irving Berlin,* p. 235.

7. Scholars have yet to adequately address the specific impact of *Oklahoma!* on Berlin's work. A number of contemporary theater critics directly referenced *Oklahoma!* in their reviews of *Annie Get Your Gun,* both positively and negatively. Praising the smooth transitions in the book, Howard Barnes of the *Herald Tribune* wrote: "Com-

parisons with *Oklahoma!* are neither necessary nor in any sense invidious. *Annie Get Your Gun* is all of a piece, as fresh as a daisy and a delight that is certain to become a hardy Broadway perennial." Lewis Nichols, of the *New York Times,* felt compelled to comment on the integration of songs, commending Berlin for writing a score "with numbers which fit the events and the story." Robert Garland, of the New York *Journal American,* who raved about the show, made a direct comparison to *Oklahoma!* "Not since one March night in 1943, at the St. James Theatre, have I had so high a musical time on Broadway." All of these reviews can be found in *New York Theatre Critics' Reviews* (1946): 382–385.

8. Historians, preoccupied with "integration," have criticized Berlin's work for this resistance. His biographer Laurence Bergreen writes, "Its songs failed to interrelate, as they did in the best Broadway scores. . . . The main complaint lodged against Berlin's score for *Annie Get Your Gun* by students of the American musical was that it was merely an assorted collection of hits, unlike the more operatic scores by Rodgers and Hammerstein. In a word, it was old-fashioned" (*As Thousands Cheer,* pp. 457–458). Contemporary reviewers seemed relieved, however, that the show did not insist on extended, self-important dance numbers like the "Dream Ballet" of *Oklahoma!* Kronenberger, of the New York paper *PM,* wrote: "Miss Tamiris' dances are of the lively, likeable pre–de Mille days, before Broadway tried for something better and generally came up with something worse." And William Hawkins, of the *New York World Telegram,* wrote: "There is nothing in the show that could be accused of being a ballet." *New York Theatre Critics' Reviews* (1946): 384.

9. Bergreen, *As Thousands Cheer,* p. 459.

10. Faced with the prospect of writing "hillbilly music" to compete with *Oklahoma!* Berlin was stumped. As Bergreen relates: "He knew nothing about hillbilly music, but he reached the conclusion that it had no place in *Annie Get Your Gun;* ultimately, it was a musical about show business, not hillbillies, and show tunes did have a place" (*As Thousands Cheer,* p. 451).

11. Rodgers, *Musical Stages,* p. 227.

12. The critics acknowledged and celebrated Merman's dominance of the play. Headlines in the *New York World Telegram* and the *Daily News* read "A Bull's Eye for Ethel Merman" and "Merman Scores Bull's-Eye." William Hawkins, of the *World-Telegram,* wrote, "It was Ethel's party to such an extent that it would not be a bad idea to declare an annual Merman Day of all May 16's in the future." Lewis Nichols of the *New York Times* directly acknowledges Merman's overwhelming presence: "In any Merman show the other members of the company habitually take on the harassed air of the losing horses in a steeplechase." *New York Theatre Critics' Reviews* (1946): 384–385.

13. *Oklahoma!* and *Annie Get Your Gun* can be seen as illustrations of the two kinds of pastoralism Leo Marx describes in *The Machine in the Garden:* the popular and sentimental versus the imaginative and complex. *Oklahoma!* expresses that "yearning for a simpler, more harmonious style of life, an existence 'closer to nature'" that Marx describes—a move away from the complications of the "artificial" urban world and toward an idealized rural folk scene. *Annie Get Your Gun* is far more aware of the

impact of industry and technology on the natural environment. As we shall see, it posits show business as a force in direct opposition to "the natural world." Leo Marx, *The Machine in the Garden* (New York: Oxford, 1964), p. 6.

14. *Bildung* is a German Enlightenment ideal that appeared in the later eighteenth century. David Sorkin defines *Bildung* as "a process of integral self-development on the basis of a form that was an inherent part of the individual. Form no longer resulted from imitation of an external, religious model, but from the development of what was innate. Man achieved a unity of essence and existence through a self-initiated process for which he was his own model." The notion of *Bildung* had a particular significance for Jews. *Bildung,* and indeed the German Enlightenment as a whole, proposed a new type of society based on education and merit. If religion and birth were discredited as standards of status, Jews had an opportunity to gain citizenship and civil rights. But German *Gebildeten* (those belonging to a bourgeoisie formed by education) conceived of emancipation "as a quid pro quo in which Jews were to be regenerated in exchange for rights." David Sorkin, *The Transformation of German Jewry* (New York: Oxford, 1987), pp. 15, 20.

According to Paul Mendes-Flohr, *Bildung* can be thought of as a secular religion. As German Jews became secular, they rushed to join what he calls the *Bildungs-burgertum,* or the "educated middle classes"—"those in German society that earned their status by virtue of educational attainments." Jews became the practitioners and guardians of *Bildung* par excellence. See Paul Mendes-Flohr, *German Jews: A Dual Identity* (New Haven: Yale University Press, 1999), pp. 5, 10.

Clearly, Jews transferred the meritocratic and educational ideals of *Bildung* to the American scene, where these merged with other American ideals to form the secular liberal religion described here in the chapter on *Babes in Arms.* This notion of *Bildung* subtly informs *Annie Get Your Gun,* especially in the linkage between falling in love, reading, and becoming a star.

15. Marianne Hirsch, "The Novel of Formation as Genre: Between Great Expectations and Lost Illusions," *Genre* 12 (Fall 1979): 296–301.

16. This story differs markedly from the biography of the real Annie Oakley. The most significant difference between the two accounts is that Annie Oakley actually met Frank Butler at a shooting match long before either was connected with Buffalo Bill's Wild West. They married soon after Annie won that match, and Frank quickly realized Annie's skills and marketability. He gave up his own act and became Annie's assistant and manager. When they finally joined the Wild West show, nearly ten years into their marriage, Annie performed solo. Winer quotes Dorothy Fields: "We did a lot of research on Annie Oakley and Frank Butler, and both of them apparently were about the dullest people in the world. Annie Oakley in real life used to sit in her tent and *knit,* for God's sake" (Winer, *On the Sunny Side of the Street,* p. 149). For information on the historical Annie Oakley, see Glenda Riley, *The Life and Legacy of Annie Oakley* (Norman: University of Oklahoma Press, 1994).

17. Annie's entrance was the first scene Dorothy and Herbert Fields wrote for the show, and one of the only scenes they showed to Irving Berlin before he decided to take on the project. It was clearly an establishing moment for all of the play's creators.

18. Marx, *Machine in the Garden,* p. 24.

19. Oscar Wilde, "The Decay of Lying," in *The Complete Works of Oscar Wilde* (New York: Harper and Row, 1989), pp. 985–986.

20. For an alternative understanding of the relationship between nature and art, particularly in the theater, see Brenda Murphy's discussion of dramatic realism, particularly the ideas of Howells and James, in Murphy, *American Realism and American Drama* (Cambridge: Cambridge University Press, 1987).

21. Winer, *On the Sunny Side of the Street,* p. 144.

22. John Chapman, "Merman Scores Bull's-Eye with Every Berlin Number in *Annie,*" *New York Daily News,* 17 May 1946 (*New York Theater Critics* [1946]: 382).

23. This view of the "world" of the stage differs somewhat from that described by Austin Quigley in *The Modern Stage and Other Worlds* (New York: Methuen, 1985). Quigley describes the interlocking tropes of "the theater" and "the world" in modern drama—an interrelation which he sees as emerging out of a concern for modern pluralistic perspectives. In other words, playwrights use the theater to imagine a series of "worlds"—the theater becomes a way of delineating horizons and borders of various worlds. In *Annie Get Your Gun,* the world of show business is the *only* world: all of America is theatrical, and all theater is business.

24. For the only synonym of the noun "traffic," Webster's Third Edition suggests "business."

25. Arthur Miller, *Death of a Salesman* (New York: Penguin, 1998), p. 111 (last scene of play).

26. My thanks to Jonathan Warren for this insight.

27. Ralph Waldo Emerson, *Selected Essays, Lectures, and Poems* (New York: Bantam, 1990), p. 22.

28. See the description in the stage directions given in the 1967 script, p. 78.

29. This image of the Indian as an ethnic immigrant parallels some of the late nineteenth-century burlesque plays of John Brougham, who often played King Powhatan with an Irish accent. Werner Sollors, *Beyond Ethnicity* (New York: Oxford University Press, 1986), p. 139.

30. Needless to say, the historical Sitting Bull did nothing of the sort. While Annie Oakley was, at one point, "adopted" by Sitting Bull, she rarely saw him. He was permitted by U.S. Indian Affairs agents to tour briefly with Buffalo Bill's Wild West long after his first encounter with Oakley. He had none of the financial resources implied in the play, and certainly had no interest in investing in the show. Sitting Bull was frequently depressed during the tour, concerned about the U.S. Army troops that were trespassing on reservation lands and about the meager aid that Indian Affairs agents were offering his tribe. Sitting Bull gave away most of his salary to urchins who hung around the show, and when the tour was over he told a reporter: "The wigwam is a better place for the red man." He added that he was "sick of the houses and the noises and multitude of men." See Riley, *Life and Legacy of Annie Oakley,* pp. 148–149.

31. The battle against prejudice was a popular topic in the postwar years. The film *Gentleman's Agreement* (Academy Award for best picture, 1947) offers a detailed examination of these strategies. Most Jews in the film prefer to keep quiet about

prejudice; some change their name and appearance in order to blend in. The character played by John Garfield leaps up to fight a bigot. The "fake" Jew, played by Gregory Peck, attempts to expose and eradicate antisemitic social practices among his WASP social circle. Chapter 6, which analyzes the problem of prejudice in Rodgers and Hammerstein's *South Pacific*, will treat this issue in greater detail.

32. See Edward Shapiro, *A Time for Healing* (Baltimore: Johns Hopkins University Press, 1992), ch. 4.

33. See Mailer's novel *The Naked and the Dead*, and Garfield's films such as *Body and Soul* (1947), *Gentleman's Agreement* (1947), and *Pride of the Marines* (1945).

34. Bergreen, *As Thousands Cheer*, p. 441.

35. Sitting Bull was played in both Broadway runs by Harry Bellaver, an Italian character actor. A survey of the annals of the New York stage during the 1930s, '40s, and '50s reveals that Bellaver made a career of playing Mexicans, Spaniards, Indians, Italians, and Jews. In other words, he played *ethnicity* itself. Likewise, Sitting Bull was played in the 1950 movie by J. Carrol Naish, an Irish actor who played a variety of ethnic characters including Indians, Mexicans, Italians, and Japanese. *New York Theatre Critics' Reviews* (1935–1955); Internet Movie Database (www.imdb.com).

36. Richard Slotkin, *Gunfighter Nation* (Norman: University of Oklahoma Press, 1992) p. 76.

37. James T. Patterson, *Grand Expectations* (New York: Oxford University Press, 1996), pp. 32–33. Maureen Honey, *Creating Rosie the Riveter* (Amherst: University of Massachusetts Press, 1984).

38. Adel and State Farm advertisements quoted in Honey, *Creating Rosie the Riveter*, p. 125. Review of *Saturday Evening Post* recruitment ads on p. 122.

39. Ibid., p. 133.

40. Laurence Bergreen (*As Thousands Cheer*, p. 555) reports an exchange that took place between Irving Berlin and Ethel Merman during rehearsals for the revival of *Annie Get Your Gun* in 1966 and that underscores Berlin's own understanding of Merman's gender identity:

> "'Irving!' she announced, 'You look great! What are you doing for sex?'
> "'Well, Ethel, if you can get it up, I can get it in.'"

41. Riley, *Life and Legacy of Annie Oakley*, p. 9.

42. Wilde, "Decay of Lying," p. 972.

43. D. A. Miller, *Place for Us: Essay on the Broadway Musical* (Cambridge, Mass.: Harvard University Press, 1998), p. 71.

44. The contemporaneous musical *Kiss Me, Kate* (1948) offers a similar strategy to women faced with increasingly limited options. Kate/Lilli also yields to her man at the end of the play, but does so with a theatrical flourish that belies and ultimately subverts the sexist plot line. In the 1999 Broadway revival, Kate winked at the audience at the end. As with *Annie Get Your Gun*, it is Kate's name that appears in the title of the show. And *Kiss Me, Kate* likewise had a strong Jewish woman librettist—possibly the only other Jewish woman writer working on Broadway, Bella Spewack. It is perhaps not coincidental that both plays were revived simultaneously on Broadway in 1999. One could speculate about the implications of these revivals for current attitudes about gender—particularly in relation to the backlash against

"political correctness" which characterized the late 1990s. On the idea that gender is performed, see Judith Butler, *Gender Trouble* (New York: Routledge, 1990).

6. "You've Got to Be Carefully Taught"

1. Michener quoted in Hugh Fordin, *Getting to Know Him: A Biography of Oscar Hammerstein II* (New York: Da Capo Press, 1995), pp. 270–271. In a letter to Oscar Hammerstein, a U.S. military officer complained that the song ruined the flow of the show. Hammerstein replied: "I am most anxious to make the point not only that prejudice exists and is a problem, but that its birth lies in teaching and not in the fallacious belief that there are basic biological and physiological and mental differences between races." Oscar Hammerstein to Lieutenant Commander McWhorter, 11 April 1949, *South Pacific* files, Oscar Hammerstein Collection, Library of Congress.
2. *New York Herald Tribune,* 2 March 1953. Clipping in Box 4, Folder F, *South Pacific* Correspondence Files, Oscar Hammerstein Collection, Library of Congress.
3. Fordin, *Getting to Know Him,* p. 270.
4. In his review of *South Pacific* (*New York Times,* 8 April 1949), Brooks Atkinson calls the play "a tenderly beautiful idyll of genuine people inexplicably tossed together in a strange corner of the world." Much later, Richard Goldstein summed up the general perception of these works, claiming (inaccurately) that Rodgers and Hammerstein "pioneered the inclusion of social commentary within the musical's form." See Goldstein, "'I Enjoy Being a Girl': Women in the Plays of Rodgers and Hammerstein," *Popular Music and Society* (Spring 1989): 1.
5. Paul Jacobs, who went to work for the American Jewish Committee in 1947, indicates how little-known the field of "race relations" was in those days among the sort of people who would have made up the audience for *South Pacific:*
   "'Hey Paul, I've been meaning to ask you something for a long time,' the butcher in Nyack, New York, said to me as Ruth and I stood in front of his display case. 'What do you do for a living?'
   "'I'm in the race relations field,' I answered.
   "'No kidding?' He looked around to see if his wife, who acted as the cashier, could hear him. 'Do me a favor, any time you get a tip on a good horse, give me a ring.'"
   See Jacobs, *Is Curly Jewish? A Political Self-Portrait* (New York: Atheneum, 1965), p. 140.
6. Whittaker Chambers, an FBI informant, identified Alger Hiss, an employee in the State Department, as a Communist during HUAC testimony in 1948. Hiss sued Chambers for libel, and during the lawsuit Chambers claimed Hiss was a spy. Although tried for (and convicted of) espionage in 1949, Hiss denied everything and no proof of espionage has ever been found. Gerhard Eisler was a German-Jewish refugee who had been active in the Communist Party. He was identified by FBI informants in 1946 as a key figure in the American Communist movement. Although there was no proof of his guilt, he was repeatedly arrested and indicted for contempt and perjury. Eisler escaped to Poland in 1949. In 1947, HUAC began investigating Hollywood for alleged Communist subversion. The committee called both "friendly" and "unfriendly" witnesses. The ten "unfriendly" witnesses refused to answer HUAC's questions and

were cited for contempt of court. In late 1947, a group of the major Hollywood producers adopted what came to be known as the "Waldorf Statement," which asserted
that they would not "knowingly employ a Communist." This instituted the infamous
blacklist. All of the Hollywood Ten were fired, and most of them served jail sentences in 1949–1950. All three of these cases received major press coverage. Ellen
Schrecker, *Many Are the Crimes: McCarthyism in America* (Princeton: Princeton University Press, 1998), pp. 128–129, 175, 320–327.

7. Ibid., p. 151.

8. Edward S. Shapiro describes Representative John Rankin as an outspoken antisemite who referred to Jews as "long-nosed reprobates" and blamed Jews not only
for Communism but also for "trying to undermine and destroy America." See
Shapiro, *A Time For Healing: American Jewry since World War II* (Baltimore: Johns
Hopkins University Press, 1992), p. 40. As Neal Gabler reports in *An Empire of Their
Own* (New York: Doubleday, 1988), Dies also spoke frequently of "restoring Christian
influence" in the United States and gladly used information about alleged "subversives" from known antisemites, including a member of the Ku Klux Klan (352).

9. Edward Shapiro quotes Arnold Forster, a lawyer for the Anti-Defamation League at
the time: "Jews were automatically suspect. . . . Our evaluation of the general mood
was that the people felt if you scratch a Jew, you can find a Communist." Shapiro, *A
Time For Healing,* p. 35.

10. See Stuart Svonkin, *Jews against Prejudice* (New York: Columbia University Press,
1997), especially chs. 1 and 5, on the connections between Jewish liberalism and
anti-Communism. Not surprisingly, the civil rights strategy backfired with those who
were *both* racist and antisemitic. James Patterson, in *Grand Expectations* (New York:
Oxford University Press, 1996), quotes Rankin, for example, who in an interview for
Time magazine (16 March 1950, p. 17) denounced civil rights activity as "part of the
communistic program. . . . Remember communism is Yiddish. I understand that every member of the Politburo around Stalin is either Yiddish or married to one, and
that includes Stalin himself" (189).

11. In the past decade a number of critics have questioned the assumption that *South
Pacific* is simply an antiracist tract, seeing it instead as an artifact of Cold War ideology. See Philip Beidler, "*South Pacific* and American Remembering; or, 'Josh, We're
Going to Buy This Son of a Bitch!'" *Journal of American Studies* 27 (1993): 207–222.
Beidler views *South Pacific* not as racially enlightened, but rather as promoting "a
deeply American politics of constructing the racial other" (208). Bruce McConachie,
"The 'Oriental' Musicals of Rodgers and Hammerstein and the U.S. War in Southeast
Asia," *Theatre Journal* 46 (1994): 385–398, reads *South Pacific* as a "metaphor of containment" whose popularity helped to "establish a legitimate basis for the American
war against the people of Southeast Asia in the 1960s" (385–386). Christina Klein,
"Cold War Orientalism: Musicals, Travel Narratives, and Middlebrow Culture in Postwar America" (Ph.D. diss., Yale University, 1997), also views *South Pacific* as an anti
Communist work which promotes American Cold War policy and offers popular support for American imperialist goals in Asia. Focusing largely on the 1958 film, Klein
notes that *South Pacific* "offered a romantic 'history' of the origins of the U.S. commitment to Southeast Asia in the years following the end of World War II, while it si

multaneously prefigured America's assumption of France's colonial obligations in Indochina after the French defeat at Dien Bien Phu in 1954" (185). While all of the above arguments have been useful for my own work, none of these critics directly connect the musical's antiracism with the Red Scare, investigate the Jewish implications, or analyze the mechanics of the genre of the musical as a way of understanding the ideological work this play performs.

12. Frederick Nolan, *The Sound of Their Music* (New York: Walker, 1978), p. 160. Klein, "Cold War Orientalism," p. 186. The music for *South Pacific* is by Richard Rodgers and the lyrics are by Oscar Hammerstein II. The book is by Hammerstein and Joshua Logan, based on stories from James Michener's collection *Tales of the South Pacific.* The play opened at the Majestic Theater in New York on 7 April 1949, directed by Joshua Logan and starring Mary Martin, Ezio Pinza, Myron McCormick, William Tabbert, Juanita Hall, and Betta St. John.

13. Fordin, *Getting to Know Him,* p. 269; Beidler, "*South Pacific* and American Remembering," p. 217.

14. In *Musical Stages: An Autobiography* (New York: Da Capo Press, 1995), Richard Rodgers described the process of creating *South Pacific:* "All this was against the accepted rules of musical-play construction. . . . Breaking the rules didn't bother us" (259).

15. Beidler, "*South Pacific* and American Remembering," p. 213. *South Pacific,* despite its reputation, was by no means the first Broadway musical to address issues of racial tolerance. Although neither Rodgers nor Hammerstein had touched the subject for many years, both had raised it in the earlier musicals *Showboat* (Hammerstein and Kern, 1927) and, of course, *Babes in Arms* (Rodgers and Hart, 1937).

16. Oscar Hammerstein and Richard Rodgers, *South Pacific,* in *Six Plays by Rodgers and Hammerstein* (New York: Random House, 1955), p. 295. Subsequent page references to the script will be given in the body of the text. While the concept and primary vision of the play came from Rodgers and Hammerstein, at a certain point in the script development Joshua Logan also worked with Hammerstein on the libretto and received a credit for the collaboration. Oddly, the lyrics of the song "Bali Hai" are written in a distinctly southern black dialect: "mos people long fo' anudder island / One where dey know dey would lak to be" (294). As Kenneth Tynan remarked in his review of *Flower Drum Song,* Asian characters in Rodgers and Hammerstein musicals speak with "more than a smidgen of pidgin" (*The New Yorker* [13 December 1958]: 101). This choice of dialect makes clear that Rodgers and Hammerstein see little difference between varieties of racial otherness. All are figured in terms of American black/white relations.

17. Seabee Luther Billis describes to Joe Cable how "women dance with just skirts on" (296). This description of tropical paradise has a long history in American popular culture. Most directly, as Philip Beidler points out, it refers to the rash of South Seas adventure films produced by Hollywood in the 1940s. In American literature, the history stretches back at least to Melville's *Typee* (1846). Stories of noble savages and Eden-like lands of paradise are also central to the representation of the Indian in early American fiction.

18. See, for example, the Chinese farmer in *The Purple Heart* (Twentieth Century Fox, 1944).
19. Rodgers, *Musical Stages,* p. 259.
20. James Michener, *Tales of the South Pacific* (New York: MacMillan, 1966), p. 167.
21. Despite the fact that the *Madama Butterfly* plot is reversed here—it is Joe who actually dies—the more significant "death" is Liat's. In the theater, existence is determined by stage time and performance skills. We learn at the end that Joe has died, but he lives night after night in his two songs (three in the film) and extended dramatic and comic scenes. By removing even the vestiges of Liat's theatrical and literary heritage, and leaving only the stereotype, Rodgers and Hammerstein make it impossible for her to come to life onstage. In addition, Liat is barely mentioned in the reviews, which is odd for one of the four members of the two central love stories. This absence of notice confirms her musical-theater death.
22. Fordin, *Getting to Know Him,* p. 277.
23. The Supreme Court case of *Plessy v. Ferguson* (1896) upheld segregation and endorsed the concept of "separate but equal" for blacks and whites. In 1947 this law was still in place, although the NAACP had begun agitating against it in earnest by the late 1940s. *Plessy v. Ferguson* was overturned in 1954 in the *Brown v. Board of Education* case. Many states had laws against interracial marriage on their books until 1967, when the Supreme Court ruled them unconstitutional. There *is* a case of miscegenation in *South Pacific:* Emile has had two children by a Polynesian woman. But she is long dead when the play begins. As Christina Klein argues in "Cold War Orientalism," the logic of the play suggests that racism can be eradicated by love, but that parental love is far more successful (and far less controversial) than romantic love in doing so. Hence, Joe and Liat have no future together, but Emile, Nellie, and his "Eurasian" children can form a family. Klein focuses on the role of adoption in the play and in the political rhetoric of the time, noting that the adoption of nonwhite children reinforces a sense of American paternalism and Asian immaturity while also avoiding problems of miscegenation.
24. "Ol' Man Author," Box 21, Folder B, Hammerstein Collection, Library of Congress.
25. In discussing *The King and I* in *Musical Stages,* Rodgers articulates a desire to write "real" Asian characters but reveals his inability to see that his characters are stereotypes: "Oscar and I were determined to depict the Orientals in the story as characters, not caricatures, which has all too often been the case in the musical theatre. Our aim was to portray the king and his court with humanity and believability" (274).
26. Schrecker, *Many Are the Crimes,* p. 142.
27. Anthony Heilbut, in *Exiled in Paradise* (New York: Viking, 1983), offers a description of refugees which easily could include Emile: "Many of these artists had grown up, as Jews or radicals, feeling like outsiders in their own homes, but they had come to see themselves as the vanguard of an internationalist spirit; paradoxically, they had found themselves more happily at home, more assimilated, as they assumed an increasingly critical stance toward all the traditions that had formerly served to exclude them" (21).

28. Schrecker, *Many Are the Crimes,* pp. 123, 142.

29. Christina Klein has discussed the tenets of Welcome House and other adoption programs: they fought against Communism by allowing Asians into the American family, but only as children, never as equals. "Cold War Orientalism," pp. 205–207.

30. Michael Denning, *The Cultural Front: The Laboring of American Culture in the Twentieth Century* (London: Verso, 1996), p. 63. In a 1936 letter to Hammerstein, Paramount executive Harry Myers urges Hammerstein not to change the name of the Hollywood Anti-Nazi League simply because some have implied it is a Communist front. Myers goes on to describe the assumptions surrounding Jews, artists, and Communists: "It is not possible to avoid being called a Red, if you belong to what is mistakenly called the intellectual class. May I remind you that you yourself told me that I am the type you would 'naturally' suppose to be a Communist" (Myers to Hammerstein, 7 November 1936, Box 21, Folder A, Hammerstein Collection, Music Division, Library of Congress). Correspondence showing Hammerstein's involvement in these and many other organizations exists in both the Irving Berlin Correspondence files and the Oscar Hammerstein Correspondence files in the Music Division of the Library of Congress.

31. See the Irving Berlin / Richard Rodgers Correspondence in the Irving Berlin Collection, Music Division, Library of Congress. Also Rodgers Correspondence, Box Z, in the Billy Rose Theatre Collection, New York Public Library for the Performing Arts.

32. Meryle Secrest, *Somewhere for Me: A Biography of Richard Rodgers* (New York: Knopf, 2001), p. 301.

33. Rodgers, *Musical Stages,* p. 184. Ellen Schrecker points out that the campaign to eliminate Communists from the federal government and later from the worlds of film, television, and radio was actually part of an effort by the New Deal's conservative opponents to discredit New Deal policies. *Many Are the Crimes,* pp. 109–110.

34. Richard Rodgers to Florence March, 21 March 1948, Richard Rodgers Papers, Series I, Correspondence J–M, Box 3, Folder 34. Dorothy is Rodgers' wife. Emphasis in original.

35. Rodgers, *Musical Stages,* p. 257. The importance of Rodgers and Hammerstein as artists and as public figures is substantiated by the fact that when Rodgers made the switch to Stevenson, the news appeared prominently in the major newspapers. The headline in the *New York Times* of 23 September 1952 read: "Gov. Stevenson Spends a Busy Day in City; Richard Rodgers Changes Tune, to Aid Him." Rodgers is quoted in the article as saying: "It is doubtful if General Eisenhower had a more loyal or active partisan than I was last spring and summer. I felt we wanted General Eisenhower, not Senator Taft. We wanted General Eisenhower, not Joe McCarthy. I now find we have lost a general and inherited the other two" (20).

36. Svonkin, *Jews against Prejudice,* pp. 115–121.

37. Ibid., p. 121.

38. As Ellen Schrecker has pointed out, Jewish groups were certainly not the only ones who linked American antiracism and anti-Communism (pp. 150–151). Arthur M. Schlesinger Jr., in *The Vital Center* (Boston: Houghton Mifflin, 1949), articulated this ideology for all liberals eager to find a way to espouse their patriotism without

threatening civil liberties. But Jews embraced this ideal particularly vocally and forcefully in the public sphere.

39. Mary Martin rose to fame playing just such a role in Cole Porter's 1938 satire *Leave It To Me*, where she made her name singing of the joys of marrying a millionaire in "My Heart Belongs to Daddy." As Nellie Forbush, however, she left that kittenish sexuality behind.

40. See Paul DiMaggio, "Cultural Boundaries and Structural Change: The Extension of the High Culture Model to Theater, Opera, and the Dance, 1900–1940," in Michele Lamont and Marcel Fournier, eds., *Cultivating Differences: Symbolic Boundaries and the Making of Inequality* (Chicago: University of Chicago Press, 1992), 21–57. DiMaggio describes how in the first part of the twentieth century, opera and drama in America struggled to distance themselves from commercial vaudeville and musical theater and to establish themselves using the high-culture models of symphonies and museums. They also looked to Europeans for their "aesthetic gravity and organizational structure(s)" (28).

41. Rodgers clearly believed he had arrived when his "symphonic" piece *Victory at Sea* (1952) became a bestseller in RCA's classical-records division (Rodgers, *Musical Stages,* p. 280).

42. Clement Greenberg, "Avant-Garde and Kitsch," *Partisan Reader* (1946): 378–389.

43. One of the most prominent of these critics was another Jewish refugee, Theodor Adorno, who in his 1941 essay "On Popular Music" lambasted the work of popular composers as standardized consumer products for the bored and indifferent. For an extended discussion of the impact of European refugees on American music, see David Josephson, "The Exile of European Music: Documentation of Upheaval and Immigration in the *New York Times,"* in Reinhold Brinkmann and Christoph Wolff, eds., *Driven into Paradise* (Berkeley: University of California Press, 1999), pp. 92–154.

44. Rodgers, *Musical Stages,* p. 260.

45. *South Pacific: Original Broadway Cast,* Audio CD (Sony, 1998).

46. As discussed in Chapter 5, the ideology of the postwar American family shifted women from the workplace (where they had been filling in for men at war) back to the domestic sphere. *South Pacific* seems to model this transformation, showing how, as Nellie contemplates her postwar life, she moves from a vocal position at center stage to a supportive and silent role.

Coda

1. Richard Rodgers and Oscar Hammerstein, *The King and I,* in *Six Plays by Rodgers and Hammerstein* (New York: Random House, 1955), pp. 448–449. Subsequent references to this play will be given in the text.

2. On the new relationship to Southeast Asia and the impact of the McCarran-Walter Act, see James T. Patterson, *Grand Expectations* (New York: Oxford University Press, 1996), pp. 207–242.

3. Other analyses of *The King and I* which focus on its Cold War themes are Christina Klein, "Cold War Orientalism: Musicals, Travel Narratives, and Middlebrow Culture

in Postwar America" (diss., Yale University, 1997); and Bruce McConachie, "The 'Oriental' Musicals of Rodgers and Hammerstein and the U.S. War in Southeast Asia," *Theatre Journal* 46 (1994): 385–398. Neither of these essays engages directly with the theatrical conventions of the play or raises the Jewish issues addressed here.

4. In addition to Rodgers and Hammerstein, the principals included John Van Druten (director), Jerome Robbins (choreographer), Jo Mielziner (set designer), Irene Sharaff (costume designer), Yul Brynner (King), Doretta Morrow (Tuptim), and Larry Douglas (Lun Tha). The British actress Gertrude Lawrence, who originated the role of Anna, was the only non-American in the group.

5. For examples of the moral and cultural education that immigrants received, see Lillian Wald, *The House on Henry Street* (New York: Dover, 1971).

6. Richard Rodgers, *Musical Stages* (New York: Da Capo Press, 1995), p. 273.

7. From an article by Richard Rodgers in the *New York Herald Tribune,* 25 March 1951. Clipping in the Hammerstein Collection, *King and I* scrapbook, Music Division, Library of Congress.

8. Klein, "Cold War Orientalism," p. 228.

9. Ironically, Rodgers and Hammerstein make Tuptim, a Burmese woman who comes from a country colonized by the British, into the voice for freedom and democracy. She struggles against the tyranny of the Siamese, who were never colonized by Europeans. The play subtly implies that the colonized countries are more civilized and the independent Asian states deeply in need of Western tutoring.

10. See Stephen Banfield, *Sondheim's Broadway Musicals* (Ann Arbor: University of Michigan Press, 1993).

11. Edward S. Shapiro, *A Time for Healing* (Baltimore: Johns Hopkins University Press, 1992), pp. 35–41.

12. Ken Mandelbaum, *A Chorus Line and the Musicals of Michael Bennett* (New York: St. Martin's Press, 1989), p. 171.

13. For eyewitness reports of audience reaction, see Mandelbaum, *A Chorus Line,* p. 172.

14. The star is also, significantly, figured as a woman: "every little step *she* takes." The conflation of America with a Broadway musical actress harks back to D. A. Miller's argument about the femaleness of the Broadway stage and opens up rich possibilities for exploration.

Credits

"But Not for Me"
By George Gershwin and Ira Gershwin. Copyright © 1930 (renewed) WB Music Corp. All rights reserved. Used by permission. Warner Bros. Publications U.S. Inc., Miami, Florida 33014.

"Babes in Arms"
By Lorenz Hart and Richard Rodgers. Copyright © 1937 by Chappell & Co., Inc. Copyright renewed. All rights reserved. Used by permission. Rights for Extended Renewal Term in U.S. controlled by The Estate of Lorenz Hart (administered by WB Music Corp.) and The Family Trust U/W Richard Rodgers and The Family Trust U/W Dorothy F. Rodgers (administered by Williamson Music). All Rights outside U.S. controlled by Chappell & Co. Warner Bros. Publications U.S. Inc., Miami, Florida 33014.

"Way Out West"
Copyright © 1937 by Chappell & Co., Inc. Copyright renewed. All rights reserved. Used by permission. Rights for Extended Renewal Term in U.S. controlled by The Estate of Lorenz Hart (administered by WB Music Corp.) and The Family Trust U/W Richard Rodgers and The Family Trust U/W Dorothy F. Rodgers (administered by Williamson Music). All Rights outside U.S. controlled by Chappell & Co. Warner Bros. Publications U.S. Inc., Miami, Florida 33014.

"All Dark People"
By Lorenz Hart and Richard Rodgers. Copyright © 1937 by Chappell & Co., Inc. Copyright renewed. All rights reserved. Used by permission. Rights for Extended Renewal Term in U.S. controlled by The Estate of Lorenz Hart (administered by WB Music Corp.) and The Family Trust U/W Richard Rodgers and The Family Trust U/W Dorothy F. Rodgers (administered by Williamson Music). All Rights outside U.S. controlled by Chappell & Co. Warner Bros. Publications U.S. Inc., Miami, Florida 33014.

"My Funny Valentine"
By Lorenz Hart and Richard Rodgers. Copyright © 1937 by Chappell & Co., Inc. Copyright renewed. All rights reserved. Used by permission. Rights for Extended Renewal Term in U.S. controlled by The Estate of Lorenz Hart (administered by WB Music Corp.) and The Family

"Some Enchanted Evening"

"A Wonderful Guy"

"Dites-Moi"

"I Whistle a Happy Tune"

"My Lord and Master"

"Lonely Room"

"Shall We Dance?"

"Let Me Sing and I'm Happy"

"Twin Soliloquies"

"Kansas City"

*

Girl Crazy

Annie Get Your Gun

Babes in Arms

The King and I

Oklahoma!

South Pacific

*

Portions of Chapter 2 appeared in "'Big Chief Izzy Horowitz': Theatricality and Jewish Identity in the Wild West," *American Jewish History*, 87, no. 4 (December 1999): 313–341. Reprinted by permission of the Johns Hopkins University Press.

Portions of Chapter 4 appeared in "'We Know We Belong To The Land': The Theatricality of Assimilation in Rodgers and Hammerstein's *Oklahoma!*" *PMLA* (January 1998): 77–89. Reprinted by permission of the Modern Language Association.

Portions of Chapter 6 appeared in "'You've Got to Be Carefully Taught': The Politics of Race in Rodgers and Hammerstein's *South Pacific*," *Theatre Journal* 52 (2000): 307–337. Reprinted by permission of the Johns Hopkins University Press.

Index

Adorno, Theodor, 239n43

Advertising industry, 16–17; women as depicted by, 142–143

Alexander, James, 112

"Alexander's Ragtime Band," 121

Alger, Horatio, 123, 209n21

"All Dark People," 91

Allen, Woody, 209n22

Alter, Robert, 207n2

American Student Union (ASU), 83

Anderson, Maxwell, 72, 170

Annie Get Your Gun, 25, 119–121; natural world versus theater world in, 119, 125–134; hit songs in, 122; theatricality of, 122–123; as *Bildungsmusical,* 123–124, 231n14; Sitting Bull as Annie's mentor in, 134–140, 148–149; as immigrant drama, 135–136; confusion of gender roles in, 140–142, 143–152; literacy as issue in, 140, 144, 146–147; compared with *Oklahoma!,* 229n7 230n13

Antin, Mary, 14, 23

Antisemitism, 7–8, 21–22, 24–25, 69, 174, 196–197, 212n60. *See also* Jews; Racism

"Anything You Can Do," 122, 124

Architecture, 16–17

Asian immigrants, 185–186

Atkinson, Brooks, 220n15, 222n40, 234n4

"At the Roxy Music Hall," 73

Babes in Arms (musical), 3, 20, 26, 222n40; original script for, 66–67, 219n3; Jewish liberalism in, 69–71; as new approach to musical theater, 71–73; in historical context, 74–79; political activism in, 78–82; racial and ethnic diversity in, 82–92; as political statement, 83–92; self-conscious theatricality of, 92–100; wordplay in, 94–95

"Babes in Arms" (song), 66, 67, 81–82, 94

Balanchine, George, 73, 221n21

Barnes, Howard, 229n7

Bayes, Nora, 212n66

Beidler, Philip, 156, 235n11, 236n17

Belasco, David, 15

Bell, Jack, 224n66

Bellaver, Harry, 233n35

Benedikt, Moriz, 48

Bennett, Michael, 197–200

Bercovitch, Sacvan, 4, 6, 204n10

Bergreen, Laurence, 139, 230nn8,10

Berkeley, Busby, 216n22

Berle, Milton, 166

Berlin, Irving, 17, 27, 67, 119, 121–123, 139–140, 212n61, 230nn8,10. See also *Annie Get Your Gun*

Bernhardt, Sarah, 15

Bernstein, Leonard, 196

Blackface, 214n7, 223n52; Jews in, 32–39, 46–47, 54, 217n45

Black performers, 24, 214n8; and Jewish artists, 26, 212n58; in *Babes in Arms,* 88–92

Blackton, Jay, 226n20

Blazing Saddles, 58, 215n16

Blitzstein, Marc, 9, 72, 220n17

Bloom, Harold, 207n2

Boorstin, Daniel, 41–42

Bordman, Gerald, 213n70, 225n9

Boyarin, Daniel, 47

Brahm, Otto, 15, 208n14

Brandes, Georg Morris Cohen, 208n14

Braudy, Leo, 226n15

Brecht, Bertolt, 8–9, 10, 72, 93, 96, 223n60

Brice, Fanny, 29, 30, 196

Brinkley, Alan, 77

Broadway theater, 18–19; as reflective of American culture, 19–20; Jews involved in, 26–28; women in, 53, 97, 151–152, 217n38, 240n14; *Babes in Arms* as new approach to, 71–73; labor unions as influence on, 72–73; segregation in, 87. *See also* Musical comedy; *entries for specific musicals*

Brooks, Mel, 58, 206n20, 215n16, 218n49

Brown, John Mason, 88, 222n40

Brynner, Yul, 192, 193, 195

Buber, Martin, 18, 210n26

Buffalo Bill. See *Annie Get Your Gun*

Buloff, Joseph, 109

Burnham, Louis, 86

Bush, Frank, 23–24

"But Not for Me," 43

Cahan, Abraham, 16

Calloway, Cab, 83

Cantor, Eddie, 1, 6, 26, 29, 32, 40, 43, 47, 54, 55, 56, 67, 157, 215n15

Capra, Frank, 74–75

Carnegie, Dale, 98

Carousel, 103, 153

Cather, Willa, 22

Chambers, Whittaker, 234n6

Chapman, John, 128

Chevalier, Maurice, 1

Chorus Line, A, 197–200

Circumcision, 47, 49

Citizenship Act of 1924, 60

Civil rights, 70–71, 86–87, 228n32

Clurman, Harold, 72

"Cockeyed Optimist, A," 178, 180

Cody, William F. (Buffalo Bill), 140. See also *Annie Get Your Gun*

Cohan, George M., 64, 98

Cohen, Robert, 79, 83, 222nn33,34

Coleman, Robert, 223n55

Comden, Betty, 196

Communist Party, 20, 75; Jews accused of association with, 154–155, 171–172, 173–174, 185–186, 235nn8,9,10; Asians associated with, 185

Congress of Industrial Organizations (CIO), 75

Coughlin, Father Charles, 69, 75

Cradle Will Rock, The, 4, 9, 72, 75, 220n17

Crawford, Cheryl, 72

Cross-dressing, 47, 49, 52–53, 166

Cuddihy, John Murray, 207n2

"Dance Ten, Looks Three," 199

Davis, Owen, 43

Death of a Salesman (Miller), 131

Deleon, Michael, 182

Denning, Michael, 19, 83–84

Dies, Martin, 154

DiMaggio, Paul, 239n40

"Doin' What Comes Natur'lly," 122, 124, 126–127, 132, 145–146

Donaldson, Walter, 42

Donovan, Timothy, 103

Dorsey, Jimmy, 43

Douglas, Ann, 212n58

Drake, Alfred, 82

DuBois, W. E. B., 14

Durante, Jimmy, 30

Eisler, Gerhard, 171–172, 234n6

Eldridge, Florence, 173–174

Eliot, George, 15

Ellison, Ralph, 216n21, 223n54

"Embraceable You," 43

Emerson, Ralph Waldo, 132–134

Ethnicity, 25–26; in popular culture, 101–102, 214n6. *See also* Black performers; Indians; Jews; Race

Euchel, Isaac, 15

"Farmer and the Cowman, The," 105–106

Faulkner, William, 22

Federal Theatre Project, 72, 87, 177, 220n17, 223n51

Feingold, Henry, 7, 70, 205n17
Fiddler on the Roof, 192, 196
Fields, Dorothy, 27, 119, 122, 139, 144, 229n3, 231n16. See also *Annie Get Your Gun*
Fields, Herbert, 27, 119, 139, 144. See also *Annie Get Your Gun*
Fields, Lew, 229n3
Fiorello, 224n69
Fitzgerald, F. Scott, 22
Flower Drum Song, 186, 236n16
Forster, Arnold, 235n9
Foucault, Michel, 10
Frankenberg, Ruth, 228n32
Freud, Sigmund, 10, 13–14, 228n31
Frueh, Alfred, 40
Frye, Northrop, 204n8, 205n10, 206n21
Funny Girl, 196

Garfield, John, 139, 233n31
Garland, Robert, 230n7
Gender roles: confusion of in *Annie Get Your Gun,* 140–142, 143–152; in postwar America, 142–143. *See also* Women
Gentleman's Agreement, 232n31
Gershwin, George, 32, 42, 67, 212n66
Gershwin, Ira, 9, 32, 42, 67, 212n66
Gesamtkunstwerk, 9, 225n7
"Getting to Know You," 184, 188
Gilbert, Douglas, 23–24
Gilbert and Sullivan, 29
Gilman, Sander, 47, 48, 205n13, 207n2, 228n31
Girl Crazy (film), 216n19
Girl Crazy (musical), 1, 3, 4, 5, 27, 41, 42–47, 52–53, 64–65; Indians as portrayed in, 56–60, 63–65
Girl of the Golden West, The, 15
"Girl That I Marry, The," 122, 124, 141
Goethe, Johann Wolfgang von, 123
Goldman, Herbert, 215n15
Goldstein, Eric, 211n44
Goldstein, Richard, 103–104
Goodman, Benny, 43
Gordon, Richard H., 112
Gould, Charles W., 21
Green, Adolph, 196
Green, Mitzi, 82
Greenberg, Clement, 178
Greenberg, Jack, 87
Greenblatt, Stephen, 2

Grey, Zane, 60
Group Theatre, 72, 177
Gutmann, Moses Julius, 50
Gypsy, 53, 152

Habimah, 18
Hall, Juanita, 161
Hammerstein I, Oscar, 15, 208n14
Hammerstein II, Oscar, 25, 27–28, 29, 30, 87, 102, 121, 160, 212n61, 225n5; as supporter of Jewish causes, 172. See also *King and I, The; Oklahoma!; South Pacific*
Hansen, Marcus Lee, 27
"Happy Talk," 159, 161
Harby, Isaac, 15
Hart, Lorenz, 30, 67–69, 70, 71, 73, 225n5. See also *Babes in Arms* (musical)
Hawkins, William, 230n12
Hawthorne, Nathaniel, 126
Heilbut, Anthony, 237n27
Hertzberg, Arthur, 205n17
Herzl, Theodor, 18, 209n25
Hirsch, Marianne, 123
Hirschfeld, Al, 41
Hiss, Alger, 234n6
Holm, Celeste, 109, 195
Homosexuality, 50
Honey, Maureen, 143
"Honey Bun," 166, 178, 180, 181
Hoover, Herbert, 224n66
House Un-American Activities Committee, 154, 172, 173–174, 234n6
Howard, Willie, 1, 4, 5, 32, 41, 43, 44, 54, 57, 60, 61, 215n13
Howe, Irving, 7–8, 33

"I Cain't Say No," 105
"I Can Do That," 199
I'd Rather Be Right, 70, 73, 224n69
"If I Were a Rich Man," 192
"I Got Lost in His Arms," 122
"I Got Rhythm," 43
"I Got the Sun in the Morning," 122, 132, 134
"I'm an Indian Too," 122, 124, 138
I Married an Angel, 73
"I'm Bringing a Red, Red Rose," 43
"I'm Gonna Wash That Man Right Out of My Hair," 155, 162, 163, 178, 179, 180
Immigrants, 208n16, 208n17. *See also* Asian immigrants; Jews, as immigrants

Immigration quotas, 24, 211n45
Indian plays, 62–63, 134
Indians: as portrayed in Broadway musicals, 44–45; and Jews, 55–64, 139; as portrayed in *Annie Get Your Gun,* 134–140
Israel, Menasseh ben, 62
"It's a Scandal! It's a Outrage!" 113
"I Whistle a Happy Tune," 184, 188–189
"I Wish I Were in Love Again," 67

Jacobs, Paul, 234n5
Jacobson, Matthew Frye, 25, 210n38
Jaffe, Sam, 37
Jazz Singer, The (film), 32
Jazz Singer, The (play), 22, 27, 28, 32–39, 185, 191
Jenkins, Henry, 215nn14,19
Jessel, George, 1, 37, 38
Jesus Christ Superstar, 196
Jewishness: as emblematic of difference, 45–47; and femininity, 47, 52–53, 216n23, 216n25
Jews: in American culture, 1–11, 40–42, 196–200; socioeconomic mobility of, 2–3, 26–27; and musical comedy, 8–11, 23–24, 40–42; theater as significant for, 13–15, 17–19, 100; split consciousness of, 14–15, 209n22; as immigrants, 15–16, 17, 27, 68, 171–172, 176, 185–186, 209n23; and black performers, 26, 212n58; in blackface, 32–39, 46–47, 54; and Indians, 44–45, 55–64, 139; liberalism of, 69–71, 220n13; and government aid, 77–78; and the civil rights movement, 86–87, 228n32; accused of Communist sympathies, 154–155, 171–172, 173–174, 185–186, 235nn8,9,10. *See also* Antisemitism
"Johnny One Note," 73
Johnson-Reed Act of 1924, 22, 40–41, 60, 211n45
Jolson, Al, 1, 26, 32, 34, 67
Jones, David C., 153
Jones, Shirley, 110

Kahn, Gus, 42
Kallen, Horace, 22
"Kansas City," 116
Kearns, Allen, 41
Kent, William, 41

Kern, Jerome, 29, 121
King and I, The, 3, 25, 27–28, 103, 152, 183–185; as immigrant drama, 185–186; Siamese culture as represented in, 187–188, 237n25; theatricality in, 188–191; racial otherness in, 191–196
Kiss Me, Kate, 233n44
Klein, Christina, 188, 235n11
Krupa, Gene, 43

Labor movement, 72–73, 75, 228n27
"Lady Is a Tramp, The," 67, 95, 97–98
LaGuardia, Fiorello, 99–100, 224n68
Lahr, Bert, 43
Landon, Margaret, 184
Leibowitz, Samuel, 87
Leonowens, Anna, 184. See also *King and I, The*
Levine, Lawrence, 77
Lhamon, W. T., 33
Lincoln, Abraham, 186
Lipset, Seymour Martin, 203n2
Literacy, as issue in *Annie Get Your Gun,* 140, 144, 146–147
Lloyd Webber, Andrew, 196
Lockridge, Richard, 88
Logan, Josh, 160
"Lonely Room," 116
Long, Huey, 69, 75
Lost in the Stars, 170
Lott, Eric, 5
Love and Theft, 5
"Love Me or Leave Me," 43
Lubitsch, Ernst, 170
Luna, Barbara, 182

Mackay, Ellin, 121
Madama Butterfly, 15, 159
Mailer, Norman, 139
"Making Whoopee," 43
Mamoulian, Rouben, 170
March, Frederic, 174
Marcus, Jacob R., 208n14
Marrano culture, 13, 207n3
Marshall, Louis, 87
Martin, Mary, 155, 162, 163, 165, 167, 170, 171, 178, 182, 239n39
Marx, Chico, 23
Marx, Leo, 125, 126, 230n13

Mast, Gerald, 203n5, 213n69
May, Lary, 205n17
McCarran-Walter Act, 185
McCarthy, Joseph, 174, 196
McCarthyism, 20, 154, 162, 172, 174,
    222n33
McConachie, Bruce, 235n11
McCormick, Myron, 167
McGowan, John, 61
McNamara, Brooks, 220n15
Meehan, Thomas, 206n20
Melnick, Jeffrey, 32
Melting Pot, The, 22
Mendelssohn, Moses, 15
Mendes-Flohr, Paul, 231n14
Menken, Adah Isaacs, 15, 208n13
Merman, Ethel, 41, 43, 44, 53, 120, 122, 128,
    133, 137, 143, 152, 230n12
Michaels, Walter Benn, 21–22, 60,
    218nn46,47,48
Michener, James, 153–154, 155, 159, 234n1
Miller, Arthur, 131
Miller, D. A., 53, 97, 151, 240n14
Miller, Glenn, 43
Minstrel performers. *See* Blackface
Mordden, Ethan, 103, 217n38
Morrison, Paul, 10
Murray, Wynn, 82
Musical comedy, 8–11, 29–31, 204n7; black-
    face in, 34, 54; Wild West as backdrop for,
    39–65; gender issues in, 47–54. *See also en-
    tries for specific musicals*
Musical theater. *See* Broadway theater
"My Baby Just Cares for Me," 6, 43, 54
"My Defenses Are Down," 124
Myers, Harry, 238n30
"My Funny Valentine," 67
"My Girl Back Home," 178

NAACP, 86–87, 211n57
Naish, J. Carrol, 233n35
National Origins Act. *See* Johnson-Reed Act
    of 1924
Nervous Wreck, The, 43
New Deal, 70, 74–76, 86, 172, 219n3
Nicholas, Harold, 88, 89–90
Nicholas Brothers, 82–83, 88, 89, 91–92,
    223n55
Nichols, Lewis, 230nn7,12

Noah, Mordecai Manuel, 15, 62, 208n12
"Nothing," 199

Oakley, Annie, 213n16. See also *Annie Get
    Your Gun*
Of Thee I Sing, 4
"Oh, What a Beautiful Mornin'," 105
Oklahoma! (musical), 4, 25, 27–28, 131, 153,
    227n21; as transitional moment in theater,
    30, 102–107, 225n9; otherness in, 107–118;
    "Dream Ballet" sequence in, 110, 114; com-
    pared with *Annie Get Your Gun,* 229n7,
    230n13
"Oklahoma" (song), 107, 226n20
"One," 199–200
O'Neill, Eugene, 72
On Your Toes, 221n21
Operettas, 29

Peck, Gregory, 233n31
Phillips, Jonas B., 15
Pins and Needles, 72–73, 75, 220n18
Pinza, Ezio, 156, 171, 177, 178, 182
Plessy v. Ferguson, 237n23
Popular Front, 20, 83–84
Porgy and Bess, 72
Porter, Cole, 203n5

Quigley, Austin, 232n23

Race: concept of, 20–21, 25–26; stereotypes
    of, 25–26, 33–34, 90–91, 157–159, 160–162;
    as performance, 138. *See also* Blackface;
    Black performers
Racism, 20–26, 101, 224n2, 237n23; as issue
    in Broadway musicals, 4–6; as issue in
    South Pacific, 153–154, 156–182. *See also*
    Antisemitism; Civil rights
Randolph, Philip, 87, 224n2
Rankin, John, 154, 235n8
Raphaelson, Samson, 22, 32, 34. See also
    Jazz Singer, The (play)
Raymond, Dorothy, 37
Reade, Jeanette, 56
Reinhardt, Max, 15, 208n14
Revues, 28–29
Rice, Tim, 196
Riggs, Lynn, 117, 225n6
Rivers, Chief, 57

Rodgers, Richard, 12–13, 25, 27–28, 30, 67–69, 71, 102–103, 121, 212n61, 219n5, 219n6; as supporter of Jewish causes, 172. See also *Babes in Arms; King and I, The; Oklahoma!; South Pacific*
Rogers, Ginger, 41, 43, 44, 53, 61
Rogin, Michael, 33, 217n45
Romberg, Sigmund, 29
Rome, Harold, 72–73
Roosevelt, Eleanor, 86, 90
Roosevelt, Franklin D., 70, 74, 86, 98, 172, 224n66, 226n17
Rosenberg, Ethel, 185
Rosenberg, Julius, 185
Rosenwald, Julius, 87
Roth, Philip, 209n22

Sabbatianism, 13, 207n3
St. John, Betta, 161
"Sam and Delilah," 43
Sarna, Jonathan, 61, 208n12, 218n50
Schlesinger, Arthur M., 238n38
Schoenberg, Arnold, 170
Scholem, Gershom, 13
Schrecker, Ellen, 162, 171, 238nn33,38
Scott, Elizabeth, 90
Scottsboro Boys, 87
"Shall We Dance," 184, 193–194, 195
Shapiro, Edward S., 235nn8,9
Shaw, Bernard, 72
Show Boat, 28, 29, 87
Shubert Brothers, 15
Siegfried, André, 21
Sitting Bull, 232n30, 233n35. See also *Annie Get Your Gun*
Smith, Gerald L. K., 69, 75
Smith Act, 154
Sollors, Werner, 39, 62, 134, 212n58, 214n6
"Some Enchanted Evening," 176, 177, 178, 179, 180, 181
Sondheim, Stephen, 196
Sorkin, David, 231n14
Sound of Music, The, 103, 186
South Pacific, 3, 4–5, 6, 25, 103, 152; as viewed by Georgia legislators, 153, 154; racism as issue in, 153–154, 156–182; success of, 155–156; difference as issue in, 162–165
Spewack, Bella, 233n44
Spingarn, Arthur, 87

Stanislavsky, Konstantin, 213n72
Steiger, Rod, 110
Stevenson, Adlai, 174, 238n35
Stoddard, Lothrop, 21
Strasberg, Lee, 72, 227n24
Straus, Oscar, 61
Stuyvesant, Peter, 77–78

Tabbert, William, 161
Teleny, 10
Tevye, 192, 196
Theatre Guild, 72
"There's No Business Like Show Business," 119, 122, 124, 128–130, 144, 150–151, 152
"They Say It's Wonderful," 122, 124, 135
This Is the Army, 121, 139
"This Nearly Was Mine," 177, 178
Threepenny Opera, The, 9, 220n17
Tin Pan Alley, 28, 122, 212n66
Trachtenberg, Alan, 17, 209n21
Tucker, Sophie, 26, 32
Twain, Mark, 123
Tynan, Kenneth, 236n16

Uncle Tom's Cabin, as dramatized in *The King and I*, 185, 186–187, 190–191

Vaudeville, 28, 71, 220n15
Veblen, Thorstein, 16
Verfremdungseffekt, 9

Weaver, Jace, 228n33
Weill, Kurt, 9, 72, 170
Weingart Institute, 69
Weininger, Otto, 47
Wenger, Beth, 77–78
West. *See* Wild West musicals
West Side Story, 4, 152
"Where or When," 67
White, Walter, 86
White, William Allen, 224n66
Whitfield, Stephen J., 207n2, 213n67
Whoopee, 3–4, 6, 27, 29, 40, 42–43, 45, 46, 53, 55, 64–65, 214n12, 215n19; gender identity in, 47–54; Indians as portrayed in, 55–56, 58
Wilde, Oscar, 10, 127, 149–150
Wild West musicals, 215n14; as backdrop for musical comedy, 39–65; Jewish characters in, 42–52; Indian characters in, 44–45, 55–

64. See also *Annie Get Your Gun;*
Oklahoma!
Witmark and Sons, 15
Wolfsohn, Aaron, 15
Woll, Allen, 87
Women: in Broadway theater, 53, 97, 151–
152, 217n38, 240n14; changing role of, 142–
143. *See also* Gender roles
"Wonderful Guy, A," 178, 179, 180, 181

Yiddish theater, 18, 210n32
"You Are So Fair," 94
"You Can't Get a Man with a Gun," 122, 124,
141–142, 149

Young Communist League, 79
"Younger Than Springtime," 159
Youth movements, 78–79, 222nn33,34
"Youth Will Arrive," 68
"You've Got to Be Carefully Taught," 4–5,
153, 157, 188

Zangwill, Israel, 18, 22, 209n25
Zevi, Shabbetai, 207n3
Ziegfeld, Florenz, 43
Ziegfeld Follies, 29
Zionists, 18, 227n22